THE CAMPAGNA TABLE

THE

CAMPAGNA

TABLE

BRING THE STYLE AND COOKING OF THE ITALIAN COUNTRYSIDE INTO YOUR OWN HOME

MARK STRAUSMAN

PHOTOGRAPHS BY EVAN SKLAR

WILLIAM MORROW AND COMPANY, INC.

New York

IN LOVING MEMORY OF JOSEPH SOLOMON STRAUSMAN.
TO MY MOTHER AND IVAN, EACH OF WHOM RAISED ME TO UNDERSTAND AND RESPECT
THE MEANING OF HOSPITALITY.

FRONTISPIECE: **A COUNTRY TABLE SET FOR A LATE SPRING WEEKEND DINNER**

It is the policy of William Morrow and Company, Inc., and its
imprints and affiliates, recognizing the importance of
preserving what has been written, to print the books we
publish on acid-free paper, and we exert out best efforts
to that end.

Library of Congress Cataloging-in-Publication Data

Strausman, Mark.
    The campagna table: bring the style and cooking of the
Italian countryside into your own home/Mark Strausman.
        p.   cm
    ISBN 0-688-13474-2
    1. Cookery, Italian.   I. Title.   II. Title: 1st ed.
TX723..S799 1999
641.5945–dc21   99-30743
                                                    CIP

Printed in the United States of America

First Edition

1 2 3 4 5 6 7 8 9 10

BOOK DESIGN BY MARYSARAH QUINN

www.williammorrow.com

ACKNOWLEDGMENTS

Special thanks

To Susan Littlefield, who helped create so many of the moments in Italy, and whose patience and hard work brought this book through its first life.

To Justin Schwartz, for taking the project over and going to bat for me every time.

To Ron Konecky, for negotiating two deals and treating me like a star.

To Ann Bramson, who first believed in me and knew there was a book somewhere inside.

To Carrie Weinberg, for all her time and talent in promoting this book.

To Susan Rike, for endless effort in making Campagna and me successful—sometimes it seems thankless but it's not.

To Julia Moskin, for helping my voice ring true.

To Reuben Gutoff, for all the support on this project and on other ones I have done.

To my investors, for making Campagna possible.

To Evan Sklar, for taking the project and helping me in creating the feeling of Campagna through pictures.

To Kevin Crafts, for styling the food, always making me feel that I was the chef, and helping me capture the Campagna spirit.

To Aletha Soulé, for the table settings and helping me to develop the Campagna table feeling.

Thanks to Gary Page, Rita Dobry, and Ron Guialdo at G Page for helping me pick the most beautiful flowers that spoke country.

Thanks to Serine Hastings and Maureen Missner at the Loom Co. for all their help and support with setting the Campagna table.

To Stuart Alpert, Grant Pezeshki, Daniel Rodriguez, and Miguel Herdex for all their help.

CONTENTS

INTRODUCTION

CAMPAGNA MEANS COUNTRY IN ITALIAN. EVEN THOUGH my home and my restaurant are in New York City, my mind, my sensibility, and my taste buds are firmly rooted in the country. I come from peasant stock (both my parents are from Eastern European families) and I have always been fascinated by country cuisine.

I grew up in New York City, and went all the way through hotel school here. But when I graduated in 1982, I decided to take an apprenticeship

at the Heissischer Hof hotel in Frankfurt, Germany. It took only three months there before I realized not only that my calling was in the kitchen but that the hospitality aspect of restaurants was just as important to me as the food. The combination of superb cooking and excellent service is essential for a successful restaurant. Many chefs feel that the food is the single most important part of the dining experience. In reality, a delicate balance between food, service, and the ambiance in the dining room is what makes a meal come together into a great experience.

I decided to learn more about the European tradition of service and ended up staying another four years, working at the Montreux Palace in Switzerland and the Amstel Hotel in Amsterdam. The service in these five-star hotels was warm on all levels, not snooty. That has been my inspiration ever since and is the back-

bone of the experience I have created at Campagna.

Country cooking has been my passion ever since I became a head chef in 1986. My training was in Continental haute cuisine, but there is a point in every career when choices have to be made. After returning to New York I had a few jobs and soon had to say to myself: "Toto, I don't think we're in Kansas any more." The level of service in hotel kitchens just didn't compare with the European standards I had learned, and I was miserable in them. Instead, I found a small bistro on the Upper East Side, Jacqueline's, where the Swiss owner shared my ideas about food and service. Jacqueline did a bustling business in caviar and champagne (remember, this was the mid-eighties) but she wanted to expand her menu to include the European classics from her own background.

In the midst of all the conspicuous consumption of the 1980s, when a lot of her customers were even richer than royalty, Jacqueline's European sensibility meant that she had special ways of making a customer feel like a king. I can still see her waltzing up to a regular customer, saying "Oh, Monsieur, bonsoir," as she led him to his table, then placing a little pillow behind his back and bringing him his usual drink. That level of hospitality is what I still try to achieve today. I could see that her caretaking was the reason her restaurant was full night after night; everyone wants to be treated nicely.

I've always liked bucking the trends and it's always worked for me, so being friendly and service-oriented in the eighties, when other restaurants were all about the appearance of the food, really turned me on. The star chefs were making towers out of greens and using chives as long as antennas for garnishes, but I wanted to stay focused on the quality of the food. I decided to start cooking classic country foods, relying on fresh seasonal ingredients, as I had learned to do in Europe.

Since Jacqueline's was my first job as head chef, I chose to work with as small a staff as possible: there were only two cooks with me in the kitchen. We made tons of good food, serving sixty to eighty dinners a night. The experience proved to me that all a good chef really needs is a stove, a knife, and a few pots and pans: you can make big music in a tiny kitchen. A spacious kitchen with all the luxury appliances is a fun thing to have but not a necessity for making great food. Of course, everyone who knows me knows that I love my toys. I'm no minimalist, but I am a realist and a romantic. Love, passion, and caring are the most important ingredients in cooking. And kitchen appliance manufactur-

ers like Sub-Zero and Wolf don't include those in their warranties.

During my time at Jacqueline's, I developed the foundations for the style of cooking and entertaining that became my trademark later on. In my next stage, I put down the butter and picked up the olive oil, moving from French cuisine to country Italian cooking. In the summer of 1988, I became the chef of Sapore di Mare in East Hampton, New York. This was the first time I had lived outside New York City (except when I was living in Europe). For a boy who grew up in an apartment in Queens, East Hampton was a breath of fresh air and also a chance to get connected with the ingredients and the people who worked the land. I survived that first crazy summer and spent the winter visiting the duck farms and farmstands, and studying every form of peasant cooking. The cooking of the European peasants, especially Italian and French, became my passion and my addiction.

With help from Maria, a real Italian grandmother who cooked with me at Sapore di Mare, I turned the restaurant into a country kitchen. It had the pantry of a Tuscan farmhouse in the 1800s. We had homemade sausages and duck prosciutto hanging in the cellar. We salted, pickled, preserved, and canned everything that walked, grew, or swam. We used the best local poultry, vegetables, and fish as they came into season. We even made our own mozzarella by hand and macerated fruit in grappa to complete the experience.

And it all worked. Every weekend, my customers came to see what the mad scientist had come up with this week. Sapore di Mare soon rivaled anything Manhattan had to offer and a lot of restaurants in Italy as well, because we used only the best products. A large part of being a chef is the ability to purchase the best ingredients, then use them in a simple and respectful way. Working on this principle, and combining it with my ideas about service and hospitality, I continued to grow at Sapore di Mare as a chef and restaurateur.

Finally, the city boy in me took over and I got the itch for buildings, people, culture, and a kitchen that was busy seven days a week. In 1990, I moved back to the Upper East Side to open Coco Pazzo.

In the restaurant business, you never stop learning until the day you retire—there's always something new, and I love it. Revisiting the Upper East Side, this time as the chef of a restaurant that was in the limelight, was an awakening. At Coco Pazzo, I cooked for every mover and shaker in New York and the world. The energy of Manhattan was intoxicating and motivating, pushing me to continue my education in the best country cooking. So I took everything I knew, and learned to produce it on a large scale. I had seen in Europe that the great chefs could cook brilliantly for sixty people as well as six hundred, and I knew that was the next step in my evolution as a chef.

During my three years at Coco Pazzo, I also spent a lot of time in Italy, researching recipes and ideas to bring my cooking to the next level. Being in Italy was the only way a Jewish boy from New York could learn to cook real Italian food. Every year I spent weeks in Italy, searching out classic recipes that I could adapt, oh so respectfully, to my palate and those of my cus-

tomers. (Of course, a lot of the food I discovered was so good that no adaptation was needed.)

Again, this formula worked and Coco Pazzo received three stars from the *New York Times,* making it the first Italian restaurant to do so. You can imagine how proud I was. After three years of keeping Coco Pazzo at the center of the New York restaurant scene, my maturation (as a chef, at least) was finally complete, and I was ready for my own restaurant.

I opened Campagna in 1994, and was pleased that my Upper East Side clientele followed me downtown to the Flatiron district. These days Campagna is full every night, with new media types, film and TV celebrities, Wall Streeters, and executives from the music, fashion, and publishing industries, all enjoying the country cooking and atmosphere. I love living and cooking in New York City, but the idea of *campagna,* the country, has also become a big part of my life. Experience has taught me that living in the city, but keeping my mind-set and my kitchen in the country, is what works for me. Campagna is about reconnecting with what's essential (in your life and in your cooking), usually with family and friends and often around a table. It's about keeping it simple but having the best, and about caring what goes into your family's mouths without being pretentious or fussy about it. In this book, as at Campagna, I try to cook for that lifestyle. I always hope that everyone who eats at Campagna or cooks from this book gets a little taste of the passion and love I've put into it.

THE KITCHEN
AND THE TABLE

THE KITCHEN
AND THE TABLE

PEOPLE ALWAYS GRAVITATE TO A KITCHEN. IT SEEMS TO hold a certain fascination. The kitchen is always the busiest room in the house and the place where people feel most secure. It belongs to the whole family. No matter how fancy the appliances and design, the kitchen is also the most practical room in the house. Even in a big house with a separate dining room, the kitchen is the most comforting and friendly place to eat. The kitchen table is a meeting place,

not only for meals but for late-night talks, family conferences, and all kinds of big and small celebrations.

Even Kennedy and Khrushchev hammered out their deals around a kitchen table, after the formal state dinners were over. I have always felt most comfortable in the kitchen, even long before I became a chef. When I used to go to parties (before I had kids!), I always noticed that everyone spent most of the night in the kitchen. I remember my parents discussing the Vietnam War and Watergate around our kitchen table.

Now that I'm a parent myself, I find that we make all of our important decisions at the table. One of the most important decisions is: "What should we feed the kids?" We try to uphold the baby-boomer commandment: Thou shalt not feed thy children take-out seven nights a week.

OVERLEAF: **PERSIMMONS IN AN EARTHENWARE *COMPOTIER* AS A CENTERPIECE INSTEAD OF FLOWERS.**

But somehow, a lot of us never learned to cook. This doesn't apply to baby boomers only. Lots of people now go to school, get advanced degrees, get big jobs—all without learning to cook. But when you grow up and realize it's time to take better care of yourself, your family, your friends, and your kids, you're going to have to learn to cook.

We all want the best. For the kitchen, that means learning to cook and serve great meals. The key isn't cooking: The key is planning. As they teach you at Harvard Business School, "piss-poor planning gives piss-poor results." Good planning makes cooking fun, not a chore. Cooking for family, friends, lovers, and even coworkers can be creative and satisfying. Learning simple cooking techniques is the first step to making great food. In this book, you'll learn the basic methods of classic cuisine, plus country Italian recipes, and together they will help you develop your own repertoire of dishes and

2

memories. Every child remembers later in life the dishes his dad cooked on weekends, whether it's scrambled eggs or rack of lamb. Eventually you'll be able to use the methods and principles to cook with more spontaneity, creating your own recipes.

The time to start cooking is when you understand that food and eating are serious parts of a relationship. You will always have someone to love you if you can cook! What could be more romantic than cooking dinner for a new "friend"? It's a promise of more fun on the way. When you settle down, you eat with your mate more than anyone else, so feeding that person can be an important way of showing your feelings. Since we all work so hard, it's nice to make a special dinner for two or gather friends at your table on the weekend. When everyone has kids (and going to a restaurant becomes an ordeal), cooking and entertaining at home are a necessity. When we make new friends through our kids, we have new entertainment responsibilities. We want to cook and serve wholesome dishes with clean flavors, in a comforting setting. We don't want to make uneducated food.

We need to learn not only how to cook but how to put meals on the table. In your home, you're more than just a cook. You're the executive chef, planning meals, purchasing ingredients, seating the guests, and serving the food. The pressure on a restaurant chef is to do it for two hundred different people in one night; the pressure on you is to do it for the same four people one night, and the next night, and the night after that. This book helps you meet that challenge. As your skill level and your family grow together, cooking will become more pleasurable and the kitchen will become a safe

COUNTRY TEA TOWELS, WHICH CAN BE USED AS NAPKINS.

haven. Many psychologists believe that children who eat dinner as part of a family grow up more well-adjusted and happy. And it's good for everyone to slow down the pace of life and work by relaxing and taking the time to set a table, sit down, and break bread together.

To increase that feeling of security and comfort, I think the atmosphere around the table is very important. What makes a good table is a certain civilized formality and tradition. Even if you didn't grow up with setting the table and serving dinner, these rituals will enhance your mealtime experience and also your children's

memories of family meals. It's more fun to cook and serve when you have nice everyday things like Provençal platters, bistro plates with soft rolled edges, and real silverware. Cloth napkins and placemats are key. Using colored serving dishes, bread plates, and painted pitchers adds a lot to your table, and collecting them is fun. Setting a table can be as simple as fork on the left, knife on the right, wineglass just touching the point of the knife. For special occasions, a more elaborate table is festive and appropriate. For more ideas about tables for entertaining, see the Al Fresco, Antipasti, and Holidays chapters.

I find that a country aesthetic, even in a city kitchen, gives the most comfortable feeling. It's good for family meals and the kind of informal but elegant entertaining we usually prefer. I like a big wooden table in a rustic style. The Tuscan or Provençal farmhouse is the vision I keep in mind for my restaurant, home store, and house.

In traditional farmhouses in Italy, the table was always in the kitchen, the warmest room in the house. The large plank table was used for conversation, meals, making pasta, doing homework, and even bathing and changing the baby. It was a place to celebrate joyous occasions and to receive comfort and shelter when times were hard. We have a wooden table just like that at Campagna, covered with inviting platters of antipasti, glowing jars of preserved vegetables and fruits, and a wheel of Parmigiano-Reggiano cheese. In my travels in Italy, I've seen countless tables like that, and they are always in constant use—whether in a Sicilian farmhouse or in a Roman kitchen. The feeling from the table is as important as the food.

One of my favorite books, *The Tuscan Year* by Elizabeth Romer, chronicles a year in the life of a Tuscan peasant family in the mid-1900s. The book focuses on Silvana, a wife and mother, whose cooking and preserving abilities help keep the family together and happy. Their life is not luxurious but it is simple, wholesome, and honest. Traditional peasants, whether or not they owned their land, worked jobs of great physical and mental strain. They were at the mercy of uncontrollable forces, with no economic protection, and they rarely were able to stop working and just relax. They worried constantly about their children's welfare and future.

Sometimes I think that modern urban life is frighteningly similar. We all work so hard, barely stopping for meals and always scrambling to get dinner on the table. Time has become a luxury. Today's parents have the same worries about their children, and the same responsibility to nourish them and care for them. At the same time, they need to nourish and comfort themselves. When I look at my life, I realize that I am a modern-day peasant. Okay, maybe I don't till the land—but I work my tail off. If you do the same thing, keep reading.

ALETHA SOULÉ VASES WITH DAFFODILS AND ROSES, TRIMMED CLOSE TO THE VASE.

THE PANTRY

THE PANTRY

IF PEASANT LIFE EVOLVED AROUND THE WARMTH OF THE kitchen, then the pantry is where the fuel for that warmth came from. The hearth gave off heat to warm the family and the house and to cook all the food. Off the kitchen, the cool pantry was the place to store the fruits of the family's labors. Preserved vegetables, dried fruits, cured hams, dried herbs and mushrooms, aged cheeses, and almost everything the family needed to eat well year-round could be stored there.

The idea of the pantry comes from the natural rhythms of the agricultural year. All summer long, the garden produces beans, tomatoes, zucchini, and peppers for the family to eat. But as autumn approaches, it's time to empty the garden of crops before the first frost. And what do you do with two hundred pounds of tomatoes? You can them. In an Italian country farmhouse, September and October are dedicated to canning and preserving the harvest.

All winter long, Mamma can go to the pantry for her canned tomatoes and dried oregano, boil some dried pasta, and make a lunch for her family that reminds them of sunny summer days. Her well-stocked pantry is the inspiration for this chapter. Americans today work as hard as any peasant. Traditional peasant cooking was limited by the seasons: there was no way to get a ripe tomato from Sicily to Tuscany two hundred years ago. Now we have the technology to make it possible. We can get a ripe tomato from Sicily or Israel or Holland at the supermarket any time of year. But we are limited by our schedules. Most days, we don't even have the time to stop at the supermarket!

We need the same thing the peasants had: a well-stocked pantry. The pantry ensures that we, too, can put clean, wholesome, nourishing food on our tables every night. Traditional peasants canned, brined, dried, cured, and preserved their own food. Today the same healthful staples (olive oil, tomatoes, garlic, pasta) are more likely to come from the supermarket. They're already in your kitchen, so you just have to come home with vegetables and a protein to put dinner on the table in no time.

When I was in cooking school, I didn't understand the value of the pantry. I would buy all the ingredients each time to make special

OVERLEAF: **CAMPAGNA HOMEMADE *SOTTOLIO*, OR PICKLED VEGETABLES.**

RIGHT: **LIGURIAN OLIVE OIL.**

meals for my girlfriends. It was no fun, not to mention expensive, to have to shop for olive oil, onions, wine, and so on every time I wanted to cook. Keeping the following ingredients on hand will make it possible for you to whip up sautés, pan sauces, dressings, risottos, and most other dishes faster than ever.

Your pantry should ideally be separate from the kitchen, as the kitchen's heat and light can affect your ingredients. If that's not possible, keep your pantry as far from the stove as you can, and make sure it is dark or dimly lit.

The pantry is limited only by the size of the cook's passion and spirit for cooking. Don't let small cupboards or closet kitchens keep you from preparing good food for your family. Besides basic pantry ingredients, all you really need to keep in your kitchen is a good knife and a few pans. And a couple of tools that don't take up any room at all: care and love. Those are stored in the pantry of your soul. These human ingredients, plus a little help from your pantry and a few minutes to spare, are all you need to make the recipes in this book.

Here's what you need to stock your pantry:

OLIVE OIL

Olive oil is the ingredient at the epicenter of Italian cuisine, and my passion for collecting and using olive oil shows at Campagna Home, where I stock at least fifteen different extra-virgin oils from Italy. Tuscany has the best reputation, but oils from Umbria, Liguria, Lake Garda, and parts of the south can also be excellent. What's really important is not where the oil is made, but how they make it. There is nothing better than real stone-pressed extra-virgin olive oil, and you can taste the difference. Most oils (even extra-virgin oils from Italy) are now pressed with a centrifuge system. It does get all the oil out of the olives, but it also heats the oil and ultimately sacrifices quality in favor of quantity.

It's important for every home cook to have an ample supply of olive oil. Italian oils are officially regulated and graded; each used for a different purpose. Even within the "extra-virgin" grade, it makes a difference if your oil is cold pressed, stone pressed, and/or bottled where it is made. Ideally, you should have a bottle of each of the following kinds in your pantry.

Olive oil should not be hoarded like fine wine, but used within a year. The more expensive the oil is, the better reason to taste it at its peak. Olive oil releases its perfume at room temperature, so never store it in a cold place like the refrigerator. And store it away from the light, which will cause it to deteriorate (that's why good oil is always bottled in dark glass).

Premium extra-virgin olive oil comes from Italy in small bottles and is even more expensive than extra-virgin olive oil. You'll find it in gourmet stores. It is always pressed in small batches, from the first pressing of olives, and has a rich, strong flavor. It should never be used for cooking, but drizzled on foods such as Pasta e Fagioli or plain cooked vegetables as a garnish.

Extra-virgin olive oil is the "ordinary" variety you'll find at the supermarket. It's very fine oil, if not as intense and rich as premium oil. I use it for most purposes, such as pasta sauces, salad dressings, and stews. At the restaurant we use Monni brand oil from outside Spoleto; they are master blenders, and every bottle is consistently good.

Pure olive oil is from the second pressing of the olives, so it is slightly less flavorful, but it is still perfectly good oil. I use it for frying and sautéing, as it can be heated to higher temperatures than extra-virgin oils.

A warning about "light" olive oil: This is an invention of American food distributors, not an official Italian grade. Light olive oil is no lower in fat than any other olive oil. It is supposed to have a lighter flavor, but pure olive oil is much the same, and a lot cheaper. These

PROVENÇAL *CARRE* (SQUARE) DISH WITH SPICED TUSCAN OLIVES.

light oils are just as expensive as extra-virgin oils.

I also like some French, Spanish, and Greek olive oils; they tend to be lighter than the green Italian oils. They are made from riper olives and are more buttery in flavor.

VINEGAR

Good vinegars have distinctive flavors and aren't overly acidic. They add much flavor and zing to cooking and I use them often. It's a bonus that they contain no fat at all. It's an old wives' tale that vinegar is made from spoiled wine. Any real vinegar producer would take offense at that statement: It takes time and knowledge to make great vinegar. It's all in the vinegar's "mother," a substance that creates the fermentation process (like a sourdough starter). Good vinegar producers know exactly how to ferment their product into mellow, balanced vinegars for salads and cooking.

Red wine vinegar is my favorite all-purpose vinegar. Where it comes from is less important than how much acidity it has: 6 to 8 percent is best. My rule of thumb is if you can't drink half a teaspoon of vinegar without coughing and tearing up, it's too strong.

Balsamic vinegar has of course become very popular in recent years. It's a very strong seasoning that permeates a dish, so I use it very carefully. All good-quality balsamic vinegar comes from Modena in northern Italy and will say so on the

bottle. I use it for making salad dressings and drizzling over cooked vegetables. Balsamic vinegars aged for two to ten years fit into this category.

Traditionally aged balsamic vinegar is a very special product from Modena, and it isn't really vinegar. To make it, producers begin with the must, a concentrated sweet juice from white grapes. The must is cooked down slowly, then placed in wooden barrels for the long aging process. It is aged for either twelve years or twenty-five years and the age will be marked on the bottle. As it ages, the must is rotated into barrels made of different woods and the product gradually takes on its distinctive character. In Modena, there is a ruling body to oversee the quality and to ensure that the name *Aceto Balsamico Tradizionale di Modena* stays special for the whole world to enjoy. It's almost like a fine aged port or sherry in flavor and is used in tiny amounts. It's sweet and rich, and I use it for drizzling on strawberries or a special salad. Aged balsamic also makes wonderful sauces when you use it to deglaze a pan in which you've cooked chicken or veal.

WINE

Red and white wine belong in the kitchen as much as they belong on the table. Cooking wine must be real wine, but it should not be an expensive or subtle wine. It would be a waste to use expensive wine for cooking, even if you could

afford it. White wine for cooking should be dry, crisp, and clean. Red wine should be dry and full-bodied. You should be able to find perfectly good cooking wines for around five dollars a bottle, if not from Italy and France then from Chile and Spain.

KOSHER SALT

Most chefs strongly prefer kosher salt to table (iodized) salt. It is coarser than table salt, so it is easier to add by hand. As you add it, you can see the crystals in the pot and gauge how much you've added. All professionals keep a bin of kosher salt by the stove and they add it pinch by pinch. You quickly learn to feel with your fingers how much you're using.

BLACK PEPPERCORNS

I recommend investing in a good pepper mill for the stove. There's no substitute for freshly ground pepper. Buy a mill with an adjustable grinder so that you can make coarse cracked pepper for encrusting steaks. Whole peppercorns are often added to soups and stocks, so that they can be strained out later on.

HOT RED PEPPER FLAKES

The supermarket product is fine, but if you can get your hands on whole dried Italian hot peppers I highly recommend them. They have more full pepper flavor, not just heat. They are small and red and can be chopped with a knife or crushed with a mortar and pestle. For less heat, use more of the red skin and fewer white seeds (which contain the heat).

HERBS

A few dried herbs are excellent, even preferable to fresh: bay leaves and oregano. Dried rosemary and thyme are acceptable. But dried "soft" herbs like parsley, basil, chives, and sage are useless. They must be bought and used fresh.

GARLIC

In one form or another, garlic appears in most of these recipes. I use it at three different "temperatures," depending on how much garlic flavor I want in the dish.

Italians usually use whole smashed cloves, which lend their flavor during the cooking but can be removed at the end. It leaves behind a sweet, nutty garlic flavor.

Thickly sliced garlic adds more pungency, but can still be removed from the dish before serving.

Minced garlic lends the most flavor, almost a "hot" garlic taste. I use it only in dishes that will be cooked for a long time, so that it has a chance to mellow. Pre-minced garlic in jars is not a good substitute for fresh.

CANNED TOMATOES

Canned plum tomatoes from Italy taste better than fresh tomatoes for most of the year. And even when fresh tomatoes are available, canned tomatoes are often a better choice in cooking. Italian plum tomatoes are naturally low in moisture, ripened on the vine, and pre-peeled. They behave very predictably in the pot, which is important to ensure consistently good cooking. Before cooking them, whole canned tomatoes should be put through a food mill (which will remove the seeds) until crushed; or pour them into a bowl and break them up with your fingers, removing the stems and seeds. The seeds can be left in if you're in a hurry.

CHEESE

In my home kitchen, I'm lost without a chunk of Parmesan cheese. In addition to providing a finishing touch for pastas, many salads, and soups, it's a vital ingredient in risottsos, soups, and stews. Parmigiano-Reggiano is the official name of this carefully regulated cheese from Parma, and the real product will always have that name stamped on the rind in indelible ink. There is no substitute for freshly grated cheese—it is absolutely worth the small investment. However, if you can't bring yourself to buy real Parmesan, a slightly cheaper and good alternative is Grana Padano cheese,

also from Italy. It, too, must always be freshly grated. Commercial "cheese products" are no substitute.

Pecorino Romano cheese is also a good grating cheese, but it is made from sheep's milk and has a much sharper, almost spicy flavor compared to Parmesan. It should be used with strong and salty ingredients like broccoli rabe and pancetta.

For grating cheese, it's worth buying a small hand grater with a turning blade: Your hands will thank you! When a recipe calls for slivered cheese, you can rub a chunk of cheese over a truffle slicer or cheese slicer. Or, peel off very thin slices with a vegetable peeler or sharp knife.

DRIED PASTA

I like dried pastas from Italy best. Dried pasta should have only two ingredients listed on the package: durum wheat flour and water. Barilla and DeCecco are excellent products, but I also like the "artisan" pastas that are beginning to show up in American gourmet stores, such as Morelli and Pastifico Umbrio, which is sold under the Campagna Home label. These handmade dried pastas are more rough and porous than commercial ones, which gives them a great texture. Keep several long pastas (like spaghetti) and short pastas (like penne and orecchiete) on hand at all times. See the Pasta chapter for a discussion of fresh pasta.

RICE

For risotto, keep Italian arborio, vialone, or carnaroli rice on hand. Other short-grain rices, such as Japanese or Spanish, will not work in the same way as Italian rices that have been developed for risotto-making.

POLENTA

Polenta is simply cornmeal, and even American supermarket brands of cornmeal can be successfully used to make Classic Soft Polenta (page 153). Imported Italian polenta is usually of a very high quality. Any variations are usually in the size of the grind, not the quality of the corn. The only polenta I would hesitate to recommend is quick-cooking polenta, which is very finely ground but which never takes on the creamy texture of real polenta. But it is practical and can still be very delicious.

DRIED BEANS AND LEGUMES

Dried cranberry beans (borlotti) and white kidney beans (can-nellini) are the Italian favorites. Stock them for soups, stews, and salads. I also keep French lentils on hand for salads and soups.

To cook dried beans, soak them for 12 to 24 hours in four times their volume of water, changing the water at least one time. Drain, rinse, and drain again. Cover with cold water, bring to a simmer, and cook until tender, adding water as necessary to keep the beans well covered. This will take anywhere from 45 minutes to 2 hours. Most beans double in size when cooked, so if a recipe calls for 2 cups cooked beans, soak 1 cup dried beans.

FROZEN FOODS

Frozen spinach and frozen peas from the supermarket are a very high-quality product, and I often use them in home cooking. But the most useful pantry-freezer items are the soups, pasta sauces, and stews you have made yourself and frozen in portion-size containers. Freezing is a great way to have homemade dinners during the week and keep your sanity at the same time. Vegetable dishes like Real Eggplant Parmigiana (page 185) and Pasta e Fagioli (page 113) freeze especially well and last for a long time. Anything with meat should be used within six months. To thaw, transfer food to the refrigerator 24 hours before using.

STOCKS

Stock is an absolute necessity in any kitchen. Chicken stock is the most versatile, but veal stock is ideal for a few classic dishes. Vegetable stock, which is easy to make, can often be substituted. Recipes for homemade stocks appear on pages 15 to 17. But canned stocks (usually labeled broth) can be okay, especially those that are reduced in salt and fat, and contain no artificial flavors or colors. Canned consommé, which is very "clean" (it has been repeatedly clarified), is also a good choice for soups.

CHICKEN STOCK

IF I COULD HAVE ONLY ONE STOCK IN MY *kitchen, this would be it. Chicken stock is the basis for so many great soups, stews, sauces, risottos, and even pasta sauces. I often use it as the cooking medium for vegetables like broccoli rabe and escarole. When choosing the herbs, select a balance between strong ones like oregano and rosemary and gentle ones like marjoram and parsley. Be especially careful with rosemary; its strong flavor can take over a whole stock.*

For food safety, it's important to cool stock quickly. Rather than waiting for it to cool in the pot, which can take hours, divide the finished stock among smaller containers and cool in the refrigerator.

MAKES ABOUT 4 QUARTS

5 pounds chicken necks and backs, or other fresh chicken bones
1 onion, peeled and quartered
1 carrot, cut into chunks
2 stalks celery, cut into chunks
1 leek, split lengthwise, well washed, and coarsely chopped
6 black peppercorns
2 bay leaves
6 sprigs assorted fresh herbs, such as thyme, rosemary, sage, parsley, oregano, and marjoram

Place all the ingredients in a large stockpot. Add water to cover completely. Heat uncovered, over medium heat, until almost boiling. Reduce the heat to medium-low and simmer gently 4 to 6 hours, until golden and flavorful. Skim off any impurities that rise to the top.

During the first 3 hours of cooking, add simmering water as needed to keep the ingredients covered. Do not add water during the last hour of cooking or the stock may taste watery.

Remove the pot from the heat and let cool slightly. Strain the stock through a medium-mesh strainer. Divide the stock among smaller containers and refrigerate until cold and gelatinous and the fat has collected on the top. When the stock is cold, remove the congealed fat from the top.

Use immediately, or refrigerate for 3 to 4 days or freeze for up to 6 months until ready to use.

VEAL STOCK

VEAL STOCK IS CLASSICALLY USED FOR ALL *kinds of meat dishes and sauces. I use it in stews and soups when a deep, but light, meat flavor is desirable. Veal bones have lots of protein, which makes for a stock with lots of body. In this book, I use only "pale" veal stock, made from blanched veal bones. The other kind is "brown" veal stock, for which you roast the bones before making the stock. Brown veal stock has a strong roasted flavor and is used mainly for classic brown sauces.*

Small bones will yield their proteins and gelatin much more easily than large ones, and your stock will be done sooner. Veal stock is strong enough to handle the flavor of garlic. Simmered in the stock, even a whole head of garlic is sweet and pungent, not strong. This stock must be cooled within 2 hours of being cooked.

MAKES ABOUT 8 QUARTS

10 pounds small or cut up veal bones, cracked if possible (your butcher will do this for you)
4 carrots, cut into chunks
3 onions, thickly sliced
3 stalks celery, cut into chunks
2 leeks, split lengthwise, well washed, and roughly chopped
1 large handful parsley sprigs
4 sprigs fresh rosemary
4 sprigs fresh thyme
12 black peppercorns
3 cloves
2 bay leaves
1 head garlic, cut vertically in half (do not peel)
2 cups dry red wine
2 cups milled or crushed canned Italian plum tomatoes
2 tablespoons tomato paste

Place the bones in a large stockpot. Cover with water and heat to a boil. Remove from the heat, drain out the water, and put the pot back on the stove.

Add all the ingredients to the bones in the pot. Add water to cover completely. Heat, uncovered, over medium-high heat until almost boiling. Reduce the heat to medium-low and simmer gently for about 8 hours, until flavorful.

During the first 7 hours of cooking, add water as needed to keep the ingredients covered. Do not add water during the last hour of cooking or the stock may taste watery.

Remove the pot from the heat and let cool slightly. Remove any large pieces of bone and strain the stock through a fine strainer to clear it. As you strain, press down on the debris to squeeze out all the juices.

Use immediately, or divide the stock among smaller containers and refrigerate for 3 to 4 days or freeze for up to 6 months until ready to use.

VEGETABLE STOCK

VEGETABLE STOCK CAN BE USED IN SOUPS, *stews, and risottos when you don't want to use meat but still want plenty of flavor and body. This is easy to make and freezes beautifully. There's no need to peel the vegetables, but they should be well washed.*

MAKES ABOUT 4 QUARTS

2 bay leaves
2 cloves
12 black peppercorns
1 cinnamon stick
5 quarts water
1 head celery (about 12 stalks), cut into chunks
4 onions, cut into chunks
1 pound button mushrooms, thickly sliced
2 bulbs fennel, cut into chunks
4 large carrots, cut into chunks
2 turnips, cut into chunks
2 parsnips, cut into chunks
3 leeks, cut into chunks
2 large handfuls parsley sprigs
1 head garlic, cloves separated (do not peel)
8 fresh rosemary sprigs
8 fresh sage leaves

Tie the bay leaves, cloves, peppercorns, and cinnamon stick in cheesecloth and place in a large stockpot. Add the remaining ingredients and heat, uncovered, over medium-high heat until almost boiling. Reduce the heat to medium-low and simmer gently for about 1 hour, until flavorful and the vegetables are very soft.

Remove the pot from the heat and let cool slightly. Strain the stock through a medium-mesh strainer. If you like, push down on the vegetables to squeeze all the liquid and some vegetable pulp into the stock, which will give it more body (and make it a bit cloudy).

Use immediately, or refrigerate for 3 to 4 days or freeze for up to 6 months until ready to use.

FISH STOCK

FISH STOCK IS CERTAINLY EASY TO MAKE SINCE *it cooks for only an hour. In fact, you must not cook it any longer, or it will turn bitter. Be sure to simmer it very gently.*

To make a nice, rich, gelatinous stock, use bones only from flat saltwater fish like sole, flounder, fluke, cod, and halibut. Rinse the bones well before adding them to the pot. During the cooking, you want to crack the bones to release the gelatin and proteins. To do this, press down on them with a sturdy spoon or ladle.

MAKES ABOUT 4 QUARTS

5 pounds bones from white fish such as sole, snapper, cod, bass, grouper, tilefish
3 carrots, cut into chunks
3 celery stalks, cut into chunks
2 onions, thickly sliced
1 leek, split lengthwise, well washed, and thickly sliced
1 fennel bulb, quartered
1 handful parsley sprigs
4 cloves garlic (do not peel)
1 teaspoon black peppercorns
2 bay leaves
2 cloves
2 sprigs fresh thyme
1 cup dry white wine
5 quarts water

Place all the ingredients in a large stockpot. Heat, uncovered, over medium heat until almost boiling. Reduce the heat to medium-low and simmer gently for 1 hour. Remove from the heat and let cool slightly. Remove any large pieces of bone and strain the stock through a fine strainer to clear it. As you strain, press down on the debris to squeeze out all the juices.

Use immediately, or divide the stock among smaller containers and refrigerate for 1 to 2 days or freeze for up to 6 months until ready to use.

BASIL PUREE

INSTANT FLAVOR FOR SOUPS, STEWS, SALAD *dressings, and almost anything you can think of. This freezes very well, so you can make it during the summer and use it all winter.*

MAKES ABOUT 3 CUPS

2 pounds fresh basil
2 cups extra-virgin olive oil

Separate the basil leaves from the stalks and rinse them under cold running water. Drain well and pat dry.

Put a handful of basil leaves in the bowl of a food processor and process until finely chopped. Add another handful and repeat until all the basil is chopped. With the machine running (at low speed if possible), drizzle in the olive oil and process just until smooth.

Use immediately, or refrigerate for 4 to 5 days or freeze for up to 6 months until ready to use. Squeeze a teaspoon of lemon juice over the top if storing.

BAKED CROUTONS

THESE HOMEMADE CROUTONS REALLY MAKE *your homemade soups irresistible.*

Day-old crusty bread, such as peasant, sourdough, or pumpernickel
Extra-virgin olive oil

Preheat the oven to 400°F. If you like, cut the crusts off the bread. Cut the bread into 1-inch cubes and spread on a baking sheet. Sprinkle lightly with olive oil, toss to evenly coat, and bake until evenly toasted and hard. Watch the croutons carefully to be sure they do not burn.

MOROCCAN COLORED GLASSWARE.

AL FRESCO

AL FRESCO

AL FRESCO LITERALLY MEANS "IN THE AIR," AND AN outdoor dinner party is my idea of a great time. The summer just isn't long enough for all the great dinners I want to have. So for this chapter, I figured out how you and I can host parties that are al fresco in spirit any time of year. Whether the guests are eating around a big table on your porch, in your backyard, or in your dining room, an al fresco party is always easygoing, cheerful, and friendly. People break bread

together, literally and figuratively. Instead of sitting and waiting for arranged food on individual plates, they just share from platters on a colorful table. There's nothing better than watching people get to know each other over satisfying, simple food you've cooked for them. Al fresco is absolutely my favorite way to eat and entertain.

It's no coincidence that Italian weddings are almost always al fresco affairs, with long tables covered with food set in meadows or even in the streets of a town. Children run from table to table. Guests get up and wander, wineglasses in hand, exchanging hugs and toasts. No one has to choose between the prime rib and the salmon; there's lots of different food, and peo-

ple eat what they want. That's what I think all parties should be like.

What makes a party al fresco? Well, the best ones are usually summer gatherings, in the late afternoon or evening. There's something about eating in the open air that just feels right. After all, that's where all the vegetables come from! Al fresco dinners offer plenty of food, but not in a strict appetizer-entrée-dessert order. This kind of meal is easy on the eye, the cook, and the guests. Colorful platters of (for instance) roasted peppers, *caponata,* sliced steak, and tomato-mozzarella salad are set out in advance. You can have a cold watercress soup and a dish of Vitello Tonnato chilling in the fridge, then go take a shower, have a glass of wine, and feel like a human being. You aren't a slave; you're a guest at your own party.

An al fresco bonus: Your guests will appreciate not being tied to their chairs for three hours. When I go to a party, even a small one, I like

OVERLEAF: **AN AL FRESCO BUFFET TABLE, WITH SICILIAN PEPPERS STUFFED WITH RICE, GRILLED TUNA WITH GRAIN SALAD, POLLETTO ALLA MATTONE, INVOLTINI DI POLLO AL TAORMINA, AND RAW MUSHROOM SALAD WITH LEMON AND PROSCIUTTO DI PARMA.**

moving around, nibbling at a chunk of Parmigiano here, a stuffed pepper there, and talking to everyone as much as possible.

One subject I can talk about for hours is room-temperature food. I've been told that I should get off my soap box—but I'm short, and no one would be able to see me! I think food tastes best at room temperature. The antipasti tables in Italian restaurants are in the dining room partly so that you can admire the food, but also because the flavors of the vegetables, olive oil, and herbs keep getting better. The refrigerator stops flavors dead in their tracks. Cheese, cured meats, and country sausages taste real only after they've warmed up a little. That said, do exercise common sense when leaving food out. As a rule of thumb, the USDA recommends that food be left out for a maximum of two hours.

For an al fresco meal, not everything has to be room temperature. If the weather is getting cool, add a tureen of hot stew to the table; on a hot day, chilled soup makes a great extra. The recipes in this chapter are particularly suited to room-temperature service, but you can also mix them with the antipasti, side dishes, soups, and stews.

I don't want to shock you, but I like presenting food even more than cooking it. I like simple food, cooked right. To me, cooking is about learning and following the best methods. Presentation is the creative part. The only rule for setting a buffet table is the order of the dishes: appetizers and salads first, then cold fish and meats, then hot food, reading from left to right on the table. Serve soup first, as a separate course. And have fun with your food! Presentation isn't architecture. Presentation is about showing that you care, not about showing off. You don't have to build fish-shaped mounds of seafood salad or leaning towers of celery sticks. Just fan your thinly sliced prosciutto or slices of ripe red tomatoes and fresh mozzarella on a platter. Pile your bright-red *peperonata* in a deep blue bowl. Add a few figs, sliced melon, olives, and a seafood salad, and you've got dinner and dessert on the table. Add biscotti and dessert wine at the end of the meal. As you look through the following recipes, you'll see that they are totally flexible. They work as salads, antipasti, sides, and main dishes; serving sizes depend only on how many dishes you're planning to put out.

To make it all look great, choose dishes of different colors, sizes, and shapes for serving. Arranging them at different heights, instead of all on the flat tabletop, is easy and looks very professional. The day before, experiment with using boxes or cake plates on the table to hold the dishes up. Cover the boxes with a tablecloth, or put the cloth over some of them and wrap the small ones in pretty linens.

Decide in advance which bowls, platters, and tureens you want to use. Don't be afraid to mix and match your platters and linens, colors and neutrals. All-white platters are a safe choice, but remember that your house isn't a Calvin Klein boutique! Minimalism is cool in theory, but a minimalist buffet table isn't exactly welcoming. Mix white, solid color, and patterned pieces in your collection. Rustic Provençal, Italian, and Portuguese pieces are perfect for al fresco serving, since they echo the outdoors and the naturally arranged food. Bright bowls of dressings, chopped herbs, and baskets of sliced bread fill in the empty spaces on the buffet.

Whether I decide on a buffet or table service, I always like to set the tables where people will be eating with flatware and placemats. A wooden table always looks best. I fold a tablecloth (linen is my favorite, for its rustic elegance) into a strip of fabric and use it as a runner down the length of the table, so that the table doesn't look bare. Give each person a water glass and a wineglass, and set pitchers of ice water on the table. Set flatware at each place, so that the guests have only to carry their plates at the buffet. If you're feeding a crowd, you can roll flatware in pretty napkins. People often think that they need to cram in their entire meal on one trip to the buffet table. If you set out both appetizer and dinner plates, they'll get the message: Slow down, take your time.

I have a thing about flowers. I really like to see flowers on a dining table, on a buffet, in the kitchen—everywhere. Put them wherever your guests are likely to wander. You want to keep the bunches small, since there's nothing more annoying than squinting through a centerpiece when you're trying to have a conversation. The flowers in the dining room at Campagna add a lot of atmosphere and color to the room. We always make bouquets that have only one kind of flower in them (a dozen miniature yellow roses, for example). I personally give a lot of credit to Mother Nature, and stiff, artificial-looking flower arrangements make no sense to me.

Serving wine in nice-looking pitchers is a great touch for the table. Of course, that's what Italians of all classes do in the country. They buy inexpensive local wine in large quantities and pour it into pitchers as it is needed. The American corollary is to choose a basic, light-bodied red and a white and buy them by the case; most stores offer a 10 percent discount. Having a "house wine" isn't only for restaurants. Slightly chilled, easygoing wines like young Tuscan Chianti and Nebbiolo reds or French Sancerre and Chablis whites complement almost anything you're likely to cook. An al fresco dinner isn't the time to bring out your fancy Barolos. In Italy, such wines are saved for special occasions—even by rich people who can afford to drink big wines at every meal. Eating in harmony with the seasons and the rhythms of life means that simple meals call for simple wines.

Entertaining at home is pretty much optional these days. Wives don't have to make roast beef for their husbands' bosses any more. Everyone wants to save time, and eating in restaurants is certainly quick and easy. I know that you're not going to cook every night, and that you're not entertaining every weekend. But summer is my favorite time to do both. With ripe summer vegetables, an outdoor grill, and the recipes in this chapter, it's hard to go wrong. When you are cooking, this is the way to do it—simply, but with great flavor, fresh ingredients, and loving presentation. Rustic Italian food evolved to suit the lives of people who worked hard all day and restored themselves at night with family and food. We're not that different. So here they are—the shortcuts to a great life.

INSALATA CAPRESE

IS THERE ANYTHING BETTER? I DON'T THINK *so. I've seen more variations on this salad in the past years than I can remember, but the fact is: None of them is better than the original, and most are worse. You don't have to push the mozzarella up the tomato's nose just to be "creative"! Why mess with perfection?*

Caprese salad is always part of summer meals at our house, and to tell you the truth, I serve it whenever I can get my hands on good tomatoes and basil. It's getting easier to find good-quality fresh mozzarella cheese, too. Polly-O fresh mozzarella is now sold in tubs in the dairy case or at the deli counter. It's so much better than the shrink-wrapped kind. To serve Insalata Caprese as a light entrée on a hot day, just add some thinly sliced Prosciutto di Parma or a few roasted red peppers.

If you can find fresh mozzarella di bufala from Italy, made with water buffalo milk, you have to try it in this salad. Outside Naples, where the tangy mozzarella di bufala comes from, we bought tomatoes and fresh mozzarella by the side of the road and slapped them together on the spot—wow!

MAKES 4 TO 8 SERVINGS

3 large, ripe tomatoes
1 pound very fresh mozzarella cheese
Salt and freshly ground black pepper
¼ cup extra-virgin olive oil
12 to 16 whole leaves fresh basil

Slice the tomatoes ½ inch thick and fan out on a platter or on individual serving plates.

Slice the mozzarella ½ inch thick or, if using small mozzarella balls, cut into quarters. Divide on top of the tomatoes.

Sprinkle with salt and pepper to taste, drizzle with olive oil, and top with basil leaves.

PRO TIP: *Vinegar should never be used in this salad. That's why using ripe tomatoes is so important: The juices provide the sweetness and acid "bite" of vinegar. If your tomatoes are ripe and the salad still tastes bland, sprinkle more salt on it.*

PANZANELLA

HERE'S THE PROOF THAT A PEASANT WITH A *kitchen garden is a better and more creative cook than almost any restaurant chef. Panzanella is just your basic garden salad—made from the tomatoes, cucumbers, basil, and onions that flourish all summer—with a great twist: vinegar-laced cubes of bread. Bread is the traditional staple of Tuscany. Many recipes using stale bread were invented over the decades. A hallmark of peasant cooking is that nothing is ever wasted. Panzanella is one of my favorite bread recipes. (Pappa al Pomodoro is another, page 108.)*

MAKES 6 TO 10 SERVINGS

½ loaf 1- or 2-day-old Tuscan or other dense,
    crusty peasant bread
4 tablespoons red wine vinegar
8 large, ripe tomatoes, diced
1 large cucumber, peeled, halved lengthwise,
    seeded, and sliced ¼ inch thick
1 small red onion, peeled, halved, and thinly sliced
6 scallions, trimmed and thinly sliced
1 cup washed and dried basil leaves
½ to ¾ cup extra-virgin olive oil
Salt and freshly ground black pepper

Cut the crusts off the bread and discard. Cut the bread into ½-inch cubes. Spread out on a tray and set aside for 1 to 3 hours to dry.

Transfer the bread cubes to a large bowl and

sprinkle with 2 tablespoons of the vinegar. Toss well. The bread should be wet but not dripping or soaked; add the remaining vinegar slowly, as necessary, until the bread is just wet.

Add the tomatoes, cucumber, onion, and scallion to the bowl and mix gently. With your hands, tear the basil leaves into small pieces and add to the bowl. Drizzle with the olive oil, sprinkle with salt and pepper to taste, and mix again. Serve immediately or refrigerate up to 4 hours before serving.

PRO TIP: *Stale bread absorbs the dressing without becoming slimy, as fresh bread might. If you only have fresh bread, cut it into cubes and dry it out in a 175°F oven.*

RAW MUSHROOM SALAD WITH LEMON AND PROSCIUTTO DI PARMA

I HAVE A REAL SOFT SPOT FOR THIS RECIPE. *How many times in your life does a salad buy you a trip to Italy?*

The makers of Prosciutto di Parma, the finest prosciutto in Italy (or anywhere), invited a group of American chefs to Giuliano Bugialli's Manhattan town house to make their best dishes using prosciutto; the prize was a trip to Parma. As instructed, we arrived at 9 A.M.; the judging was to start at noon. As the other chefs whipped out their tools and started working, I settled down to read a book. By 11:30, everyone thought I was nuts. At 11:45, I minced a stalk of celery, sliced a few mushrooms, arranged the prosciutto on the plate, and shaved a little Parmigiano on top. A squeeze of lemon juice,

a drizzle of olive oil, and I had the prizewinning salad!

The combination of Prosciutto di Parma and Parmigiano-Reggiano cheese makes perfect sense; they come from the same region and are often used together. In fact, the Parmigiano cheesemakers are the ones who raise the pigs for Prosciutto di Parma; the pigs are fattened on whey and other by-products of cheesemaking, then sold to the makers of prosciutto.

MAKES 4 TO 6 SERVINGS

12 large cremini mushrooms, cleaned
1 stalk celery, peeled and minced (see Pro Tip)
½ cup crumbled or shaved Parmesan cheese
Freshly squeezed juice of 1 lemon
¼ cup extra-virgin olive oil
Salt and freshly ground black pepper
About 18 paper-thin slices Prosciutto di Parma (about 8 ounces)
4 to 6 sprigs fresh basil

Slice the mushrooms as thin as possible and transfer to a medium mixing bowl. Add the celery, Parmesan cheese, lemon juice, olive oil, and salt and pepper to taste. Mix gently, then taste for seasonings.

Place three slices of prosciutto on each serving plate. Spoon the mushroom mixture over the prosciutto, then top with a sprig of basil. Serve immediately.

PRO TIP: *When using raw celery in a salad, peel the back of each stalk with a vegetable peeler before mincing it. This removes the tough fibers and strings.*

CLASSIC ITALIAN SEAFOOD SALAD

I ALWAYS REMEMBER THE MEALS THAT I'VE *had right after arriving in Italy. One evening we flew into Rome and had a long drive to Naples ahead of us. Spending the night on the coast, in Anzio, seemed like a good idea. When we walked into the local trattoria, al fresco platters of poached seafood caught our eye. The chef came out with a skillet and tossed handfuls of octopus, squid, shrimp, and mussels into it. He squeezed a lemon over it, broke off a few dried peppers and crumbled them in too, then doused the whole thing with Tuscan olive oil. And then he made it even better: He warmed the salad in the skillet just to body temperature, to release the perfume of the oil. When I think about this recipe, I can still taste it. Walk into any restaurant on the long, long coast of Italy, and you'll find some version of this fantastic salad.*

The method is important here: The octopus is boiled in unsalted water because it is cooked for a long time and could become too salty; salt and wine are added for the quick cooking of the calamari, shrimp, and scallops. If necessary, you can adjust the seafood choices to suit your taste; or use precooked calamari and octopus. The salad is best made and served the same day; refrigerating it won't ruin it, but it's much better held at room temperature. And of course, you can warm it in a skillet just before serving if you like.

MAKES 6 TO 10 SERVINGS

FOR THE SEAFOOD
- ½ pound cleaned octopus
- 3 tablespoons salt
- 1 bay leaf
- 1 bottle (750 ml) light, dry white wine

- 1 pound cleaned small calamari, cut into rings
- 8 sea scallops
- 16 medium-size shrimp, peeled and deveined
- 1 clove garlic, smashed and peeled
- 3 tablespoons extra-virgin olive oil
- 24 littleneck clams
- 24 small cultivated mussels
- Pinch of hot red pepper flakes

FOR THE SALAD
- 1 stalk celery, minced
- ¼ red onion, minced
- Pinch of hot red pepper flakes, or more to taste
- Salt
- ¼ cup freshly chopped Italian parsley
- Freshly squeezed juice of 2 lemons
- ½ cup extra-virgin olive oil
- Freshly ground black pepper

To cook the seafood, bring a large pot of unsalted water to a boil. Add the octopus and boil for 45 minutes, or until tender when pierced with a knife. Lift out of the pot, drain, and set aside to cool.

Add the salt, bay leaf, and ½ cup of the wine to the boiling water. Add the calamari to the pot and boil for about 5 minutes, or until tender when pierced with a knife. Lift out of the pot, drain, and set aside to cool.

Reduce the heat to a bare simmer. Add the scallops and poach until just firm, about 5 minutes. Lift out of the pot, drain, and set aside to cool. Add the shrimp to the pot and poach until just firm, about 4 minutes. Lift out of the pot, drain, and set aside to cool.

In a large skillet with a lid, combine the garlic and olive oil. Heat over medium-high heat until the garlic begins to turn golden brown, then add the clams and mussels, hot red pepper flakes, and remaining wine. Reduce the heat to a simmer, cover, and cook until the shells have opened, about 5 minutes. Let cool in the liquid, then remove from the shells and transfer to a large serving bowl. Reserve about ¼ cup of the liquid. Discard the shells and any mussels and clams that don't open.

To finish the salad, cut the octopus, scallops, and shrimp into 1-inch pieces and transfer to the serving bowl. Add the calamari, celery, onion, hot pepper flakes, salt to taste, and parsley, and mix well. Add the lemon juice and about 3 tablespoons of cooking liquid (the mixture should not be too wet). Mix again and add the oil a little bit at a time, mixing after each addition and tasting as you go. There should be plenty of olive oil, but the salad shouldn't taste greasy. Taste for salt and pepper. Mix thoroughly and serve at room temperature, or warm in a skillet just before serving.

VITELLO TONNATO WITH ROSEMARY WHITE BEANS

ONE THING I NOTICED WHEN COOKING IN *Europe is that while we prefer our mayonnaise hidden in a sandwich or mixed into a salad, Europeans love it nice and thick as a sauce for chilled vegetables, meat, or fish.* Vitello tonnato *is an extremely popular Italian summer entrée, and is considered very classy. It may sound a little strange—sliced cold veal with a tuna-flavored mayonnaise on top— but it really works and is very refreshing with a tomato salad.*

I developed this recipe at first by roasting the veal instead of poaching it, as in the classic recipe. Poaching is hard to do perfectly, takes some flavor

out of an already mild meat, and leaves you with no tasty crust on your slices.

MAKES 4 TO 8 SERVINGS

2 cups dried white beans, such as cannellini or Great Northern
¼ cup extra-virgin olive oil
2 teaspoons chopped fresh rosemary leaves
Salt and freshly ground black pepper
One 2-pound veal loin, tied for roasting (your butcher will do this for you)
½ to 1 cup dry white wine
1 cup mayonnaise
One 2-ounce can imported Italian olive oil–packed tuna, drained
1 tablespoon brine from a jar of capers
Dash of Worcestershire sauce
1 tablespoon brine-cured capers
¼ cup minced celery
2 tablespoons minced fresh chives

To cook the beans, put them in a pot and cover with 8 cups cold water. Soak overnight or up to 24 hours, changing the water every 8 hours or so. Drain, rinse, and transfer to a large pot with a lid. Cover the beans completely with cold water. Cover and bring to a boil. Reduce the heat and simmer until the beans are cooked through but not falling apart. Start checking them for doneness after 45 minutes; add boiling water as needed to keep the beans covered as they cook. When cooked, drain thoroughly and transfer to a mixing bowl. Add the olive oil, rosemary, and salt and pepper to taste and mix gently. Set aside to cool to room temperature.

To roast the veal, preheat the oven to 350°F for thirty minutes. Season the veal with salt and pepper. Place it in a roomy, heavy-bottomed roasting pan and roast for 5 minutes. Remove from the oven and pour the white wine over the veal, then return to the oven and continue roasting for 10 to 15 minutes more, basting every 5 minutes with the wine in the bottom of the pan or adding more wine. Roast until the meat reaches an internal temperature of 140°F. Remove from the oven, cover with foil, and let rest at least 15 minutes to let the juices settle. If possible, let cool to room temperature before slicing.

To make the tuna sauce, combine the mayonnaise, tuna, brine, and Worcestershire sauce in a food processor and blend until smooth. Refrigerate until ready to serve.

Slice the veal as thin as possible and fan the slices out on serving plates or on a platter. Spread each slice with a dab of tuna sauce and place a mound of beans at the base of the fan. Sprinkle the whole plate with capers, celery, and chives.

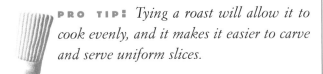 **PRO TIP:** *Tying a roast will allow it to cook evenly, and it makes it easier to carve and serve uniform slices.*

GRILLED BEEF "CARPACCIO" WITH TOMATO AND RED ONION

IN MY EXPERIENCE, FOOD TASTES BEST AT THE *end of an unpleasant trip to a great place, when you're exhausted, excited, and relieved to have gotten where you're going. On one summer vacation in Italy, we decided it was time to see some of the south. We headed for the heel of Italy's boot, but we hit a blister: a smoggy town on the Adriatic. The sea had warmed to the temperature of a* bathtub, *the city was hot as hell, and we couldn't wait to get out. I drove north like a maniac and made it to Orvieto, in Umbria, before collapsing at a villa with a quiet courtyard, a small restaurant, and a hammock. The short lunch menu included this dish, which sent me off to the hammock for the best nap of my entire life.*

The carpaccio, *normally top-quality beef sliced and served raw, was cooked on just one side, making it firmer and more flavorful; serving sliced tomato and onion together reminded me of the classic New York steakhouse salad I love. This would make a substantial summer appetizer with a simple pasta afterward, or a light entrée on its own. If you don't want to grill the meat, sear it in a very hot grill pan or nonstick pan. Have all of the ingredients prepared before you cook the meat.*

MAKES 4 SERVINGS

Four 2-ounce filet mignons, pounded thin and layered between pieces of butcher paper or wax paper (your butcher will do this for you)
Salt and freshly ground black pepper
2 ripe tomatoes, thinly sliced
½ red onion, very thinly sliced
1 cup thinly sliced Parmesan cheese
4 small handfuls arugula
4 tablespoons extra-virgin olive oil
2 lemons, halved

Heat a nonstick or cast-iron frying pan over medium-high heat until very hot. Peel the paper off one filet, season it on both sides with salt and pepper, and place in the hot pan. Sear on both sides, cooking each side no more than 1 minute. Transfer to a serving plate. Repeat with remaining filets.

Divide the tomatoes, onion, Parmesan, and

arugula on top of the filets, working in that order. Season with salt and pepper to taste. Drizzle each plate with 1 tablespoon olive oil and serve immediately, garnished with the lemon halves.

PRO TIP: *Ask your butcher to pound the meat thin (as for scaloppine) and layer it between pieces of butcher paper. Keep it refrigerated until the last minute and it will be easy to peel it off the paper.*

ROASTED PEPPERS

PRESENTING AN AL FRESCO BUFFET IS ALL *about color, and a platter of gleaming red peppers is just what I like to see (not to mention the fact that they are delicious and go with every dish known to man). Roasted peppers preserved in olive oil (sott'olio) perk up winter meals all over Italy. Roasted peppers are so easy to make that there is no recipe for them. But there is a method and a couple of pointers.*

Roast as many red peppers (or yellow peppers; green peppers aren't sweet enough) as you like on a grill, or over a gas flame, or even on a hot griddle, turning them occasionally, until the skins are black all over. You can also bake them on a sheet pan in a 550°F oven. Don't rush the cooking: the more the skins are cooked, the easier it will be to get them off later. As they are roasted, put them in a paper bag and close the top, so the peppers will steam their skins loose. Leave them for 20 minutes or so.

Now comes the hard part: peeling them. Yes, it's tempting to run them under water. But if you do that, you'll watch the beautiful red and yellow oils swirling down the drain. They should be in your

mouth. There are many shortcuts in good cooking, but you can't do anything that compromises the dish: Rinsing peppers ruins them. Rub the skins off, and don't worry if some flecks of black skin remain on the peppers. (For your own sake, have a fingernail brush handy afterward.)

To serve, slice the peppers into 1-inch-wide strips and arrange on a platter. Drizzle them with extravirgin olive oil (or warm the oil with a couple of smashed garlic cloves first). Serve at room temperature, preferably without refrigerating them first.

PEPERONATA

WHEN RED PEPPERS AREN'T ROASTED IN AN *Italian kitchen, it's usually because they're being cooked in olive oil into a sweet, bright red concentrate called* peperonata. *Southern Italians like them cooked until very soft, almost a jam, called* pasticce de Dante *after the poet, who supposedly wrote the recipe. This recipe has the Sicilian touch of capers, and you can cook it less or more, as you prefer. It is great as part of an antipasto platter, or with grilled meats and fish as a kind of* condimento, *or relish. This can be made up to three days before you plan to serve it and refrigerated or even frozen. Bring to room temperature before serving.*

MAKES ABOUT 12 SERVINGS

½ cup extra-virgin olive oil
1 large red onion, diced
2 large cloves garlic, thickly sliced
2 anchovies, rinsed of oil or salt and boned if necessary

CONTINUED

ROASTED PEPPERS WITH FRESH BASIL LEAVES IN A BURNT ORANGE TERRA-COTTA DISH.

4 red bell peppers, cored, seeded, and cut into
    1-inch pieces
4 yellow bell peppers, cored, seeded, and cut into
    1-inch pieces
2 green bell peppers, cored, seeded, and cut into
    1-inch pieces
2 teaspoons capers, rinsed of vinegar or salt
10 ripe plum tomatoes, diced, or 2½ cups milled
    or crushed canned Italian tomatoes
Pinch of hot red pepper flakes
Salt and freshly ground black pepper

In a large skillet, heat the olive oil over medium heat. Add the onion and garlic and cook, stirring, until the onion is wilted, about 3 minutes. Add the anchovies, peppers, capers, tomatoes, and red pepper flakes, stirring to break up the anchovies. Reduce the heat to a simmer and cook for about 45 minutes, until the peppers are very soft.

Taste for salt and pepper. Serve warm or at room temperature.

PRO TIP: *When cooking with anchovies, add them to the pot after you've sautéed the onion and garlic but before adding the other ingredients. This gives them a chance to "melt" in the oil and flavor the dish smoothly and evenly.*

TOMATOES PROVENÇALE

EVERY SUMMER, PEOPLE FROM ALL OVER THE *world flock to the French Riviera for fun, sun, bouillabaisse, and tomatoes Provençale. The south of France is the only resort area in the world that also has a terrific local cuisine. I had the best bouillabaisse of my life at a restaurant near Nice called Tatou, which is also famous for its tomatoes Provençale. These are halved tomatoes, gently baked for almost 5 hours, reducing them to a light casserole of pure tomato, incredibly rich in flavor. If you had told me that I had died and gone to heaven while I was scooping this up with chunks of bread, I wouldn't have been at all surprised. The chef was kind enough to share the recipe with me.*

MAKES 6 TO 10 SERVINGS

8 large, ripe round tomatoes (plum tomatoes will
    not work)
Salt
3 tablespoons extra-virgin olive oil, divided
2½ cups Traditional Tomato Sauce (page 133)
3 tablespoons plain dried bread crumbs
Parmesan for sprinkling
8 slices fresh goat cheese (optional)

Preheat the oven to 250°F.

Cut the tomatoes in half and arrange them, cut side up, on a sheet pan with sides. Sprinkle salt over the tops. Bake for 2½ hours, until the tomatoes are somewhat dry. Do not turn off the oven.

Use 2 tablespoons of the olive oil to grease a baking dish just large enough to hold the tomato halves in a single layer and place them in it (or divide them in threes or fours among individual baking dishes). Gently pour the tomato sauce evenly over the tomatoes. Sprinkle on the bread crumbs, then the Parmesan. Bake, uncovered, 2 hours more. If desired, lay the slices of goat cheese on top for the last 15 minutes of cooking. Drizzle the remaining tablespoon of olive oil over and let cool slightly before serving, or serve at room temperature.

PRO TIP: *When cooking whole or halved tomatoes, move them as little as possible during the cooking. As they heat, the skins become very delicate and the tomatoes can easily fall apart.*

CAPONATA

WELL, I'M NOT GOING TO LIE TO YOU. Caponata *isn't one of those speedy weeknight dishes you can start cooking at 7:00 P.M. and have on the table at 7:30 (you'll find those on page 175). But it is one of the great recipes of the Italian tradition, a slow-cooked mix of ripe summer vegetables flavored with the contrasts of vinegar and sugar, capers and raisins, olives and sweet peppers. It turns eggplant into something like a jam and something like a salad. Trust me. It's wonderful. Every time I give someone a spoonful to taste, they come back for a plateful.*

Caponata *belongs to a family of dishes that we don't eat much of anymore—home-preserved vegetable relishes and chutneys. In traditional Italian home cooking, they take the form of vegetables preserved in jars with spices and salt, called* condimenti *(roasted peppers and marinated artichoke hearts are also in the family). All winter long, the flavors keep getting deeper as they're brought out to serve with simple grilled meat or fish meals, or dinners of cheese, salame, and bread. Caponata, with*

its sweet and sour flavors, is a classic Sicilian condimento; *the combination of raisins, sugar, and vinegar gives away the Arab origin of the dish.*

MAKES ABOUT **10** SERVINGS

2 medium eggplant (do not peel), cut into
    ½-inch dice
2 teaspoons kosher salt
1 cup all-purpose flour
2 cups vegetable oil
½ cup olive oil
1 medium onion, diced
1 clove garlic, thickly sliced
4 stalks celery, sliced ¼ inch thick
2 red bell peppers, cored, seeded, and cut into
    1-inch pieces
2 yellow bell peppers, cored, seeded, and cut into
    1-inch pieces
One 16-ounce can Italian plum tomatoes,
    crushed or milled, or 6 ripe plum tomatoes,
    diced
2 teaspoons sugar, or to taste
¼ cup red wine vinegar, or to taste
1 teaspoon capers, rinsed of vinegar or salt
½ cup pitted green olives, chopped
½ cup golden raisins
Salt and freshly ground black pepper

Place the eggplant cubes in a colander and sprinkle with the kosher salt to draw out the juices. Place the colander in a larger bowl or on a tray to catch the juices, cover with a towel, and refrigerate 2 to 24 hours. Do not rinse; pat the cubes dry on paper towels.

Place the flour in a shallow bowl. Line a baking sheet with paper towels. In a deep, heavy skillet, heat the vegetable oil over medium-high heat until hot but not smoking. Working in batches to avoid crowding the pan, roll the eggplant pieces in the flour, shake off any excess, and add to the hot oil. Fry until golden brown, turning once, remove with a slotted spoon, and drain on the prepared baking sheet.

Preheat the oven to 400°F.

In an ovenproof pot with a lid, heat the olive oil over medium heat. Add the onion, garlic, celery, and peppers, and cook, stirring, until the onion is translucent, about 5 minutes. Add the tomatoes, reduce the heat to a simmer, and cook, uncovered, 15 minutes. Stir in the sugar, vinegar, capers, olives, raisins, cooked eggplant, salt and pepper to taste, and mix well. Cover and bake 10 minutes. Taste for sugar, vinegar, salt, and pepper, let cool, and serve at room temperature.

VIDALIA ONION CONFIT

AT THE MONTREUX PALACE, THE FIVE-STAR *hotel where I worked in Switzerland, we served incredible amounts of pâtés and terrines each day. The clients loved the rich, traditional flavors, but I was just as interested in the savory pickled vegetables we served alongside. I come from the Jewish pickle-loving tradition, but I never knew that pickled onions could taste so fancy—and so good. This confit (the word has about eighteen different meanings, but it generally refers to some kind of slow-cooked pickle or preserve) is great with fish, meat, or vegetables, making it a regular on my buffet tables.*

In the Montreux Palace kitchen, we simmered the onions in wine until they were almost reduced to a paste. Back in the States, I use our naturally sweet Vidalia onions from Georgia, balancing out their sweetness with a little stock. The amount of sugar you add will depend on how naturally sweet

the onions are. White wine gives a more oniony result, but red wine would also be a great cooking medium here.

MAKES ABOUT 12 SERVINGS

½ cup extra-virgin olive oil
6 large Vidalia white or red onions, thinly sliced
3 cups dry white wine
1 cup Chicken Stock (page 15), Vegetable Stock (page 17), or low-sodium canned broth
Salt and freshly ground black pepper
2 tablespoons sugar, or to taste

In a large heavy pot with a lid, heat the olive oil over medium heat. Add the onions and cook, stirring, until translucent, 8 to 10 minutes.

Add the wine, stock, salt and pepper to taste, and sugar, reduce the heat to a bare simmer, cover, and cook about 1 hour, until the onions are meltingly soft. Check the pot occasionally; if the mixture seems to be drying out, add more liquid 1 tablespoon at a time. Taste for salt, pepper, and sugar and serve hot or at room temperature.

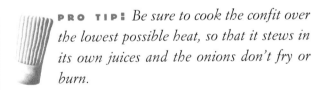 **PRO TIP:** *Be sure to cook the confit over the lowest possible heat, so that it stews in its own juices and the onions don't fry or burn.*

ITALIAN POTATO-BASIL SALAD

WHEN I BEGAN COOKING RUSTIC ITALIAN FOOD, *I have to admit I was a little inhibited. I was so afraid of violating some sacred peasant recipe that I followed every tradition to the letter! It wasn't until I'd made several serious eating trips to the Italian countryside—especially the great food regions of Tuscany, Emilia-Romagna, and Sicily— that I realized that I could cook their classics as well as an Italian chef. That's when I started developing recipes for a few of my own dishes within the Italian tradition.*

This dish is a great example. Pesto and potatoes are traditionally served together in trenette al pesto, *a classic dish of Liguria that combines long flat pasta with potatoes, green beans, and pesto. And the combination of fish and potatoes is true to the traditions of the Tuscan coast. I developed this recipe for Sapore di Mare, a Tuscan-inspired seafood restaurant; frankly, it's the best summer side dish for fish I've ever had. Without the cheese and nuts, which would make the pesto too rich (not to mention making it slide off the potatoes), the dressing is absorbed.*

MAKES ABOUT 6 SERVINGS

24 small new red, yellow, or white potatoes, scrubbed (do not peel)
½ cup extra-virgin olive oil
2 cloves garlic, smashed and peeled
1 medium red onion, minced
12 large leaves fresh basil
2 tablespoons chopped fresh chives
¼ cup freshly chopped Italian parsley
3 tablespoons red wine vinegar
Salt and freshly ground black pepper

Put the potatoes in a medium pot and cover with salted water. Cover, bring to a boil, and boil until tender but not falling apart, about 12 minutes. Drain and let cool at least 10 minutes. When cool enough to handle but still warm, peel the potatoes and slice them ½ inch thick. Transfer to a large mixing bowl.

In a blender or food processor, or using a hand blender, puree the remaining ingredients. Pour over the potatoes, mix gently, and set aside for at least 1 hour to let the flavors meld. Taste for salt and pepper. Serve at room temperature.

PRO TIP: *After boiling the potatoes, let them cool for at least 10 minutes before peeling or slicing them—not only so that you can touch them but to let the starch settle back into the potatoes. If you peel and slice them too soon, the starch could make your salad gummy.*

FUNGHI ALLA GRIGLIA

IF YOU SPEND ENOUGH TIME IN TUSCANY, *you rarely have to look at a menu. Depending on the season, you'll already know exactly what everyone is eating—and any time of year, you know it will probably be cooked* alla griglia, *on the grill. Fall is the time for* Funghi alla Griglia: *perfectly grilled, moist and smoky samples of the region's plentiful mushroom crop. I love mushrooms cooked this way.*

Although a squeeze of lemon and a dribble of oil are all you really need to dress them, this anchovy-garlic dressing (a Roman classic) pairs well with mushrooms. Lemon and oil are still the main ingredients, but the salinity of anchovy and the punch of garlic really wake up the dish, especially if you're using cultivated mushrooms, which are more subtly flavored than the wild ones. Serve over greens for a substantial appetizer or a light entrée—or add a platter of fennel salad and one of grilled tuna, and you have a buffet.

MAKES 6 SERVINGS

FOR THE DRESSING

   1 anchovy, rinsed of oil or salt, deboned if
      necessary
   2 cloves garlic, smashed and peeled
   Freshly squeezed juice of 2 lemons
   10 tablespoons extra-virgin olive oil
   2 tablespoons freshly chopped Italian
      parsley
   Salt and freshly ground black pepper

FOR THE MUSHROOMS

   6 to 12 large mushrooms, such as portobello,
      cremini, oyster, porcini, or hen-of-the-woods,
      wiped clean and left whole
   ¼ cup extra-virgin olive oil
   Salt

To make the dressing, blend the anchovy and garlic into a paste in a food processor or mortar. Transfer to a small bowl and stir in the lemon juice, olive oil, parsley, and salt and pepper to taste. Set aside to let the flavors meld.

Heat a grill or broiler, or preheat the oven to 475°F. Lightly brush the mushrooms with the olive oil and sprinkle with salt.

If using a grill, place the mushrooms, cap side down, on the grate. Grill 1 minute, then rotate ¼ turn to create X marks on the cap. Grill 2 more minutes, then turn the mushrooms over and continue cooking until tender. Test by piercing the mushrooms with the tip of a knife.

If using a broiler or the oven, place the mushrooms, cap side up, on a baking sheet. Broiled mushrooms should be turned every 2 minutes; baked mushrooms need not be turned at all.

When cooked, drizzle with the dressing (or just extra-virgin olive oil) and serve immediately. Or let cool to room temperature and serve.

PRO TIP: *Mushrooms have so much natural moisture that I prefer very hot, dry cooking methods for them, such as grilling, broiling, or baking. The moisture evaporates into steam instead of seeping out into a pan and making the mushrooms soggy.*

SUMMER TOMATO SOUP

I LOVE TOMATO SAUCE MADE WITH FINE SAN *Marzano tomatoes as much as the next chef, but for tomato soup, give me a good old American beefsteak. I can't resist buying tons of ripe local tomatoes at summer's end, knowing that I won't see them again for an eternity. This quick soup is like the best tomato juice you can imagine; I like it cold or hot. Slightly fortified with basil and stock, it's barely cooked at all, so the tastes are fresh tomato and fresh basil, and the color is bright red. There's nothing simpler or more perfect. As often happens in three-star Michelin restaurants, you'll be overwhelmed by how underwhelming—yet incredible—this soup is.*

Of course, if you have ripe yellow or orange tomatoes to mix with the red, that would also make a great soup.

MAKES **8** TO **10** SERVINGS

¼ cup extra-virgin olive oil
1 large onion, minced
1 clove garlic, thickly sliced
16 large, very ripe tomatoes, quartered, with
    their juices
1 cup Chicken Stock (page 15), low-sodium
    canned broth, or tomato juice
Salt and freshly ground black pepper
¼ cup fresh basil leaves, julienned, plus extra for
    garnish

In a large, heavy pot, heat the olive oil over medium heat. Add the onion and garlic and cook, stirring, until the onion is wilted, about 3 minutes. Add the tomatoes with their juices. Heat to a simmer and simmer about 15 minutes, until the tomatoes lose their raw look. Add the stock, salt and pepper to taste, and basil. Simmer gently until the

tomatoes have melted slightly into the soup, about 10 minutes.

Remove the soup from the heat. When the soup has cooled enough to work with safely, pass it through a food mill or rub it through a fine sieve to remove the skins and seeds. Reheat over a low flame or chill until very cold. Taste for salt and pepper. Serve garnished with basil.

 PRO TIP: *This is a case where a hand blender can't be used to puree the soup—it will not remove the tomato skins.*

WATERCRESS SOUP

A GOOD WATERCRESS SOUP IS LIKE YOUR *favorite black dress or suit—understated, but it makes you look truly fabulous, slightly European, and elegantly mysterious, not to mention thin.*

Watercress soup is where classic cooking started for me. The traditional recipe calls for a butter-and-flour velouté base that is both rich and difficult to make. I was lucky enough to get one of my first looks at French cuisine by working with Michel Guérard at New York's Le Train Bleu, when his lightened cuisine minceur *was all the rage. That's why this near-classic is thickened with potatoes. It's a terrific combination: peppery, bitingly pungent cress with floury, earthy potato. I add spinach to preserve the bright green color. Cold or hot, this soup is one of my favorites, and it goes with everything.*

MAKES 8 TO 10 SERVINGS

¼ cup extra-virgin olive oil
1 onion, minced
1 clove garlic, minced
1 leek, trimmed, split, well rinsed, and cut into
    1-inch pieces
2 medium potatoes, peeled and cut into eighths
2 quarts Chicken Stock (page 15), Vegetable
    Stock (page 17), low-sodium canned broth,
    or water
8 bunches watercress, coarsely chopped
1 bunch fresh spinach, coarsely chopped or one
    10-ounce box frozen spinach, thawed,
    drained, and chopped
Salt
Baked Croutons (page 18)

In a large, heavy pot, heat the olive oil over medium heat. Add the onion, garlic, and leek and cook, stirring, until the onion is wilted, about 3 minutes. Add the potatoes and cook, stirring, 2 minutes more. Add the stock, half of the watercress, the spinach, and salt to taste. Reduce the heat and simmer about 45 minutes, until the potatoes are very soft. Add the remaining watercress and cook 10 more minutes.

In a blender or food processor, or using a hand blender, puree the soup. Return to the pot and either reheat or cool to room temperature, then refrigerate until very cold. Taste for salt. Serve hot or cold, garnished with croutons.

PRO TIP: *Saving half the watercress for the end of the cooking ensures that the soup will have the bright green color you want.*

GRILLED VEGETABLE FEAST

IN MY COOKING CLASSES, I GET ASKED MORE *questions about grilled vegetables than anything else. People who think nothing of throwing a steak or some swordfish on the grill get all shy when I introduce them to an eggplant. Well, I'm here to tell you that it's no miracle. It's just a little bit different.*

Grilling vegetables has to be done over lower heat, since crusty on the outside and rare on the inside is not the goal here. Vegetables are not steak. Vegetables should always be cooked all the way through, and in the case of grilling, it's better to risk overcooking than undercooking. Keep the vegetables cooking slowly on the perimeter of the grill, or wait until the fire has died down to a medium heat. Be patient.

Some vegetables are oiled before cooking, some after, depending on how long they take to cook. Thinly sliced soft vegetables like zucchini or eggplant will be incinerated if you oil them.

To make your grilled vegetable feast even more festive, set out bowls of different dressings, such as garlic-anchovy (page 215), Basil Puree (page 18), or Fresh Herb Dressing (page 77). You can grill all the vegetables in advance, set them out on platters, and be a guest at your own party.

Asparagus must be precooked before grilling. Boil in salted water with a tablespoon of butter. Trim spears and boil 3 minutes, then remove to a bowl filled with ice water. Drain and pat dry, then grill 4 to 5 minutes, rotating every 2 minutes and cooking until the spears are tender at the center and lightly charred on the outside. Drizzle with extra-virgin olive oil immediately after cooking.

Beets must be precooked before grilling. Boil unpeeled beets in unsalted water 25 to 30 minutes, until tender. Drain and set aside until cool enough to handle. Peel and slice about ½ inch thick. Brush with olive oil and sprinkle with salt. Grill 1 minute, rotate 45 degrees to make an X mark, and grill 1 minute more. Turn and repeat, cooking until heated through and lightly charred on the outside. Drizzle with extra-virgin olive oil immediately after cooking.

Eggplant must be cooked over medium heat; hotter temperatures will burn it without cooking the center. To prepare eggplant for grilling, slice them lengthwise into ½-inch-thick slices at least 3 or up to 24 hours before grilling. Sprinkle generously with salt on both sides and let drain on paper or kitchen towels. Keep refrigerated. Just before grilling, rinse off the salt under running water and pat dry. Place on the grill without oil or salt. Cook 3 minutes, then rotate 45 degrees to make an X mark and cook 3 minutes more. Turn and repeat, cooking until dry on the outside and soft in the center; test by pressing a slice with your finger. Drizzle generously with extra-virgin olive oil, salt, and pepper immediately after cooking.

Fennel need not be precooked, but it's important to keep the slices thin so they cook through. Trim the stems and leaves to about 1 inch from the bulb; do not core. Slice lengthwise into ¼-inch slices, trying to keep the slices whole. Brush with olive oil, sprinkle with salt, and place on the grill. Cook 2 minutes, then rotate 45 degrees to make an X mark and cook 2 minutes more. Turn and repeat, cooking until limp, tender, and very slightly charred. Drizzle generously with extra-virgin olive oil, salt, and pepper immediately after cooking.

Mushrooms with large caps, such as portobello, cremini, porcini, and large button mushrooms, are best for grilling. Mushrooms with small or no caps, such as oyster or hen-of-the-woods, are fine as long as they are large enough not to fall through the grill. Snap or slice off the stems, then prebake: Preheat the oven to 350°F, place the caps on a baking sheet, brush the tops with olive oil, sprinkle with salt, and bake until soft, 10 to 15 minutes. (This can be done up to a day ahead; store prebaked mushrooms tightly wrapped in the refrigerator until ready to grill.) When ready to grill, brush with olive oil and sprinkle with salt and pepper. Cook 2 to 3 minutes, then rotate 45 degrees to create an X mark and cook 2 to 3 minutes more. Turn and repeat, cooking until limp and slightly charred around the edges. Drizzle with extra-virgin olive oil immediately after cooking.

Onions can be grilled raw, but it does take some time, 30 to 45 minutes. It's best to keep the onions cooking slowly around the edges of the grill while other things cook in the hot center. Use large onions and cut them in half crosswise, without peeling. Sprinkle the cut sides with salt and place them cut side down on the grill. Without turning, cook them slowly until the cut side is very brown to black and the flesh within is soft, sweet, and translucent. Drizzle with extra-virgin olive oil immediately after cooking.

Tomatoes must be large to grill well. Stem and core the tomatoes, then cut in half horizontally. Sprinkle with salt and pepper and rub with olive oil. Place cut side down on the grill and grill 2 to 3 minutes without moving. Turn the tomatoes over and cook about 10 minutes, until soft. Remove carefully and drizzle with extra-virgin olive oil immediately after cooking.

Zucchini grill beautifully. Tiny ones should be cut in half lengthwise; larger ones cut lengthwise into ¼-inch-thick slices. Do not oil or salt the slices; place them directly on the grill. Cook 1 minute, then rotate 45 degrees to create an X mark and cook 1 minute more. Turn and repeat, cooking until limp and slightly charred around the edges. Drizzle with extra-virgin olive oil and sprinkle with salt and pepper immediately after cooking.

Bruschetta, grilled bread with olive oil, is a perfect accompaniment to grilled vegetables. Start with 1- or 2-day-old peasant bread. If using a round loaf, cut into quarters. Slice ½ to ¾ inch thick. Grill 1 minute, rotate 45 degrees to make an X mark, and grill 1 minute more. Turn and repeat, cooking until heated through and lightly charred on the outside. Rub the edges of the bread with a cut clove of garlic on one or both sides of the bread, as you like. Drizzle with extra-virgin olive oil immediately after cooking, or top with chopped tomato and basil, chopped tomato and onion, or anything you like.

SICILIAN PEPPERS STUFFED WITH RICE

THERE'S REAL ITALIAN FOOD, AND THEN *there's what I call "Brooklyn Italian," the Italian food my family used to go out for on special occasions. Whatever borough the restaurant was in, it always had the same Italian-American menu, with plenty of meat, cheese, peppers, and tomato sauce. I wasn't into Jewish traditions like chopped liver and gefilte fish; even then, I liked Italian comfort food best.*

The food at those restaurants was never "authentic" (it is a version of southern Italian home cooking, with more meat and huge portions), but it sure was good. When I was growing up, the Italian family next door ate this all the time; the hallway always smelled great. Stuffed peppers are a classic dish from the region around Naples, and I had this version on the nearby Amalfi coast in Salerno.

MAKES 6 TO 12 SERVINGS

¼ cup extra-virgin olive oil
2 cloves garlic, minced
1 red onion, diced
1 small green bell pepper, cored, seeded, and diced
1 pound ground veal, or a combination of veal and beef
1 cup milled or crushed canned Italian tomatoes
⅛ teaspoon hot red pepper flakes
1 cup cooked white rice
3 tablespoons freshly grated Parmesan cheese
2 large eggs, lightly beaten
½ cup plain dried bread crumbs
1 teaspoon dried oregano
2 tablespoons freshly chopped Italian parsley, plus extra for garnish
Salt and freshly ground black pepper
6 medium-size red or yellow bell peppers

3 cups Traditional Tomato Sauce (page 133), Quick and Fresh Summer Tomato Sauce (page 134), or tomato sauce of your choice

Preheat the oven to 400°F.

In a large skillet, heat the olive oil over medium heat. Add the garlic, onion, and green pepper and cook, stirring, until the onion and pepper are wilted, about 5 minutes. Raise the heat to medium-high, add the veal, and cook, stirring, 2 minutes. Add the tomatoes and red pepper flakes and simmer gently until thickened, about 15 minutes. Transfer to a large mixing bowl and set aside to cool.

In a separate mixing bowl, combine the rice, cheese, eggs, bread crumbs, oregano, and parsley. Add to the veal mixture and mix together very well. Season with salt and pepper to taste.

Slice off the tops of the peppers and reserve them. Core and seed the peppers but leave them whole. Divide the veal mixture among the peppers, stuffing lightly and mounding the filling just above the tops. Rest a reserved pepper top on each. Transfer to a baking dish, cover with a lid or foil, and bake for 45 to 50 minutes, until the peppers are very tender.

When ready to serve, heat the tomato sauce. Place the peppers on a serving dish and ladle the sauce over them. Serve immediately, sprinkled with chopped parsley.

PRO TIP: *To make the peppers in advance, let cool after baking and refrigerate. When ready to serve, slice them in half vertically as they come out of the refrigerator, arrange on a platter, and let warm to room temperature. (Once they warm up, they'll be too crumbly to slice.) Pour the hot tomato sauce over them at the last minute.*

SUMMER BUFFET ALLA PARMA

IF MY DOCTOR SUDDENLY TOLD ME THAT IT *was a great idea to eat lots of meat and salt and cheese, I would eat this meal at least once a day for the rest of my life. I'm a talker and a nibbler, so I love to eat lots of little things, contrasting them, and trying them out together in new ways. Chefs love to eat with their hands.*

Parmigiano-Reggiano cheese, prosciutto, and various salumi *(cured meats and sausages) simply arranged on a cutting board; a platter of* Insalata Caprese; *celery sticks and crusty bread add up to a great meal. This is real Italian comfort food— delicious, savory, and undemanding. However you present it, whether on a rustic wooden table or a marble counter, it always looks like a still life.*

Cheese, olives, and cured meats are at their best flavor at room temperature, so give them plenty of time out of the refrigerator beforehand. For a picnic or summer buffet, this is an outstanding choice, great for big groups, warm evenings, or a combination of the two. All you need is access to a good Italian import store or catalog. You'll need about 3 ounces of cheese and 3 ounces of meat per person. In winter, instead of Caprese *salad and vegetable antipasti, you could serve the meat and cheese with a big green salad and* condimenti *like* Peperonata *(page 30) or* Caponata *(page 33).*

Prosciutto di Parma, thinly sliced and fanned out
   on a plate
Sliced dried hot and sweet Italian sausages, such
   as *salame*, sopressata, cappicola
Parmigiano-Reggiano cheese, cut into large
   chunks
Celery sticks
Oil-cured black olives

1 recipe *Insalata Caprese* (page 25)
Assorted vegetable antipasti, such as Fennel and
   Orange Salad (page 66), Asparagus with
   Butter and Parmesan (page 215), and Beet
   and Lentil Salad (page 63)
Sourdough rolls and sliced peasant bread

ITALIAN PROSCIUTTO.

FARFALLE AL PORTOFINO

ITALIANS FIND AMERICAN PASTA SALADS VERY *strange, and I have to admit that when I see those tubs of "tortellini salad" with Elmer's-glue dressing, I have to agree. But there is a place for a well-seasoned, room-temperature pasta on an al fresco table. The secret is in the sauce.*

Some Italian pasta dishes, especially those made with summer vegetables, call for an uncooked sauce (salsa cruda), which can be as simple as chopped tomatoes marinated in herbs and olive oil. As it comes out of the pot and hits the bowl, the hot pasta heats the sauce, releasing the flavors and aromas of the tomatoes and olive oil. That's all the cooking the sauce gets. These pastas rely on plenty of top-quality olive oil for binding and flavor, and can be great at room temperature as long as they are never refrigerated. For other summery pastas, such as Spaghetti alla Pescatora or Fusilli Provençal, see the Pasta chapter (page 128).

This dish uses poached string beans and fresh shrimp, plus the punch of fresh lemon juice and sundried tomatoes, to keep the flavors alive. The arugula wilts but stays peppery; don't make the pasta until you're almost ready to serve the dish.

MAKES 4 TO 8 SERVINGS

- 1 pound raw medium shrimp, peeled and deveined, or 1 pound precooked shrimp
- ¼ pound thin string beans, trimmed
- 12 sundried tomatoes, cut into thin strips
- 8 ripe plum tomatoes, diced
- 2 bunches arugula, torn into bite-size pieces
- 2 tablespoons freshly chopped Italian parsley
- ⅓ cup fresh basil leaves, torn into small pieces
- 1 pound farfalle (bowtie) pasta
- ¼ cup extra-virgin olive oil
- Freshly squeezed juice of 1 lemon
- Salt and freshly ground black pepper

Arrange a steamer in a pot with a few inches of salted water. Bring to a boil, add the raw shrimp, cover and steam until just cooked through, about 5 minutes. (If using cooked shrimp, omit this step.) Remove the shrimp from the steamer and set aside to cool. Place the string beans in the steamer, cover, and steam until cooked through, about 10 minutes. Set aside to cool, then cut in half crosswise.

In a large serving bowl, combine the cooked shrimp and string beans, both kinds of tomatoes, arugula, parsley, and basil and mix.

In a large covered pot, heat to a boil a gallon of water with a tablespoon of salt. When it boils, add the pasta, stir well, and cover until it returns to a boil. Uncover and boil until just tender to the bite all the way through.

When the pasta is cooked, drain it well and immediately add it to the bowl. Add the oil, lemon juice, and salt and pepper to taste. Mix well and serve immediately or at room temperature.

PRO TIP: *To save time, cook the shrimp and string beans and dice up all the tomatoes ahead of time. Just before serving, cook the pasta; prepare the greens while it's cooking.*

HERB-ROASTED SWORDFISH WITH LEMON AND CAPER SAUCE

IN THE UNIVERSE OF FOOD, THERE ARE SOME *natural laws of attraction: potatoes and onions, anchovies and garlic, tomatoes and basil.*

Lemon and parsley is a another great one. Add butter and capers, and you have the perfect, simple sauce for fish. Variations of this idea are found in seafood restaurants all over France and Italy—from the northwestern tip of Brittany, where I had the perfect Dover sole à la meunière, *to the southeastern tip of Sicily, where swordfish, lemon, and capers are a perfect combination. Here's my favorite interpretation of these classic traditions—cooked in just fifteen minutes. Roasted herbs add a wonderful perfume. Summer side vegetables like tomatoes, eggplant, and zucchini are great with swordfish.*

MAKES 4 SERVINGS

8 sprigs fresh rosemary
8 sprigs fresh thyme
2 cloves garlic, thinly sliced
Four 8-ounce swordfish fillets
Olive oil
Salt and freshly ground black pepper
Freshly squeezed juice of 2 lemons
20 capers, rinsed of vinegar or salt
3 tablespoons cold unsalted butter
4 teaspoons freshly chopped Italian parsley

Preheat the oven to 450°F.

Place the whole herb sprigs in a bowl, cover with water, and soak 15 minutes. Lift them out of the water and arrange in a small roasting pan. Place the garlic slices on top. Rub each swordfish fillet with a teaspoon of the oil, then season with salt and pepper to taste. Arrange the fillets on top

of the herbs and bake 12 to 15 minutes, until cooked to your liking.

Remove the fish to a serving platter. Place the roasting pan with the herbs and garlic on top of the stove and add the lemon juice and capers. Simmer over medium-high heat for 1 minute. Remove the herb sprigs from the pan and divide on top of the fish fillets. Whisk the cold butter into the liquid in the pan until it melts and pour this sauce over the fish. Serve immediately garnished with the parsley.

PRO TIP: *Soaking the herbs well in water prevents them from burning while you cook the fish. You want the herbs to smolder and smoke, but not catch on fire.*

GRILLED TUNA WITH GRAIN SALAD

IF YOU'VE BEEN TO MY RESTAURANT CAM-
*pagna, this dish will need no introduction. It's one
of an exclusive group of time-tested dishes that
never goes off the menu. It is a great way to get your
grains. In the 70s, when I started cooking, only hip-
pies would eat wheat berries and barley. But time
has proven how nutritious grains are, and chefs
have demonstrated how good they can taste. A
nutty mixed-grain salad spiked with vegetables and
vinaigrette makes a perfect bed for tuna right off the
grill.*

*I always make this dish by preparing the grain
salad the day before (feel free to mix and match the
grains). To cook the grains, boil them separately in
plenty of salted water until just tender. Drain and
spread out on a sheet pan to cool so they don't stick
together. Wheat berries, barley, couscous, and beans
all swell to about double in size as they cook, so
start with ½ cup of each.*

MAKES 4 TO 8 SERVINGS

FOR THE GRAIN SALAD
  1 cup cooked pearl barley (see above)
  1 cup cooked wheat berries, cooled, or
      1 additional cup cooked pearl barley
  1 cup cooked couscous, cooled
  ½ cup cooked or canned white beans, cooled
  1 cup diced tomatoes
  ½ red bell pepper, cored, seeded, and diced
  ½ yellow bell pepper, cored, seeded, and diced
  1 scallion, white and pale green parts, thinly sliced
  ¼ cup freshly chopped Italian parsley
  2 tablespoons red wine vinegar
  ½ cup extra-virgin olive oil

  Salt and freshly ground black pepper
  1 teaspoon hot red pepper flakes, or to taste
  Lemon juice to taste

FOR THE TUNA
  Four 8-ounce tuna steaks
  Salt and freshly ground black pepper
  2 teaspoons extra-virgin olive oil
  Freshly squeezed juice of ½ lemon
  2 teaspoons dried oregano
  Lemon wedges

The day before you plan to serve the dish, make
the grain salad. Combine all of the salad ingredients in a mixing bowl. Mix well. Refrigerate until
1 hour before serving; let warm to room temperature. Taste for salt, pepper, hot red pepper flakes,
and lemon juice.

When ready to serve, make the tuna. Heat a
grill to very hot. Meanwhile, season the fillets with
salt and pepper and arrange them in a dish in a
single layer. Whisk together the olive oil, lemon
juice, and oregano and pour over the fish.

When the coals are hot, lift the fillets out of the
marinade, shaking to remove any excess, and
place on the grill. Grill 2 minutes, then rotate 45
degrees to make an X mark. Grill 2 minutes more,
then flip the fillets and repeat on the other side.
Grill until done to your liking. Remove to serving
plates and serve hot, with lemon wedges and grain
salad.

PRO TIP: *With practice, you can learn to
test fish for doneness without cutting into
it. Press the flesh with your finger. When it
feels plump and firm but with a little
"give," like a tire full of air, it is done.*

SALMON GRILLED OVER HERBS WITH SCALLION-BASIL DRESSING

ONE OF THE GOOD THINGS TO COME OUT OF *the nouvelle cuisine movement was the use of vinaigrettes as sauces. The deliciously rich meat glazes and butter sauces we used to cook weren't exactly low in fat! And they tended to distract you from the food underneath.*

Drizzling a room-temperature vinaigrette on hot food releases the aromas and flavors of both. Salmon is a strong-flavored fish, rugged enough to take a strong herb dressing. Salmon is a great fish for al fresco dining because it won't dry out on a buffet like other fish; the lemony vinaigrette helps on that front, too. And of course, salmon is a crowd pleaser as far as fish goes. Let the herbs burn down a little before placing the fish on the grill, so that the fish absorbs fragrant smoke, not searing flames.

MAKES 4 SERVINGS

Four 8-ounce salmon fillets
Salt and freshly ground black pepper
6 whole sprigs fresh rosemary
8 whole sprigs fresh thyme
6 whole sprigs fresh oregano
4 whole sprigs fresh sage
4 whole sprigs fresh marjoram (or use additional fresh oregano)
¼ cup balsamic vinegar
4 teaspoons extra-virgin olive oil

FOR THE DRESSING
½ cup extra-virgin olive oil
Freshly squeezed juice of 1 lemon
1 scallion, white and pale green portions, thinly sliced
2 ripe plum tomatoes, minced
8 fresh basil leaves, torn into small pieces
Salt

The day before you plan to serve the salmon, arrange the fillets in a nonreactive baking dish. Sprinkle with salt and pepper, lay the herbs on top, and drizzle on the vinegar and oil. Cover and refrigerate overnight or up to 24 hours.

Heat a grill to very hot. Lift the fillets out of the marinade (do not discard it) and transfer to a separate plate. Stir the herbs around in the marinade to make sure they are completely coated, then arrange them in 4 "beds" on the grill. Discard the marinade. Let the oil burn off and let the herbs begin to smoke and smolder. Then place the fillets, skin side up, on top of the herbs. Grill 5 to 6 minutes, then turn the fillets and grill 5 to 6 minutes more, until done to your liking. Remove the salmon to a serving platter.

Meanwhile, make the dressing. In a small skillet, warm the olive oil over medium-high heat. Add the lemon juice, scallion, tomatoes, and basil and salt to taste, simmer 1 minute to blend the flavors, and pour over the fish. Serve immediately.

PRO TIP: *Although you can vary the herbs you use for grilling, keep in mind that they must be "stick" herbs like rosemary, thyme, or oregano, not "soft" herbs like parsley or basil.*

CAMPAGNA GRILLED LOBSTER

ONE OF THE FIRST THINGS I LEARNED AT COOK-
*ing school is that you don't have to boil a lobster;
you can broil it. I was shocked by this radical idea.
But it's true: Broiling or grilling lobster in the shell
creates a hot oven for the lobster meat, and as the
shell chars, the smoky flavor is absorbed by the
meat. And that stronger seafood flavor is the perfect
complement to an herbed bread crumb stuffing.*

*I know it's tempting to use fewer, larger lobsters,
but lobsters larger than 2½ pounds tend to become
tough in the cooking. And really big ones are just
disturbing; my wife hasn't eaten lobster since the
night I cooked a 12-pounder, just to see what it
would be like. You don't have to butterfly the live
lobsters yourself. If you have the fish market do it,
just make sure you cook the lobsters within about
four hours. If you want bigger tails, ask for female
lobsters; bigger claws, ask for male. I prefer female
lobsters, because they provide roe to flavor the stuffing with, but it isn't necessary.*

MAKES 6 SERVINGS

FOR THE STUFFING
½ cup extra-virgin olive oil
6 cloves garlic, minced
2 cups plain dried bread crumbs
6 scallions, white and pale green parts, minced
⅓ cup freshly chopped Italian parsley
1 teaspoon hot red pepper flakes, or to taste
2 tablespoons chopped fresh rosemary leaves
1 tablespoon chopped fresh marjoram or
    fresh oregano leaves
1 teaspoon dried oregano
2 tablespoons balsamic vinegar
Salt and freshly ground black pepper
Lobster roe, if available

6 whole lobsters, 1½ to 2 pounds each,
    butterflied (your fish market will do this
    for you)

FOR THE SAUCE
1 cup extra-virgin olive oil
3 cloves garlic, smashed and peeled
2 tablespoons balsamic vinegar
1 teaspoon hot red pepper flakes
Salt

To make the stuffing, heat the olive oil in a skillet
over medium-high heat. Add the garlic and cook,
stirring, until golden, about 3 minutes. Set aside to
cool. In a large bowl, combine the remaining
stuffing ingredients. Add the cooled oil and garlic
and mix well.

Heat a grill to very hot or preheat the oven to
550°F. On a large baking sheet, arrange the lobster halves cut side up, with the tail meat exposed.
Season the tails with salt and pepper. Spoon the
stuffing into the cavity where the tail meets the
body.

Place the lobsters directly on the grill, or slide
the baking sheet carefully into the oven. Cook
about 7 minutes per pound of lobster, moving
them around on the grill so they cook evenly.
When the shells have turned a deep red, the meat
should be done. Don't worry if the tails start to
curl, or if the shells burn a bit. Transfer to a platter and let rest about 5 minutes before serving.

While the lobsters are cooking, make the
sauce. In a skillet, heat the olive oil over medium-
high heat. Add the garlic and cook, stirring, until
golden, about 3 minutes. Add the vinegar, red
pepper flakes, and salt to taste and remove from
the heat. Drizzle over the cooked lobsters or
transfer to individual ramekins and use as a dip-
ping sauce.

INVOLTINI DI POLLO AL TAORMINA

TAORMINA, AN ANCIENT HILL TOWN IN SICILY, *is famous for its views of Mt. Etna, its Greek theater, and its location overlooking the sea. I think it should also be famous for its eggplant.*

It was in Taormina that I realized eggplant is what separates the men from the boys as far as cooking is concerned. We walked into a restaurant and, as usual, were seriously impressed by the antipasti table. Only this time, each and every dish was made with eggplant.

Even my entrée of veal scaloppine came rolled around a spoonful of eggplant caponata. *In this recipe, the* caponata *trickles out of the* involtini, *or rolls, and mixes with the juices in the pan to create a delicious sauce with no effort. The aggressive Sicilian flavors of* caponata *are perfect with delicate chicken breast; a little black olive paste binds and thickens the sauce.* Peperonata *makes a good stuffing, too.*

MAKES 4 TO 8 SERVINGS

8 large boneless chicken breast halves, pounded
     thin (your butcher will do this for you) and
     layered between pieces of butcher or wax
     paper
Salt and freshly ground black pepper
All-purpose flour, for dredging
¾ cup *Caponata* (page 33) or *Peperonata*
     (page 30)
¼ cup extra-virgin olive oil
1 cup dry white wine
1 tablespoon fresh oregano leaves, or
     1½ teaspoons dried oregano
1 teaspoon black olive paste

Peel the paper off of a chicken fillet and season generously with salt and pepper. Spread a layer of flour on a plate. Lay the fillet on a work surface and spoon *caponata* down one side. Roll closed so that the *caponata* is in the center of the roll and secure with a toothpick at each end. Carefully dredge the roll in flour, shaking off any excess. Repeat with the remaining chicken fillets and *caponata*.

In a large skillet, heat the olive oil over medium-high heat. Working in two batches if necessary to avoid crowding the pan, brown the rolls on both sides. When all the chicken is browned, return it to the pan and add the wine. Simmer 1 minute, then add the oregano, olive paste, and salt and pepper to taste. Simmer 3 minutes, turning the rolls once. Remove the rolls to serving plates or a platter and continue to simmer the sauce until thickened, 1 to 2 minutes more. Pour over the rolls and serve immediately or let cool to room temperature.

PRO TIP: *Although closing your* involtini *with a toothpick is not absolutely necessary and may seem like an extra step, you'll find it easier to cook them when they're securely closed.*

POLLETTO ALLA MATTONE

JUST A FEW PERFECT INGREDIENTS: A CHICKEN, *a lemon, wild herbs, and a clean brick. Like many of the dishes in this chapter, the simplicity of this grilled chicken is what makes it so good. The elements are nothing special, but the method makes the dish.*

Flattening the chicken out, both before it cooks (your butcher does this part) and while it's cooking (by weighing it down with a brick or heavy pans) makes all the difference. Mattone *means brick; that's what you use to keep the chicken flat as it cooks to a perfect, even doneness. The method comes from Tuscany, where they know how to grill absolutely everything.*

Long marinating helps make up for the mild flavor of most chicken. You'll find that this method keeps the juices inside the bird, sealed inside a crisp crust. When weather chases you back to the kitchen, make the chicken in a frying pan. Some people like it even better that way.

MAKES 6 TO 10 SERVINGS

Two 2½-pound fresh chickens, halved, backbones removed, and pounded flat (your butcher will do this for you)
4 teaspoons hot red pepper flakes, or to taste
6 cloves garlic, thickly sliced
2 teaspoons dried oregano
Salt
12 whole sprigs fresh rosemary
12 whole sprigs fresh thyme
Freshly squeezed juice of 3 lemons
2 tablespoons balsamic vinegar
¼ cup extra-virgin olive oil

Place the chicken halves in a large bowl. Sprinkle the red pepper flakes over the chicken, lightly rubbing them into the skin. Add the garlic and oregano and toss well. Sprinkle with plenty of salt, add the whole herb sprigs, and toss again. Add the lemon juice, vinegar, and oil and mix until the chicken is completely coated. Cover and refrigerate overnight or up to 24 hours, turning the chickens occasionally in the marinade.

Heat a grill to very hot. When the flames have died away and the coals are glowing red, lift the chicken halves out of the marinade, shake off any excess, and place on the grill. Place a clean brick on top of each piece to weigh it down, or place a pot lid on the chicken and rest full cans on top. Grill 5 minutes, then rotate 45 degrees to create an X mark. Cook 20 minutes more, then turn the chickens over, replace the brick on top, and grill 25 to 30 minutes more, until cooked through.

 PRO TIP: *When grilling chicken, a fire that is too hot can cause flare-ups from the fat and can burn the chicken. Be patient—cook it slowly.*

COLD PEPPER-CRUSTED ROAST BEEF WITH HERB SAUCE

IT'S HARD TO RESIST COOL, SILKY, ROASTED *meat with a flavorful sauce on a summer buffet. This seductively textured dish is a classic of Continental haute cuisine, and it's also a popular summer dish in Italian resorts. Herb mayonnaise is easy to make and always delicious; this combination of seasonings is my personal favorite.*

In fact, I'd say the mayonnaise is so good that if you had a sudden moment of insanity that compelled you to go to a good gourmet store and buy preroasted roast beef instead of making it yourself, no one would notice. Why not? You're allowed. Have the deli man slice it thin, you make the sauce, salad, and a vegetable, and you're all set. Of course, this is a buffet dish that should go on the table at the last minute, to keep the mayonnaise tasty and safe.

MAKES 8 TO 12 SERVINGS

3 to 4 pounds top round of beef, in one piece
2 tablespoons olive oil
Salt and coarsely ground black pepper
2 tablespoons Dijon mustard
½ onion, minced
½ clove garlic, minced
¼ cup freshly chopped Italian parsley
24 fresh basil leaves
1 tablespoon chopped fresh dill
1 tablespoon chopped fresh rosemary leaves
1 tablespoon dried oregano
1 tablespoon dried thyme
¼ cup thawed frozen spinach
1½ cups mayonnaise
1 tablespoon Worcestershire sauce
1 tablespoon red wine vinegar
½ teaspoon ground white pepper

The day before you plan to serve the dish, roast the meat. Preheat the oven to 500°F. Rub the meat with the olive oil and season generously with salt. Firmly press pepper all over the surface of the meat. Place in a roasting pan and roast until a meat thermometer inserted in the center registers 130°F. Start checking the meat after about 30 minutes. When cooked, set aside to cool to room temperature, then cover and refrigerate.

In a blender or food processor, or using a hand blender, puree the mustard, onion, garlic, herbs, and spinach. Add the mayonnaise, Worcestershire, vinegar, and salt to taste, and blend until the mixture is smooth and green. If necessary, thin the sauce with lemon juice. Taste for salt and white pepper. Cover and refrigerate until ready to serve.

Using a long serrated knife, slice the chilled meat as thinly as possible. Arrange it on a platter and serve the sauce separately; or, spread the sauce on a platter and arrange the meat on top.

 PRO TIP: *Pressing the coarse pepper into the meat creates a crust that improves the texture, flavor, and look of the meat when it is sliced.*

GRILLED SKIRT STEAK WITH CHEF'S MARINADE

WHEN YOU WANT TO PLEASE A SUMMER CROWD, *skirt steak is the answer. Skirt steak (aka London broil) is very flavorful and very reasonably priced. Tender it's not, but this is a case where a spicy marinade really gets the chance to penetrate, soften, and flavor the meat. You wouldn't do this to prime rib-eye, but it does great things for skirt steak.*

Save your love of rare meat for prime cuts like my Tagliata alla Fiorentina (page 193); skirt steak should always be cooked through, until just pink in the center. But don't overcook it! The sliced steak can be served hot, but it's even more flavorful if you let it cool to room temperature, like most grilled foods.

MAKES 4 TO 8 SERVINGS

One 2-pound skirt steak or London broil
Salt and freshly ground black pepper
Pinch of hot red pepper flakes
Pinch of paprika
1 teaspoon dry mustard
Pinch of curry powder or cumin
1 teaspoon dark sesame oil
2 teaspoons soy sauce
1 teaspoon balsamic vinegar
1 clove garlic, thickly sliced
1 tablespoon chopped fresh cilantro
2 scallions, white and pale green parts, minced

Arrange the steak in a nonreactive baking dish just large enough to hold it. Whisk the remaining ingredients together and pour over the steak. Cover and refrigerate at least 4 or up to 24 hours, turning the steak occasionally in the marinade.

Heat a grill to very hot. Lift the steak out of the marinade, shaking off any excess, and place on the grill. Grill 2 minutes, then rotate 45 degrees to create an X mark. Grill 5 minutes, then flip and repeat on the other side. Continue grilling until cooked through but still a bit pink in the center. Do not overcook. Serve immediately or at room temperature.

PRO TIP: *When making marinades, combine the dry spices in advance to let the flavors meld. You can make them in large batches; they will hold until you add "active" ingredients like oil, vinegar, or garlic.*

POPPIES GROW WILD IN TUSCANY IN THE SPRING.

SALADS,
DRESSINGS,
AND GREENS

French String Bean Salad

Asparagus, Tomato, and Beet Salad

Beet and Lentil Salad

Sautéed Mushrooms on Tricolore Salad

Fennel and Orange Salad

Salad of Fava Beans with Pears and Pecorino Toscano

Warm Shrimp Salad with White Beans, Basil, and Arugula

Spicy Squid and Octopus Salad

Club Salad

Madison Salad

Warm Chicken Salad with Capers, Olives, and Tomatoes

Seared Breast of Duck with Potato-Basil Salad

French Mustard Vinaigrette

Italy's Simple Vinaigrette

Fresh Herb Dressing

No-Fat Balsamic Vinaigrette

SALADS, DRESSINGS, AND GREENS

F YOU WANT TO ANNOY A YOUNG CHEF JUST OUT OF cooking school, assign him to the salad station. He thinks grilling and sautéing are macho and tossing salad is boring. But we've all got to know how to make a great salad. After all, we're going to be making a lot of them. People just love salads.

For some reason (probably because I like to be a little difficult), I've always liked making salads and all through my training in Europe, I

worked the "cold kitchen" whenever I could. It's one of the most interesting areas of a restaurant kitchen, where salads and cold appetizers are assembled. You get to work with all kinds of greens, the freshest and most exotic raw and cooked vegetables, beans, lentils, fish, poultry, meat, and cheese. You learn all about dressings and cold sauces; it's incredible how many different ones there are, covering all the seasonal ingredients like asparagus, tomatoes, green beans, and mushrooms.

The first big thing I learned is that a handful of greens is not a salad. It's just leaves. Vegetables are vegetables: A salad is a dish, with unified flavors and textures. (It's like the difference between plain rice and risotto.) The flavors should be balanced, not repetitive. It's good to mix soft, sweet lettuces like Bibb and Boston with crunchy, spicy greens like endive, arugula,

and watercress. I like to spark up salads with vegetables like fennel, peas, and red peppers.

On the other hand, the look of a salad should be fairly repetitive. Tiny lentils and big romaine leaves in the same bowl doesn't look good, and it's hard to eat. A little time spent dicing and chopping to bring all your vegetables to approximately the same size makes your salads more appetizing. Then you bind these separate ingredients into a salad with a savory vinaigrette. You'll find recipes for my favorites at the end of the chapter. I love punchy seasonings like vinegar and mustard. But remember that the dressing is there to bind it all together and bring out the flavors of the ingredients, not to overpower or soak the greens. With salads (like with clothes), it's better to be a little underdressed than overdressed.

When I started out cooking, salads were served either before or after the main course. Then, under the influence of nouvelle cuisine,

OVERLEAF: **AN ALETHA SOULÉ VASE WITH WHITE AND PINK SWEET PEAS.**

SALADS, DRESSINGS, AND GREENS

chefs started turning salads into main courses. We played with the new idea of serving hot and cold foods together, and hot "something" on cool greens was suddenly the most elegant way to cook. Grilled shrimp, sautéed mushrooms, warm goat cheese, sliced breast of duck—everything was presented on a bed of fancy greens. The warm cooking liquids make their own dressings for the salads. There's something about the combination that's very comforting. And people love the idea that they can stay thin while eating wonderful food! The main-course salads in this chapter are based on this idea; they're the favorites from Coco Pazzo and Campagna that many of my regulars eat three or four times a week.

The chapter starts with a salad I could eat every day, and sometimes do: French String Bean Salad. I'm hopelessly addicted to its mustardy dressing. But most of the other dishes are more Italian in their flavors, like my Warm Shrimp Salad with White Beans, Basil, and Arugula, Fennel and Orange Salad, and Spicy Squid and Octopus Salad. And then there're what I call my Upper East Side salads, chosen by "ladies who lunch"—Madison Salad, Club Salad, and Warm Chicken Salad with Capers, Olives, and Tomatoes. All of these depend on the quality of what you put into them. This is true of all cooking, but especially salads. Since there is little or no cooking involved, you're married to the flavors and textures of your raw ingredients.

These salads can be served in as many ways as you can think of—as appetizers, lunch main courses, or light dinners with a great soup and some bread. When the summer vegetables of the Al Fresco chapter have disappeared, these salads rescue your buffet, and they make wonderful appetizers for a dinner party. They're much more interesting than a plain green salad, and not much harder to make. Fresh, homemade salad dressings are the key. Whether you're serving a salad on a buffet or at the table, always dress it at the last minute. Tossing the ingredients and dressing together in the bowl is essential: It brings the salad together. If your guests pour dressing individually on their salads, the ingredients and dressing won't have a chance to blend together. And that's what makes a really great salad.

When I'm making a salad that needs tossing, I always like to use my wooden salad bowl. I call it an heirloom, because it will last forever. It's made from a single piece of wood; you can find them in maple, cherry, and even oak. It's used only for salad, and it's never washed with soap, just rinsed and sometimes polished with beeswax. Like your favorite leather briefcase, it just gets better and darker with age.

I love to serve vegetable and first-course salads on colorful platters and bowls. There's nothing more beautiful than vegetables in their natural state, and highlighting that with pottery is the way to go. After all, a stew is always going to look like a stew—a big, brown, delicious mess. But a salad of sunny orange pieces and fennel, speckled with fresh black pepper and golden olive oil is truly beautiful. Even a plain green salad, made with the freshest greens and tossed with a few herbs and croutons, looks refreshing. Why not let Mother Nature do the decorating work for you?

FRENCH STRING BEAN SALAD

EVERYONE KNOWS THAT THE FRENCH ARE *patriotic to the point of being arrogant. Well, they do have a lot to be proud of, especially their bistros and brasseries. French bistro classics like leeks vinaigrette, mushrooms* à la grecque, *and green beans* à la moutarde *have the strong, pungent flavors that I love. A lot of chefs prefer simple dishes when they're cooking for themselves. If you've ever eaten an early dinner in France (Americans do tend to eat much earlier than the French), you've probably caught the staff finishing their meal. It's usually a country dish like this one, eaten with a piece of crusty bread so none of the dressing goes to waste.*

You should cook the beans until tender but still green; it's better to overcook them slightly than to undercook them. This very mustardy dressing is made to stand up to a piece of aged steak or a pork roast. The salad is also great warm or chilled.

MAKES 4 SERVINGS

1 pound string beans or *haricots verts*
　　(see Pro Tip), trimmed
½ cup extra-virgin olive oil
½ cup minced onion
¼ cup French Dijon mustard
1 tablespoon mayonnaise
2 teaspoons red wine vinegar
1 tablespoon dried herbes de Provence, or
　　½ teaspoon *each* dried oregano and dried
　　thyme
Salt and freshly ground black pepper
1 plum tomato, seeded and minced

Bring a pot of lightly salted water to a boil. Add the beans and cook 3 to 5 minutes, until bright green and cooked through but not mushy. Mean-while, fill a large bowl with ice water. Drain the beans in a colander, then plunge into ice water to stop the cooking. When cool, drain well, let dry, and cut in half. Place the beans in a large serving bowl.

In a small skillet, heat 1 tablespoon of the oil over medium heat. Add the onion and cook, stirring, until wilted, about 5 minutes.

In a small mixing bowl, whisk together the mustard, mayonnaise, vinegar, herbs, and salt and pepper to taste. Drizzle in the remaining oil and whisk until emulsified.

Add the onion and tomato to the beans. Add the dressing and toss well. Taste for salt and pepper. Set aside at least 30 minutes to let the flavors blend. Serve at room temperature.

PRO TIP: *If you can find small, very slender beans, also known as French haricots verts, use them for this salad. Snip off only the stem end, leaving the "tail" at the other end, and do not cut them in half after cooking.*

same size and shape, then toss them together with a light creamy dressing. I use a teaspoon of mayonnaise or mustard to bind my vinaigrettes. If you like, you can cook and cut the vegetables and make the dressing in advance; toss them together at the last minute. Mix in some soft lettuces, or serve the finished salad on top of greens.

MAKES 6 SERVINGS

2 pounds asparagus
2 beets (do not peel)
4 plum tomatoes, diced, with their juices
2 scallions, white and pale green portions, thinly sliced
6 tablespoons red wine vinegar
I teaspoon French Dijon mustard
I cup mayonnaise
¼ cup extra-virgin olive oil
Salt and freshly ground black pepper
½ pound mixed baby salad greens (mesclun), or a mixture of at least three lettuces such as red leaf, romaine, endive, radicchio, arugula, frisee, watercress, and Boston (optional)

ASPARAGUS, TOMATO, AND BEET SALAD

WHEN YOU CAN'T EAT YET ANOTHER PLAIN *green salad, vary your vegetables with a simple composed salad. This is just one example of a good vegetable combination: sweet beets, firm green asparagus, juicy tomatoes. The trick is to combine three different vegetables into a unified taste.*

It's important to keep the vegetables balanced in size and shape: You don't want bats and balls of asparagus and beets in the same bowl. Cut cooked vegetables of your choice into approximately the

Bring 2 pots of lightly salted water to a boil. Meanwhile, cut off the woody ends of the asparagus. Peel the bottom 3 inches of each stalk with a vegetable peeler. Tie in bundles of up to 12 spears, using cooking twine.

Add the tied asparagus to one pot and boil uncovered until bright green and cooked through but not soft, 7 to 10 minutes. Prepare a large bowl of ice water. When the asparagus are cooked, transfer to the ice water and cut off the twine.

Add the beets to the other pot and boil until tender all the way through when pierced with a knife, about 10 minutes. Set aside to drain and cool.

When the asparagus are cool, pat dry and cut into ½-inch lengths. Put in a large serving bowl.

When the beets are cool, cut into ½-inch cubes and add to the asparagus. Add the tomatoes and scallions.

In a small bowl, whisk together the vinegar, mustard, and mayonnaise. Add the oil and salt and pepper to taste, and whisk to combine. Drizzle over the vegetables and mix gently but thoroughly. If using salad greens, divide them on serving plates and place the asparagus salad on top.

PRO TIP: *As with many cooked vegetable salads, both the vegetables and dressing can be prepared a day in advance, then combined and brought to room temperature just before serving.*

BEET AND LENTIL SALAD

YOU'D HAVE TO DIG DEEP TO FIND AN EARTH-*ier combination than beets and lentils. That's why they're great together, especially when the beets are cut small so they can mix with the lentils. In Italy, a little minced celery is added to almost every salad, for its crispness and refreshing flavor. This salad goes well with meat and with meaty fish like swordfish and tuna. You can also leave out the beets for a lentil salad or substitute fresh basil for the chives.*

MAKES 4 TO 6 SERVINGS

2 cups dried lentils, preferably French green
    lentils such as du Puy
3 beets (do not peel)
1 stalk celery, minced
2 tablespoons finely chopped fresh chives
2 tablespoons red wine vinegar
½ cup extra-virgin olive oil
Salt and freshly ground black pepper

French lentils do not need presoaking, but if you are using regular lentils, cover with plenty of water and soak them overnight. Drain, cover with lightly salted water, and cook until al dente, 25 to 40 minutes. Drain in a colander and set aside to cool.

Bring a pot of lightly salted water to a boil. Add the beets and boil just until tender when pierced with a knife, about 10 minutes. Set aside to drain and cool. When cool, cut into ½-inch dice.

Transfer the lentils to a serving bowl. Add the celery, chives, vinegar, oil, and salt and pepper to taste. Mix well. Add the beets and mix gently. Taste for salt and pepper. Serve at room temperature.

PRO TIP: *Small French or Italian lentils (look for the name du Puy or Castelluccio) are less likely to become mushy than supermarket lentils.*

SAUTÉED MUSHROOMS ON TRICOLORE SALAD

WHEN I WAS THE CHEF AT SAPORE DI MARE, I *learned just how much people love salads. The restaurant is in fashionable East Hampton, and many of our summer customers simply would not order any appetizer that wasn't a salad. But just how many plain green salads can you make? I created this as a quick, easy appetizer when you want a little more than routine greens. The mushrooms take minutes to cook, and the rosemary and balsamic vinegar in the skillet become the perfect dressing for slightly bitter greens. You can arrange the greens in advance and keep them refrigerated, but cook the mushrooms at the last minute for the best effect.*

MAKES 4 SERVINGS

1 endive, leaves separated
2 small bunches arugula, well washed
1 medium-size head radicchio, cored and pulled
    apart
1/2 cup extra-virgin olive oil
1 clove garlic, thinly sliced
1 pound assorted fresh mushrooms, such as
    cremini, shiitake, portobello, chanterelle, and
    white button, sliced 1/2 inch thick
1 teaspoon chopped fresh rosemary leaves
1/4 cup balsamic vinegar
Salt and freshly ground black pepper
8 large shavings Parmesan cheese

In a bowl, toss together the endive, arugula, and radicchio leaves. Cover with a damp towel and set aside.

In a large skillet, heat the oil over medium-high heat. Add the garlic and cook, stirring, until golden, about 3 minutes. Add the mushrooms, reduce the heat to low, and cook, stirring occasionally, until the mushrooms are soft. Add the rosemary, balsamic vinegar, and salt and pepper to taste and simmer until thickened, about 2 minutes.

Meanwhile, divide the greens on serving plates. While the mushrooms are still hot, spoon them over the greens. Top with Parmesan cheese and serve immediately.

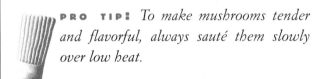 **PRO TIP:** *To make mushrooms tender and flavorful, always sauté them slowly over low heat.*

FENNEL AND ORANGE SALAD

WHEN BLOOD ORANGES ARE IN SEASON IN THE *winter, you'll see this salad in every Roman trattoria. Finocchio arancia is also a Sicilian dish that reflects the island's great agricultural fertility. Much of the citrus in Italy is grown in Sicily. What pulls this dish together is the good olive oil and fresh black pepper. It's good to make it 3 to 4 hours in advance, to let the fennel and oranges marinate together. Fennel and orange salad is easy to put together and is best served family style, from a big platter. If you like, spoon the salad over a bed of arugula at the last minute. Serve it with plenty of bread.*

MAKES **6** SERVINGS

4 navel oranges or sweet blood oranges
2 fennel bulbs, trimmed
1/3 cup extra-virgin olive oil
Salt and freshly ground black pepper
Arugula (optional)

Cut a thick slice off the top and bottom of each orange to expose the flesh. Cutting from top to bottom, following the contours of the orange, remove the outside layer of peel and white pith completely. One by one, cut the orange sections free of the white membranes and transfer to a bowl. Squeeze any remaining juice from the orange halves into the bowl and set aside.

Halve the fennel bulbs lengthwise and cut out the hard base. Thinly slice and transfer to a serving bowl. Drain any excess juice from the oranges and add the orange sections and juice to the fennel. Drizzle the salad with oil and add salt and pepper to taste. Mix well and serve or set aside to marinate up to 1 hour. Taste for salt and pepper. If desired, serve over arugula.

PRO TIP: *The oranges can be sectioned a day in advance, then refrigerated in their juices. But whenever you are making salads with vegetables like fennel and celery, which have a high water content, they should be sliced just before the salad is made, to keep them crisp and fresh.*

SALAD OF FAVA BEANS WITH PEARS AND PECORINO TOSCANO

THIS IS MY BLEND OF A PAIR OF TUSCAN *classics: a spring salad of fava beans (aka broad beans) and pecorino cheese and a fall dessert of pears and pecorino drizzled with honey and black pepper. Pears are available year-round now, and when fava beans come into season this is a wonderful way to use them. The combination of sharp, salty cheese, fresh mild beans, and sweet pears will surprise your guests, making this a great first course for a dinner party.*

Pecorino Toscano is a farmhouse cheese made from sheep's milk, but it's very different from pecorino Romano (pecora means sheep). Pecorino Romano is sharp, and though it's great on some pastas it's usually too strong to be an eating cheese. Pecorino Toscano is softer and smoother. It is available either fresh or aged, and both are good in this salad. It has become widely available in gourmet stores.

MAKES 4 SERVINGS

2 cups shelled fava beans (from about 2 pounds beans; see Pro Tip)
4 ounces pecorino Toscano, in one piece
2 ripe pears, cored (do not peel)
5 tablespoons extra-virgin olive oil
Salt and freshly ground black pepper

Place the fava beans in a serving bowl. Cut the cheese and pears into pieces about the same size as the beans and add to the bowl. Drizzle with oil, add salt and pepper to taste, and mix gently but thoroughly. Serve immediately.

PRO TIP: *Fava beans must be removed from the pod and then individually peeled before using. Use a small knife for the peeling. This is a little tedious, I'll admit: I'd recommend listening to the radio or talking on the phone while you do it!*

TUSCAN SHEEP'S MILK CHEESE AND OTHER INGREDIENTS FOR MAKING SALAD OF FAVA BEANS WITH PEARS AND PECORINO TOSCANO.

WARM SHRIMP SALAD WITH WHITE BEANS, BASIL, AND ARUGULA

IF YOU'VE EVER BEEN TO TUSCANY, YOU KNOW *that the Tuscans' nickname—*mangiafagioli, *or bean-eaters—is no joke. White beans and olive oil are fundamental to their cuisine, and they have an amazing talent for cooking white bean soup, white bean crostini, and white bean salad every day. People think of Tuscany as farm country, but it also has a seacoast. On the Mediterranean, Tuscan fishermen eat their white beans with shrimp. It's an excellent combination, and peppery arugula complements them both. This salad must be eaten at room temperature or warmer, to enhance the olive oil and black pepper that bring the dish together.*

MAKES 4 TO 8 SERVINGS

½ cup extra-virgin olive oil
1 clove garlic, thinly sliced
2 pounds small to medium-size raw shrimp,
    peeled and deveined
1 cup cooked or canned white beans (page 14)
2 tablespoons Basil Puree (page 18) or
    3 tablespoons fresh basil leaves, torn into
        pieces
Freshly squeezed juice of 1 lemon
Salt and freshly ground black pepper
4 large handfuls arugula

In a large skillet, heat ¼ cup of the oil over medium-high heat. Add the garlic and cook, stirring, until golden, about 2 minutes. Add the shrimp, stirring until just cooked through. Add the beans, basil puree, lemon juice, remaining ¼ cup oil, and salt and pepper to taste and toss to heat through.

Divide the arugula on serving plates. Spoon the shrimp mixture on top, making sure to include all the pan juices. Top with additional black pepper and serve immediately.

PRO TIP: *Dried beans should never be cooked al dente—they should be soft all the way through. Cooked beans need to be seasoned with plenty of salt, but don't add it during the cooking: It will loosen the shells of the beans.*

SPICY SQUID AND OCTOPUS SALAD

THIS DISH IS FOUND ALL ALONG THE SOUTH-*ern Italian coast, from Reggio di Calabria to Rome. Grilling octopus gives it a nice crust. I like how this dressing combines the local flavors of vinegar and hot pepper: not a subtle taste, but an addictive one. You can serve this over arugula or another peppery green if you like. Italian seafood salads are some of my favorite dishes and the recipes are generations old. There's no need to adjust the recipe for American tastes because the combinations are made in heaven.*

Cooking octopus is very simple: Just keep boiling it, adding water as needed, and it will become tender. Squid has to be cooked either very quickly or very slowly to be tender. Anything in between will result in rubber bands.

MAKES 8 TO 10 SERVINGS

2 pounds cleaned octopus, left whole
2 pounds cleaned calamari (squid), cut into
    ½-inch rings
½ cup extra-virgin olive oil
1 clove garlic, thinly sliced
Salt

1 tablespoon hot red pepper flakes, or less to
   taste
3 tablespoons freshly chopped Italian parsley
¼ cup red wine vinegar

To cook the octopus, bring a large pot of unsalted water to a boil. Add the octopus and boil for 45 minutes, or until tender when pierced with a knife. Lift out of the pot and drain. While still hot, cut into ½-inch pieces.

To cook the squid, preheat the oven to 450°F. Arrange the squid on a baking sheet, drizzle with oil, dot with garlic slices, and sprinkle with salt and hot red pepper flakes. Bake 10 minutes, until the squid begins to brown and is lightly cooked through. Let cool slightly, then transfer to a large mixing bowl, making sure to include all the garlic and oil. Add the octopus, parsley, and vinegar to the squid and mix well. Taste for salt and hot red pepper flakes. Serve at room temperature.

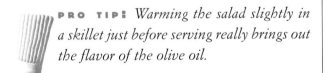 **PRO TIP:** *Warming the salad slightly in a skillet just before serving really brings out the flavor of the olive oil.*

CLUB SALAD

I'VE LOVED CLUB SANDWICHES SINCE I WAS A *kid, but when I cut bread out of my diet I thought I'd seen the last of them. Then I thought of a way to get them back. Years spent cooking on New York's Upper East Side taught me that almost anything can be made into a salad if you think about it long enough. This was an easy creation: a salad with club sandwich ingredients of turkey, tomato, and bacon. The blue cheese is optional.*

You want to make this with real roast turkey or, failing that, real roast chicken, which is getting very easy to find in supermarkets. Deli turkey has about as much taste as newspapers, and the wet texture of a stack of them left out in the rain.

MAKES 6 MEAL-SIZE SERVINGS

¼ cup French Dijon mustard
¼ cup red wine vinegar
1 small shallot, minced
¼ cup mayonnaise
Salt and freshly ground black pepper
¼ cup extra-virgin olive oil
1½ pounds roasted turkey or chicken meat,
   removed from the bone and torn into bite-
   size pieces
6 large handfuls mixed baby salad greens
   (mesclun), coarsely chopped
½ Belgian endive, coarsely chopped
1 scallion, minced
3 plum tomatoes, diced
2 strips cooked bacon, crumbled
½ cup Danish or domestic cow's milk blue
   cheese, crumbled (optional)

Whisk together the mustard, vinegar, shallot, mayonnaise, and salt and pepper to taste. Slowly drizzle in the olive oil and whisk until the dressing is emulsified.

CONTINUED

In a serving bowl, combine the remaining ingredients. Add the dressing and toss gently until evenly coated. Taste for salt and pepper and serve.

PRO TIP: Fine aged blue cheeses like Roquefort and Gorgonzola are wonderful eating cheeses, but it's a waste to use them in salad dressing: Domestic and Danish blues are fine for this purpose.

MADISON SALAD

LIKE MANY CHEFS, AFTER YEARS IN THE BUSINESS I have finally turned into my own worst customer. This salad—which I use as an affectionate tease for my pickiest customers—is the proof.

When I was cooking on the Upper East Side of Manhattan, I noticed that everyone ordered their salads chopped up into tiny pieces. People wore their best clothes to dinner, and wrestling with a big leaf of lettuce was too risky for a Chanel suit. It seemed like everyone was on a diet all the time, and no matter how many salads I put on the menu, all the customers wanted their own special blend of ingredients. So I made a salad with a little bit of everything in the kitchen, chopped up tiny—and you know what? It turned out to be a great dish.

In retrospect, I think the Madison Salad was a fork in the road in my career. I realized that "If you can't beat 'em, join 'em" was the way to go. I chose to join my customers in their own game by creating food that all of us would like, and I've never looked back. My regulars have been returning for this salad for years.

Obviously, this recipe is impossibly long; trying to follow it in a home kitchen might drive you crazy. I wanted you to get an idea of what the real dish is like, but you can use almost any combination of beans, vegetables, and greens. The constants are the Parmesan cheese and the tuna fish—I always say it's the only fish that migrates up Madison Avenue!

MAKES 12 MEAL-SIZE SERVINGS

1 clove garlic, smashed and peeled
¼ cup red wine vinegar
¾ cup extra-virgin olive oil
Salt and freshly ground black pepper

Two 6-ounce cans water-packed tuna fish, drained
  and crumbled
¼ cup cooked lentils
¼ cup cooked or canned white beans
¼ cup diced cooked beets
¼ cup diced cooked string beans
¼ cup diced cooked potatoes
¼ cup cooked fresh or frozen peas
¼ cup chopped cooked asparagus
¼ cup chopped fresh plum tomatoes
¼ cup minced red onions
4 button mushrooms, thinly sliced
¼ cup diced red bell peppers
¼ cup diced yellow bell peppers
¼ cup diced raw zucchini
¼ cup diced prosciutto (optional)
I cup slivered Parmesan cheese
I pound mixed baby salad greens (mesclun), or a
  mixture of at least three lettuces such as red
  leaf, romaine, endive, radicchio, arugula, frisee,
  watercress, and Boston
I large handful arugula
I Belgian endive
½ head radicchio

To make the dressing, in a nonreactive bowl, combine the garlic and vinegar. Set aside to infuse for 1 hour while you prepare the salad ingredients. Whisk in the olive oil and salt and pepper to taste until emulsified.

In a serving bowl, combine all the salad ingredients except the greens, arugula, endive, and radicchio. Add the dressing and toss gently until evenly coated. At the last moment, chop the remaining ingredients and mix into the salad. Taste for salt and pepper and serve.

 PRO TIP: *A good knife is the cook's best friend: Chopping with a very sharp blade is easier, quicker, and actually safer, since a sharp knife cuts rather than slips.*

WARM CHICKEN SALAD WITH CAPERS, OLIVES, AND TOMATOES

IN THE 1980s, WHEN I WAS COOKING IN *Europe, salads and vinaigrettes were rediscovered by chefs in the nouvelle cuisine movement. Quick sautés on salad greens were suddenly all the rage, especially for lunch. I immediately liked the combination of cool greens and hot food. I use that French technique with Italian ingredients, which is my favorite way to cook. It's easy: Put down the butter, shallots, and demiglace with one hand, and pick up the olive oil, garlic, and balsamic vinegar with the other!*

MAKES **4 TO 6** MEAL-SIZE SERVINGS

8 ounces mixed baby salad greens (mesclun), or a
  mixture of at least three lettuces such as red
  leaf, romaine, endive, radicchio, arugula, frisee,
  watercress, and Boston
6 large boneless, skinless chicken breast halves,
  cut into strips
Salt and freshly ground black pepper
All-purpose flour, for dredging
½ cup vegetable oil
⅓ cup top-quality balsamic vinegar,
  preferably aged
I teaspoon capers, rinsed of salt or vinegar
3 plum tomatoes, diced
12 black brine-cured olives, such as Niçoise or
  Gaeta, pitted
20 fresh basil leaves, torn into small pieces
¼ cup extra-virgin olive oil

Arrange the salad greens on serving plates.

Season the chicken strips with salt and pepper. Working in batches, spread about ½ cup of flour out on a plate and dredge the chicken in the flour, shaking off any excess. Meanwhile, in a large skillet, heat the vegetable oil over medium-high heat. Add the chicken as it is dredged and cook, stirring occasionally, until browned. Remove the chicken to a plate.

Wipe out the skillet with paper towels and add the balsamic vinegar. Heat over medium heat until simmering. Add the browned chicken and toss to coat. Add the capers, tomatoes, olives, basil, and salt and pepper to taste. Toss, add the olive oil, and toss again. Divide the chicken mixture on top of the greens, grind pepper over the top, and serve immediately.

PRO TIP: *With the state of the poultry industry today, it really does make a difference when you choose organic poultry or at least free-range—both in the flavor and in your conscience.*

SEARED BREAST OF DUCK WITH POTATO-BASIL SALAD

CHEFS WHO COOK ON THE UPPER EAST SIDE *of Manhattan, as I used to, have a special challenge: cooking elegant, light, flavorful food not once but twice a day. The lunch crowd at Coco Pazzo—also known as "ladies who lunch"—absolutely requires salad! I love to make my customers happy, so I was glad that my experience in the best European hotels had included cooking lunch for a discerning crowd. I created this combination for the Amstel Hotel's private lunch club, when I was the chef of the garde-manger, or salad kitchen. It was one of the first dishes I ever got to create for a menu, and it's still a great one.*

MAKES 4 MEAL-SIZE SERVINGS

2 double mallard or 4 double Peking boneless duck breasts, skin-on, trimmed of excess fat
Salt and freshly ground black pepper
2 teaspoons extra-virgin olive oil
2 shallots, minced
1 clove garlic, thinly sliced
2 tablespoons top-quality balsamic vinegar, preferably aged
¼ cup dry sherry
¼ cup Chicken Stock (page 15) or low-sodium canned broth
1 teaspoon chopped fresh rosemary leaves
4 ounces mixed baby salad greens (mesclun), or a mixture of at least three lettuces such as red leaf, romaine, endive, radicchio, arugula, frisee, watercress, and Boston
1 recipe Italian Potato-Basil Salad (page 35)

Preheat the oven to 450°F.

Heat an empty ovenproof skillet over medium-high heat. Rub the skins of the duck breasts with salt and pepper and place them skin side down in the hot skillet. Immediately lower the heat to medium and cook without moving the breasts until the skin crisps and the fat starts to melt, about 10 minutes.

Turn the breasts over and transfer the skillet to the hot oven. Bake 10 minutes. Remove the skillet from the oven, transfer the breasts to a plate, and pour off excess fat from the frying pan. Wipe it out with paper towels and add the olive oil. Heat over medium-high heat and add the shallots and garlic. Cook, stirring, until golden, about 3 minutes. Add the vinegar, sherry, stock, rosemary, and salt and pepper to taste. Place the breasts in the skillet, reduce the heat, and simmer until the sauce is thickened and reduced to about ¼ of its original volume.

Meanwhile, divide the greens on serving plates. Pile the potato salad on top of the greens. Cut the cooked breasts in half, then cut each half into quarters. Place four pieces of duck on the potatoes on each plate. Drizzle with sauce and serve immediately.

PRO TIP: *Duck breasts that have been removed from the bone by a professional have also had most of their fat removed, making them easier to cook and lighter to eat. Mallard duck breasts are less fatty than other breeds.*

FRENCH MUSTARD VINAIGRETTE

MAKES 1 CUP

1 clove garlic, smashed and peeled (optional)
¾ cup extra-virgin olive oil
¼ cup Dijon mustard, preferably French
1 shallot, minced
¼ cup red wine vinegar
1 lemon wedge
Salt
Freshly ground black pepper

If you want a garlic flavor, combine the garlic and oil 30 minutes before making the dressing. Discard the garlic before proceeding with the recipe.

In a mixing bowl, whisk the mustard, shallot, and vinegar together. Squeeze the lemon juice over the mixture and add a pinch of salt. While whisking, slowly drizzle in the olive oil until the dressing is thick and emulsified. Season to taste with salt and pepper. Keep refrigerated.

ITALY'S SIMPLE VINAIGRETTE

MAKES 1 CUP

1 clove garlic, smashed and peeled
¼ cup red wine vinegar
1 tablespoon fresh lemon juice
¾ cup extra-virgin olive oil
Salt and freshly ground black pepper

In a jar, combine all the ingredients and shake well before using. Season to taste with salt and pepper. Keep refrigerated and shake well before using. (This dressing will not emulsify like the French vinaigrette, because it contains no mustard.)

FRESH HERB DRESSING

MAKES ¾ CUP

¼ cup finely chopped Italian parsley
¼ cup finely chopped fresh mint
¼ cup finely chopped fresh basil
2 lemons, halved
½ clove garlic, minced
Salt and freshly ground black pepper
½ teaspoon hot red pepper flakes
⅓ cup extra-virgin olive oil

In a mixing bowl, combine the parsley, mint, and basil. Squeeze the lemons over the mixture. Add the garlic, a pinch of salt and pepper, and red pepper flakes and mix well. While whisking, drizzle in the olive oil. Season to taste with salt and pepper and set aside to marinate at room temperature at least 2 hours. Taste for salt, pepper, and lemon juice and whisk before using. Or keep refrigerated and shake well before using.

NO-FAT BALSAMIC VINAIGRETTE

MAKES 1¾ CUPS

½ cup Dijon mustard, preferably French
¾ cup balsamic vinegar
½ cup water
Salt and freshly ground black pepper

In a jar with a tight-fitting lid, combine the mustard and vinegar. Add the water and salt and pepper to taste and shake well. Keep refrigerated and shake well before using.

VENETIAN-STYLE GLASS DECANTERS WITH OLIVE OIL AND BALSAMIC VINEGAR.

VEGETABLE ANTIPASTI AND SIDE DISHES

VEGETABLE ANTIPASTI AND SIDE DISHES

WHEN I FIRST SAW MARIA, THE ROMAN CHEF WHO taught me all about vegetables, I wasn't sure if she had arrived from Rome or from Central Casting. Maria is my picture-perfect Italian mamma, right down to the slippers she used to wear, even in the dining room. She was such a character that she even upstaged *me!* Her stamp is still all over Campagna, especially in the beautiful platters filled with colorful antipasti that cover our long, wooden farmhouse table.

Maria had never been to cooking school, and she didn't have a huge repertoire of techniques, methods, and ingredients. But she taught me the single best way to cook every vegetable in an Italian kitchen. She demanded constant attention, yelled at us when we took shortcuts in the kitchen, and even did my laundry for me on occasion. She treated work like home, and the staff as if we were all her children—with a mixture of affection and scolding that made her just like a real mother.

For cooking purposes, Maria was the Italian mother I never had. I noticed in my time in Europe that most Americans don't grow up with a real sense of local produce and seasonal cooking. European chefs seem to learn the basics young, often from watching their grandmothers

correct their mothers' cooking. Working in Europe gave me some of the instincts I needed, and she was my final teacher—a real live Italian grandmother cooking in my kitchen at Sapore di Mare. To Maria, each vegetable had its own character, and its own best cooking method.

She simply couldn't stand anything less than perfect food. Perfectly chosen, perfectly cooked, and perfectly seasoned. I still remember the first time she made me Peas and Prosciutto, and Cauliflower Stained with Red Wine. It was in those moments that I understood: There's so much more to vegetables than a stack of little green beans or a pile of sautéed spinach. Before Maria, I have to admit I thought vegetables were pretty boring. I liked them, but except for seasonal delicacies like asparagus and wild mushrooms they didn't seem very inspiring.

OVERLEAF: **THE ANTIPASTO TABLE AT CAMPAGNA.**

She taught me how to slowly bake the moisture out of tender button mushrooms, then put it back by marinating them in a puree of basil, lemon juice, and olive oil. She taught me to bake beets before peeling them, and to braise bitter greens in stock to mellow them out. She taught me that there are some shortcuts you can take, like using top-quality frozen peas—and some you can't, like frying eggplant without salting it first. I can still hear the shriek she let out when she caught one of the kitchen crew rinsing roasted peppers to make seeding them easier.

Fortunately, Maria was a real home cook. Her cooking was quick, simple, flavorful, and wholesome. She used everything as long as it was real and good, right down to the ends of peppers and nubs of prosciutto. Her cooking had total integrity.

The recipes in this chapter are not only the ones Maria introduced me to. I learned the world's best recipes for potatoes in Switzerland and in Germany, where I worked in a hotel that had a separate kitchen just for the preparation of potatoes. Choosing the right potato preparation for a main course there was almost as important as choosing a wine. In Provence I discovered an eggplant gratin, and string beans braised in tomatoes that I remember as among the best dishes I've ever tasted. At Sapore di Mare in East Hampton, the fall brought quiet to the restaurant—and squash and beets to the produce stands, helping me create a fantastic Winter Vegetable Roast.

It's up to you to decide whether to serve these dishes as antipasti, before the main course, or as *contorni,* along with it. Many of them are just as good either way. A big part of being a good cook is knowing what to serve when. Menu planning is nearly as important as cooking. In terms of taste, there is simply nothing better than seasonal, local vegetables. Spring asparagus and spring lamb are a perfect flavor combination. In the fall, roasted birds and braised cabbage or escarole are the best. Summer's eggplant and tomatoes are great with grilled meat and fish.

But menu planning isn't only about seasonality. And we all have to consider a lot of other factors: what the kids will eat, what can be made quickly, and what is available at the supermarket. "What goes together?" is a question I hear all the time. Most of us can decide between beef and fish—it's harder to decide what to serve with them. So here are some other things to keep in mind.

First trick: This may seem obvious, but don't repeat a vegetable within a meal. Even if beets are in season, when you're starting with a beet and lentil salad, leave the beets out of your Winter Vegetable Roast (page 97). Second trick: Vary the colors of the vegetables you choose and you'll end up with a good variety of flavors too. Instead of asparagus, spinach, and peas, think cauliflower, spinach, and carrots. Sweet vegetables (like red peppers, beets, and carrots) should be mixed with earthy and bitter ones (like potatoes, escarole, and string beans). They look and taste better together.

There's one more element of putting menus together. I think of it as "sensibility." It is partly about texture, and partly about cooking methods. In general, main dishes that are softer and milder, or have been steamed, poached, or braised, go best with braised, boiled, or steamed vegetables. Main dishes

that are crusty, crisp, grilled, or sautéed get crunchy, roasted, or sautéed vegetables. For example: Soft fish fillets are better with tender spinach than with robust broccoli. With a crusty grilled steak, roasted potatoes are better than boiled ones.

European chefs sometimes choose side dishes by thinking in terms of "masculine" and "feminine" foods. Some dishes are robust, big-flavored, and aggressive; some subtle, delicate, and sweet. But of course strict rules are hard to follow: Mashed potatoes go both ways, and you can serve them with almost everything. The most foolproof way to choose is to taste the dishes together in your mind, before you make them. It comes easily with just a little experience.

Campagna's antipasto table is so irresistible, with its glowing colors on beautiful platters and everything shining with olive oil, that a lot of people never get past the antipasto course. An antipasto buffet is a terrific way to entertain at home, especially if there are many vegetarians in your crowd. Almost all of the dishes can be made well in advance and rewarmed or served at room temperature. With six antipasti from this chapter, plus a savory dish of *Peperonata* (page 30) or *Caponata* (page 33), bread, a piece of Parmigiano, and some *soppresata* or cured meats, you're all set for a casual dinner with friends. In winter, add a pasta course afterward or some soup beforehand. For bigger occasions, just add more kinds of antipasti (or look in the Al Fresco and Salads chapters for more great vegetable dishes).

For an antipasto buffet, think in terms of color—not only of your vegetables, but of your serving pieces. A bright vision of reds, blues, yellows, greens, flowers, vines, leaves, and vegetables gives an effect of warmth and abundance. All-white backgrounds are fine for a few plates, but mix in lots of color with them—put green vegetables on pale yellow platters, mound pink-stained cauliflower in Mediterranean blue dishes, and lay spears of asparagus, with their green-to-yellow shading, on colorful Provençal pottery. Roasted red peppers or sliced tomatoes add deep color. Arrange the table by thinking of it as a bouquet of flowers: start in the center, and work your way outward. For more ideas about arranging buffets, please read the introduction to the Al Fresco chapter.

Mostly, what I hope you'll take away from this chapter is a new appreciation of the vegetables you already know. You can cook great-tasting vegetable dishes without branching out into exotic beans or growing heirloom tomatoes (although those are great things to do). I absorbed from Maria the Italian understanding that vegetables are truly alive and a part of life. I think that helps Italians bring their vegetable dishes to life on the plate. Whether they're northern or southern, rural or urban, picking olives or designing shoes for a living, they eat far more vegetables than we do. I hope that after reading this chapter, you'll want to follow suit.

A TYPICAL ANTIPASTO APPETIZER AT CAMPAGNA.

PARMESAN-STUFFED ARTICHOKES

HERE'S A TYPICAL AND RELATIVELY EASY artichoke dish from southern Italy. Italians have been eating artichokes since ancient times, and Romans have long been famous for their artichoke recipes. Maria was a Roman cook, and she most often baked her artichokes in plenty of olive oil, with this simple stuffing of garlic, mint, and Parmesan. You could also add some minced prosciutto to the stuffing.

Baking them in a slow oven keeps the natural juices and the olive oil inside the artichokes. When they've cooled to room temperature, the artichokes are juicy and pungent. Cook these in the morning for an evening party, and serve them at room temperature. They look great on a buffet table.

MAKES 6 SERVINGS

6 large artichokes
1 1/2 cups plain dried bread crumbs
1/2 cup freshly grated Parmesan cheese
2 cloves garlic, minced
1/4 cup freshly chopped mint
2 tablespoons freshly chopped Italian parsley
Salt and freshly ground black pepper
1/2 cup extra-virgin olive oil

Preheat the oven to 325°F.

Cut off the top inch of each artichoke, removing the sharp tips of the center leaves with kitchen scissors or a sharp knife. Cut off the sharp tips of the outer leaves. Remove the outer layer of small leaves at the base, and any leaves that are torn or wilted. In the center of the artichoke, you'll see small hairy leaves; use a pointed teaspoon or small knife to remove this hairy "choke" from the center. Cut off the stem at the base so the artichoke can stand upright.

In a medium bowl, combine the bread crumbs, Parmesan, garlic, mint, parsley, and salt and pepper to taste. Mix well, then add the oil and mix until combined and moist. Stuff the mixture in between the leaves of the artichokes, packing lightly. Arrange them in a roasting pan, cover with a lid or foil, and bake 45 minutes to 1 hour, until the bottoms of the artichokes are tender when pierced with a knife. Serve hot or at room temperature.

 PRO TIP: *The artichokes can be stuffed a day ahead and baked just before serving.*

A COPPER POT OF ARTICHOKES FOR PARMESAN-STUFFED ARTICHOKES.

BABY ARTICHOKES BAKED WITH MINT AND GARLIC

ARTICHOKES ARE SERVED ON EVERY ANTIPASTO *table in Rome. I especially like the baby artichokes that come in early spring. Baby artichokes are the only artichokes that we grow in America that resemble the Italian artichokes.*

This is my version of the classic Roman dish Carciofi alla Romana, in which the artichokes are usually braised in liquid until tender. I like to remove the stems and bake them standing up, so they cook more evenly and make a better presentation. Line them up in the pan like little Roman soldiers.

MAKES 4 TO 6 SERVINGS

2 tablespoons fresh lemon juice
24 baby artichokes
2 cloves garlic, thickly sliced
¼ cup freshly chopped mint
¼ cup extra-virgin olive oil
Salt and freshly ground black pepper

Preheat the oven to 325°F.

To prepare the artichokes, fill a large bowl with cold water and add the lemon juice. Pull or cut the outer leaves off until you get to the pale greenish yellow inner leaves. Cut off the stem at the base so the artichoke can stand upright and place in the water.

Drain the artichokes and pat dry. Arrange them upright in a baking dish with a lid and sprinkle with garlic, mint, oil, and salt and pepper to taste. Cover tightly and bake 35 to 45 minutes, until the artichoke bottoms are tender when pierced with a knife. Set aside to cool to room temperature and serve.

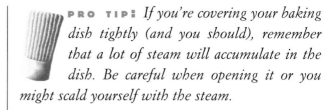

PRO TIP: *If you're covering your baking dish tightly (and you should), remember that a lot of steam will accumulate in the dish. Be careful when opening it or you might scald yourself with the steam.*

PEAS AND PROSCIUTTO

I CONFESS: I'M ADDICTED TO THESE PEAS. *Piselli e prosciutto is one of the Italian family classics that made Maria, who taught it to me, seem like my own grandmother. She took tender little peas and sautéed them in butter with onion and prosciutto—and amazed me with the simplicity of the recipe. In the spring, Roman restaurants always serve roast pork with artichokes and* piselli e prosciutto. *It has been a staple at Campagna since we opened, and I eat it pretty much every day, often added to my salad. It makes the salad sweet and interesting.*

Go ahead and use frozen tiny green peas or petits pois *in this dish: Maria often did!*

MAKES 4 TO 6 SERVINGS

¼ cup extra-virgin olive oil
1 teaspoon unsalted butter
½ onion, minced
2 ounces Prosciutto di Parma or other best-quality prosciutto, minced
1 pound shelled fresh or frozen peas
¼ cup Chicken Stock (page 15) or water
Salt and freshly ground black pepper

In a large skillet with a lid, heat the oil and butter over medium-high heat until the butter is melted and foamy. Add the onion and prosciutto and cook, stirring, until the onion is wilted, about 2 minutes. Add the peas and stock, lower the heat to medium, cover, and cook, stirring occasionally, until the peas are tender, 5 to 10 minutes. If the mixture becomes too dry, add more stock 1 tablespoon at a time; the finished dish should be moist but not soupy. Season with salt and pepper to taste and serve or set aside to cool to room temperature.

PRO TIP: *When sautéing fresh peas, don't parboil them—use their own natural moisture for cooking and the flavor will be great.*

STRING BEANS WITH BROWN BUTTER AND ALMONDS

THIS DISH IS FROM MY HOTEL AND RESTAURANT *school days, and it's still great for a dinner party. I was trained in classical French cooking, but I left butter behind and switched to olive oil when I began my career as an Italian chef. A trip to England reminded me of how good vegetables cooked in butter can be. The English often serve beans cooked in butter with their Sunday roasts.*

Browning the butter gives it a special nutty flavor. Lemon juice makes a good contrast. To do as the French do, add the almonds, and serve with a steak or roast chicken.

MAKES 4 TO 6 SERVINGS

3 tablespoons sliced almonds
1 pound string beans, trimmed
2 tablespoons unsalted butter
1 lemon half
Salt

Preheat the oven to 350°F.

Spread the almonds on a baking sheet and bake, watching carefully to make sure they do not burn, until golden brown and toasty, 5 to 10 minutes.

Meanwhile, bring a pot of lightly salted water to a boil. Add the beans and boil until bright green and cooked through but firm to the bite (they will cook a little more later in the recipe), about 5 minutes. Meanwhile, prepare a large bowl of ice water. When the beans are cooked, transfer them to the ice water. When cool, drain and pat dry.

When ready to serve, melt the butter in a large skillet over medium-high heat. It will melt completely, then foam up, then settle down and turn golden. Watching carefully, cook the butter just until the white milk solids turn light brown. Add the beans and lower the heat to medium. Cook, stirring, until the beans are heated through and coated with butter, 2 to 3 minutes. Squeeze the lemon half over the beans. Add salt to taste and the almonds, mix well, and serve immediately.

 PRO TIP: *This dish is also great without almonds: Browned butter has plenty of nutty flavor.*

STRING BEANS À LA FRANCOISE

IF YOU WANT PROOF THAT AL DENTE IS NOT *the be-all and end-all of cooking vegetables, brew a pot of these beans. I had them for the first time at the wedding of my friend Francoise in the French alpine city of Grenoble (site of the 1968 Olympics). Since it was a typical three-day French wedding with lots of food and drink, I have to admit that these beans and many glasses of the local Chartreuse is about all I remember. After that weekend, I fell immediately in love with every French girl who knew how to make this dish.*

Don't be afraid to cook the beans for a long time over low heat. Let them get soft and tender while you make the main course. Serve them with steak and you'll know why Jean-Claude Killy flew down those mountains in 1968.

MAKES 6 TO 8 SERVINGS

¼ cup extra-virgin olive oil
2 cloves garlic, thickly sliced
I small onion, minced
2 cups milled or crushed canned Italian plum tomatoes
½ teaspoon dried herbes de Provence, or ¼ teaspoon *each* dried oregano and dried thyme
1½ pounds string beans, trimmed
Salt and freshly ground black pepper

In a large skillet, heat the oil over medium-high heat. Add the garlic and cook, stirring, until golden, about 3 minutes. Add the onion and cook until wilted, about 3 minutes. Add the tomatoes and herbes de Provence, bring to a simmer, and cook 1 minute, then add the string beans and salt and pepper to taste. Mix well.

Reduce the heat to a simmer, cover, and simmer until the beans are very tender, about 25 minutes. Taste for salt and pepper and serve or set aside to cool to room temperature.

PRO TIP: *If you don't have a food mill, pour the tomatoes from the can into a bowl and use your fingers to gently crush them.*

MARIA'S DROWNED ZUCCHINI

MY FRIEND MARIA, A ROMAN CHEF, TAUGHT *me all there is to know about zucchini. In Italian, this dish is called zucchini* affogate, *drowned zucchini. You slowly stew the vegetable with onion and garlic until it becomes soft and concentrated, almost like a relish.*

This is a perfect recipe for the end of the summer, when gardens and farmer's markets are overflowing with zucchini. You can make lots of it and freeze it for when you have no time to cook. Serve it as an antipasto or side dish, or toss it with pasta to make a quick lunch.

MAKES 6 TO 8 SERVINGS

¼ cup extra-virgin olive oil
2 cloves garlic, thickly sliced
I small red onion, sliced
4 medium zucchini, sliced into ½-inch rounds
2 teaspoons freshly chopped thyme
I teaspoon dried oregano
½ cup Chicken Stock (page 15), Vegetable Stock (page 17), low-sodium canned broth, or water
Salt and freshly ground black pepper
3 tablespoons freshly grated Parmesan cheese

In a large skillet, heat the oil over medium-high heat. Add the garlic and onion and cook, stirring, until the onion is wilted, about 3 minutes. Add the zucchini and cook, stirring, until browned, about 5 minutes. Add the thyme, oregano, stock, and salt and pepper to taste. Cover and simmer until the zucchini is very tender and the sauce is thickened, 5 to 10 minutes. If the mixture becomes too dry, add stock or water 1 tablespoon at a time; the finished dish should be quite wet. Taste for salt. Add the Parmesan, taste for salt and pepper, and serve immediately or set aside to cool to room temperature.

ROMAN BROCCOLI RABE

EVER SINCE CAMPAGNA OPENED, PEOPLE HAVE *been begging me for this recipe. It's the only way you need to know how to cook broccoli rabe. Broccoli rabe—also called rapini, or broccoli di rape—is a strong bitter green that tastes great with fruity olive oil and garlic. Many cooks blanch broccoli rabe before cooking, but that just makes it soggy. I sauté it raw, then add the liquid so the texture is firm and the color bright. The bread makes the dish more substantial, almost like a soup. You'll need extra bread to* scarpa, *or scrape, the juices from the bottom of the bowl. The crusty heel of the loaf is the best part. Watching people* scarpa *your food is the best compliment a chef can get.*

MAKES 6 TO 8 SERVINGS

⅓ cup extra-virgin olive oil
2 cloves garlic, thickly sliced
1½ pounds broccoli rabe, cut into 2-inch lengths
½ cup Chicken Stock (page 15), Vegetable Stock (page 17), low-sodium canned broth, or water

¼ teaspoon hot red pepper flakes
Salt
6 slices peasant bread (optional)
1 clove garlic, halved (optional)

In a large soup pot, heat the oil over medium-high heat. Add the sliced garlic and cook, stirring, until golden, about 3 minutes. Add the broccoli rabe and stir vigorously to coat evenly with oil. Add the stock, red pepper flakes, and salt to taste, cover, and simmer until the broccoli rabe is tender, 10 to 15 minutes. If the mixture becomes too dry, add stock or water 1 tablespoon at a time; the finished dish should be quite wet. Taste for salt.

Meanwhile, if using, toast the bread. Rub the crusts with the cut sides of the garlic. Place a slice of bread in each serving bowl. Ladle the broccoli rabe and its juices over the bread and serve immediately.

PRO TIP: *There's a reason why you'll find thick slices of garlic in many Italian dishes. They are not meant to be eaten, but to flavor the dish while cooking. Big slices can be easily spotted and pushed aside on the plate, while minced garlic can't.*

ESCAROLE BRAISED IN TOMATOES AND HERBS

ESCAROLE IS SOUTHERN ITALY'S STAPLE VEG-
*etable. It's strong and easy to grow year-round. A
quick wilting in hot oil, garlic, and spicy red pepper,
then a slow braising in tomatoes makes escarole
into a deliciously rustic and easy dish. Cooked escarole is tender and flavorful, not bitter and tough as
the raw product can be. Serve this over grilled or
toasted bread, as we do at home, or as a side dish for
Italian Roast Chicken with Vegetables (page 183).
You can add stock and soaked beans to make an
easy soup, then add stale bread the next day to
make a typically Tuscan bread soup.*

MAKES **6** TO **8** SERVINGS

¼ cup extra-virgin olive oil
2 cloves garlic, thickly sliced
¼ teaspoon hot red pepper flakes, or more to
    taste
3 heads escarole, leaves separated and cut into
    2-inch lengths
1 cup milled or crushed canned Italian plum
    tomatoes
1 teaspoon dried oregano
Salt
3 tablespoons freshly grated Parmesan cheese
6 slices peasant bread (optional)
1 clove garlic, halved (optional)

In a large soup pot, heat the oil over medium-high
heat. Add the sliced garlic and cook, stirring, until
golden, about 2 minutes. Add the red pepper
flakes and cook 1 minute, then add the escarole
and stir vigorously to coat evenly with oil. Add the
tomatoes, oregano, and salt to taste. Cover and
simmer until the escarole is very tender, about 30
minutes, adding water if needed to keep the mixture moist. Transfer to a serving dish, sprinkle
with Parmesan cheese, and serve immediately or
set aside to cool to room temperature.

Meanwhile, if using, toast the bread. Rub the
crusts with the cut sides of the garlic. Place a slice
of bread in each serving bowl. Ladle the escarole
and its juices over the bread and serve immediately.

PRO TIP: *Evenly distribute the heat of
hot red pepper flakes in a dish by adding
them after you have browned the garlic, but
before adding the other ingredients. Mix
thoroughly and continue with the recipe.*

EGGPLANT GRATIN À LA PARADOU

WHENEVER I READ A DESCRIPTION OF A GREAT *restaurant experience in a guidebook, it's like I'm making a movie of it in my head. I can picture the whole place and imagine my meal long before I get there. Usually the reality can't live up to my movie, but at the Bistro du Paradou it did. From the moment I saw the owner, who looked like he came straight from Central Casting, that tiny Provençal bistro was perfect.*

It was a real bistro, where everyone eats the same meal. The guidebook had politely warned us that the Paradou was a quirky place, where everyone keeps his mouth shut and eats what he's given. It almost killed us that we couldn't get seconds on this appetizer, but we were too scared of getting thrown out to speak up.

After dinner, we sat outside with a Cognac and watched the residents play boules *and drink* pastis *late into the night. I decided that night that the people of Paradou didn't have to die—they already lived in heaven.*

MAKES 6 TO 8 SERVINGS

4 medium-size eggplant (do not peel)
Salt
3 to 4 cups pure olive oil
All-purpose flour, for dredging
3 cups Traditional Tomato Sauce (page 133)
1 teaspoon dried herbes de Provence or
    ½ teaspoon *each* dried oregano and
    dried thyme
½ cup grated French Gruyère cheese
2 tablespoons heavy cream
Pinch of white pepper

Cut off the top and bottom of each eggplant. Slice ½ inch thick and lay a single layer of slices on a baking sheet. Sprinkle generously with salt (about ¼ teaspoon per slice), then turn and salt the other side. Repeat with the remaining eggplant, putting a sheet of wax paper between each layer. Rest another baking sheet on the very top and weigh it down with full cans (or anything heavy). Set aside to drain for 2 to 4 hours. Rinse under running water and drain on paper or kitchen towels.

In a large, deep skillet, heat 2 inches of the olive oil until very hot but not smoking. Spread the flour out on a plate. Working in batches to avoid crowding the pan, dredge the eggplant slices on both sides in flour. Shake off any excess and immediately slip into the oil. Cook until golden brown on both sides. Drain on paper towels.

Preheat the oven to 350°F. Arrange the eggplant slices in overlapping rows in a baking dish. In order, add the tomato sauce, herbs, cheese, cream, and white pepper, distributing them evenly over the eggplant. Cover and bake until the cheese is browned and the eggplant is soft, about 45 minutes to 1 hour. Uncover the dish for the last 15 minutes of cooking. (The gratin can be made up to a day in advance and reheated in a 325°F oven before serving.)

 PRO TIP: *When deep-frying, always bring the ingredients to be fried to room temperature beforehand. Cold ingredients will lower the oil temperature, giving soggy results.*

BAKED BUTTON MUSHROOMS WITH PESTO

A MAINSTAY ON THE ANTIPASTO TABLE AT *Campagna, these mushrooms are dried out in the oven, then brought back to life with a garlicky pesto. They're best when you give them time to marinate; the dish is better the day after you make it. Keep it refrigerated and wrap it well to keep the flavors from escaping out of the mushrooms. Serve this pungent vegetable dish with plenty of bread, so none of the dressing is wasted.*

MAKES 8 TO 12 SERVINGS

3 pounds white button mushrooms, preferably of uniform size
3 cloves garlic, peeled
1 cup fresh basil leaves
⅓ cup fresh Italian parsley leaves
Juice of 1 lemon, or more to taste
1 cup extra-virgin olive oil
Salt
Pinch of hot red pepper flakes

Preheat the oven to 450°F.

Arrange the mushrooms in a large baking dish or roasting pan. Cover with a lid or foil and bake 30 minutes. Carefully uncover the pan, making sure not to burn yourself with the steam, and set aside to cool to room temperature.

Combine the garlic, basil, and parsley in a food processor. With the machine running, add the lemon juice and then slowly drizzle in the oil, until the mixture emulsifies. Add salt to taste and the red pepper flakes, and pulse just to mix. Taste for salt and lemon juice.

Drain any liquid from the mushrooms and transfer to a serving bowl. Add about half the pesto (basil mixture) and mix well. Add more pesto as desired, until the mushrooms are thickly coated but not swimming in dressing. Serve at room temperature.

OVEN-BRAISED FENNEL

FENNEL HAS SO MUCH FLAVOR AND NATURAL *sweetness that you don't want to do much to it. The light anise flavor really comes out with slow, simple cooking. Cooked fennel should be very soft and sweet; only raw fennel should be crisp. This vegetable goes with many main dishes; fennel and fish are a wonderful combination straight from the south of France, and fennel with roast pork is an Italian classic. No wonder this dish sells out every night at Campagna Home.*

MAKES 6 SERVINGS

3 fennel bulbs, trimmed and sliced lengthwise ¼ inch thick
⅓ cup extra-virgin olive oil
Salt and freshly ground black pepper

Preheat the oven to 400°F.

Arrange the fennel slices in a single layer in a baking dish or roasting pan. Drizzle with olive oil and sprinkle with salt and pepper to taste. Cover with a lid or foil and bake until the fennel is lightly browned and tender at the base when pierced with a knife, 35 to 45 minutes. Serve immediately or set aside to cool to room temperature.

PEARL ONIONS BAKED IN RED WINE

THESE ONIONS ARE ALWAYS ON THE ANTIPASTO *table at Campagna. They're a little showy, with a deep red-wine syrup, and people always notice them and order them. I think of them as one of my "hooks," and you can use them that way, too. Any time you serve whole onions as a vegetable, people are surprised and happy.*

Braising is one of my favorite techniques, because of how it concentrates flavors. When braising in wine, you usually have to cut the liquid with something lighter like stock or water. But in this recipe, the onions are strong enough to stand up to the red wine. This assertive dish is great with meat, poultry, and fish, especially roasts. Let it develop flavor by making it in advance, then serving it at room temperature.

MAKES 10 TO 14 SERVINGS

4 pints (8 cups) whole pearl onions or shallots, trimmed and peeled
2 cups dry red wine
¼ cup sugar
¼ cup extra-virgin olive oil
Salt and freshly ground black pepper

Preheat the oven to 325°F.

Arrange the onions in a deep baking dish or roasting pan, pour the wine, sugar, and oil over and sprinkle with salt and pepper to taste. Stir gently, cover with a lid or foil and bake until the onions are tender and the liquid is thick, 45 minutes to 1 hour. If the onions are cooked but the liquid is still thin, use a slotted spoon to transfer the onions to a serving bowl and simmer the liquid uncovered on top of the stove until syrupy. Taste for salt, pepper, and sugar. Pour over the onions and mix well. Set aside to cool to room temperature and serve.

LEEK GRATIN

I WAS TRAINED IN CLASSICAL FRENCH CUISINE, *but for eating, my favorite French food definitely comes from bistros. Leeks, a peasant winter staple, are a perfect example of simple bistro food, either poached and topped with vinaigrette or gratinéed with a little cream and cheese.*

Leeks are hardy vegetables that can grow almost year-round. They have lots of protective membranes to insulate them from the cold, and that's what can make them slimy. You want to wash them very, very well, forcing out the grit and removing the outer layers, which contain most of the membranes. Like any tough vegetable, leeks should be cooked long and slow, until very tender. You can make them well in advance, then reheat them just before serving.

MAKES 4 TO 6 SERVINGS

6 leeks, trimmed, split lengthwise, and well rinsed
Salt and freshly ground black pepper
1 tablespoon unsalted butter, cut into pieces
½ cup heavy cream
6 tablespoons grated Gruyère cheese

Preheat the oven to 350°F.

Arrange the leeks cut side up in a single layer in a baking dish. Sprinkle with salt and pepper to taste, dot with butter, and gently pour the cream over the top. Sprinkle with the cheese, cover with a lid or foil, and bake 35 minutes. Carefully uncover and bake 5 to 10 minutes more, until the top is golden brown and the leeks are tender.

 PRO TIP: *Whenever you are baking with cream, do not let the oven temperature exceed 400°F, or the cream will separate, leaving curds and an oily residue—not at all what you want in your dish!*

OVEN-BAKED BROCCOLI

BROCCOLI IS ONE OF AMERICANS' FAVORITE *vegetables, but I was a late convert; I didn't really love it until I tasted it cooked this way. Broccoli should be either very crisp, as in Chinese stir-fries, or very soft and sweet, as in this dish. Slowly baking broccoli in liquid, so that it cooks in its own juices, makes it tender and flavorful. The florets become almost crispy on top, and a golden glaze of Parmesan cheese pulls the whole thing together.*

MAKES 4 TO 6 SERVINGS

4 large heads broccoli, florets only, cut into
    2-inch pieces
2 cloves garlic, thinly sliced
2 tablespoons extra-virgin olive oil
¼ cup Chicken Stock (page 15), Vegetable Stock
    (page 17), low-sodium canned broth, or water
Salt and freshly ground black pepper
3 tablespoons freshly grated Parmesan cheese

Preheat the oven to 350°F.

Arrange the broccoli in a single layer in a baking dish or roasting pan. Dot with garlic, drizzle with oil and stock, and sprinkle with salt and pepper to taste. Cover with a lid or foil and bake about 25 minutes, until the broccoli is tender at the stalk when pierced with a knife. Uncover the dish and raise the heat to 425°F. Sprinkle with cheese and bake about 5 minutes more, until the cheese is melted and browned. Serve immediately or set aside to cool to room temperature.

PRO TIP: *There are times when "al dente" is not desirable for vegetables, and this is one of them. The broccoli should be cooked until very soft—this will concentrate the flavors.*

CAULIFLOWER STAINED WITH RED WINE

THIS DISH FROM THE ANTIPASTO TABLE AT *Campagna is one of the first vegetables my Roman friend Maria cooked for me—and the one that made me realize that she was a great cook. Cauliflower has a strong flavor (it's part of the cabbage family), but it can be watery if you steam or boil it. Maria solved that by baking it in red wine, giving it a deep, tangy flavor that is totally addictive. The purple and pink colors of the finished dish are also pretty impressive. You'll never go back to plain boiled cauliflower, that's for sure.*

MAKES 4 TO 6 SERVINGS

1 head cauliflower, cut into 2-inch chunks
1 clove garlic, thinly sliced
¼ cup extra-virgin olive oil
¾ cup dry red wine
Salt and freshly ground black pepper

Preheat the oven to 450°F.

Arrange the cauliflower in a single layer in a baking dish or roasting pan. Dot with the garlic, drizzle with the oil and wine, and sprinkle with salt and pepper to taste. Cover with a lid or foil and bake about 30 minutes, until the cauliflower is tender at the stalk when pierced with a knife. Set aside to cool to room temperature and serve. If desired, simmer the pan liquids in a separate pan until thick to make a sauce for the cauliflower.

PRO TIP: *Vegetables are at their most flavorful at room temperature. Be sure to make this ahead so that it can cool properly. If you must refrigerate it in advance, let it warm up before serving.*

SPINACH SAUTÉED WITH OLIVE OIL AND GARLIC

OLIVE OYL MADE POPEYE EAT HIS SPINACH, *right? Extra-virgin olive oil makes me eat mine. The flavor of a fruity olive oil is a perfect match for the strong flavor of spinach in this side dish, a companion to many dishes at Campagna. Spinach and fish are great together; so are spinach and lamb. And this is also the classic accompaniment for my favorite steak,* Tagliata alla Fiorentina *(page 193). You can apply the same cooking method to escarole, chard, and other greens, but you will have to cook them longer.*

MAKES 6 TO 8 SERVINGS

¼ cup extra-virgin olive oil
2 large cloves garlic, thickly sliced
2 pounds fresh spinach, well washed
Salt

Preheat the oven to 250°F.

In a large skillet, heat the oil over medium-high heat. Add the garlic and cook, stirring, until golden, about 3 minutes. Working in batches to avoid crowding the pan, add a large handful of spinach, with the water that clings to the leaves, to the skillet, using tongs to move it around in the hot pan. When it wilts, remove to a baking dish and place in the oven to keep warm. As each batch is finished, remove to the baking dish. When all the spinach is cooked, sprinkle with salt to taste, mix together gently, and serve immediately.

PRO TIP: *Keeping things moving in the pan is one of the most valuable tricks of the chef trade. To let the spinach sauté rather than steam in its own water, you need a hot pan with not too much spinach in it.*

FRENCH-STYLE SAUTÉED SPINACH

SPINACH IS ONE OF THE FEW VEGETABLES *that's equally at home in Italy and France. That's because it adapts well to both Italian and French cooking styles. Italians cook raw spinach in a matter of seconds, with olive oil and garlic; the French blanch and then sauté it with butter and nutmeg. My son loves the French kind the most. Maybe there's a little French chef in that boy! (Dad wouldn't mind.)*

MAKES 6 TO 8 SERVINGS

2 pounds fresh spinach, well washed
6 tablespoons unsalted butter
1 clove garlic, smashed and peeled
Pinch of ground nutmeg, preferably freshly grated
Salt

Bring a large pot of salted water to a boil. Prepare a large bowl of ice water. When the water boils, add ¼ of the spinach and cook 1 minute. Using a slotted spoon, transfer to the ice water. Repeat until all the spinach is cooked, adding ice to the water in the bowl as needed to keep it very cold. When all the spinach is cooked and cooled, lift out of the ice bath in batches and squeeze firmly (do not wring) to remove excess water. Lay on kitchen towels to drain.

When ready to serve, melt the butter in a large skillet over medium heat. Add the garlic and cook, stirring, until golden, about 3 minutes. Add a handful of spinach to the skillet and use tongs to move it around in the hot pan, separating the leaves. Working quickly, as soon as each handful heats through, add another handful. Lower the heat to medium if the butter starts to brown; add a tablespoon of water if the pan becomes too dry.

CONTINUED

Sprinkle with nutmeg and salt to taste, mix well, and serve immediately.

PRO TIP: *When sautéing with butter, heat the pan over medium-high heat before adding the butter. This lets the butter fry for a moment and take on a nutty flavor. Then reduce the heat to medium to finish melting.*

A FRESH OLIVE BRANCH, THE SYMBOL OF PEACE.

SPICED BEET PUREE

CAMPAGNA IS A COUNTRY ITALIAN RESTAURANT, *but many non-Italian cooks have influenced me throughout my career. I worked with a Jamaican chef who made a spicy puree he called "Granny's beets." Like a lot of dishes named after grandmothers (see Lasagne della Nonna, page 180), it was terrific. It uses the natural sweetness of beets, spicing them up with a little brown sugar and cloves. I think it's important to stiffen the texture of these beets with a couple of potatoes, which add the starch you need for a silky puree. Serve this island favorite with poultry or fish.*

MAKES 8 SERVINGS

8 large beets (do not peel)
2 medium potatoes (do not peel)
¼ cup heavy cream
2 tablespoons unsalted butter
2 tablespoons dark brown sugar
⅛ teaspoon ground cinnamon
Pinch of ground cloves
Salt and freshly ground black pepper

Bring two pots of lightly salted water to a boil. Separately boil the beets and potatoes until tender all the way through, about 15 minutes. Remove to a colander and set aside until cool enough to handle.

Meanwhile, in a saucepan, heat the cream just until it simmers. Turn off the heat, add the butter, sugar, cinnamon, cloves, and salt and pepper to taste, and stir. Set aside to infuse.

When the beets and potatoes have cooled slightly, peel and place in a food processor or food mill. Puree just until smooth, add the cream mixture, and mix well. Serve immediately.

WINTER VEGETABLE ROAST

WHEN YOU'RE GOING ALL OUT FOR A FALL OR *winter dinner, this is the ultimate side dish. The earthy flavors are great with roasted meat or poultry. For a stunning presentation, spoon the finished vegetables around the roast on a serving platter.*

The vegetables used in this recipe aren't written in stone. You could use only two or three of them, or substitute diced sweet potatoes or carrots for the orange squash and pumpkin.

MAKES 6 TO 10 SERVINGS

1 pint Brussels sprouts, outer leaves removed
2 large beets (do not peel)
1 large butternut squash or 2 acorn squash
1 small pumpkin
¼ cup extra-virgin olive oil
4 tablespoons unsalted butter, cut into pieces
2 tablespoons sugar
Salt
⅛ teaspoon nutmeg

Bring two pots of salted water to a boil. With the tip of a small knife, cut an X into the base of each Brussels sprout. Cook the beets and Brussels sprouts in separate pots until just tender. Prepare a bowl of ice water. When the vegetables are cooked, plunge them into ice water to stop the cooking. While the beets are still warm, peel them and cut them into ½-inch dice. Cut the Brussels sprouts in half and set aside.

Meanwhile, cut the stems out of the squash and pumpkin. Peel them with a sturdy peeler or sharp paring knife. Cut in half, scoop out the seeds, and cut into ½-inch dice.

Preheat the oven to 450°F.

When all the vegetables are prepared, toss them together and spread on cookie sheets or in earthenware baking dishes. Drizzle with olive oil and dot with butter. Sprinkle with sugar, plenty of salt, and nutmeg. Bake until tender all the way through and a little crusty, 30 to 45 minutes. Start checking the vegetables after 30 minutes.

If you want to make the vegetables more crusty, raise the heat at the end of the cooking to 550°F. Bake until browned and serve immediately or at room temperature.

SAUTÉED POTATOES AND ONIONS

MY FIRST MEMORY OF EUROPE IS ABOUT POTA-*toes. When I arrived at the Heissischer Hof in Frankfurt, I was still nervous about the decision I'd made to uproot myself. When I was asked if I wanted to see the kitchen, of course I said yes. The first stop was the* kartoffel kuche, *potato kitchen. Later that day, I called home and my mother asked how I liked it there. My reply was "Mom, this place is serious. They even have a separate kitchen just for potatoes." And the rest is history.*

I learned all about potatoes in Germany. Germans almost always boil potatoes before sautéing them; it's much easier to get boiled potatoes to brown evenly. If you've ever tried to make lyonnaise potatoes (which is similar to this dish), you know what I mean: If you try to brown the raw potatoes, the onions burn; if you reduce the heat, the potatoes won't cook. Here's the solution. It's called brat kartoffel *in German. Using clarified butter prevents the potatoes and onions from burning.*

MAKES 4 SERVINGS

6 medium potatoes
2 tablespoons clarified butter (see Pro Tip)
4 tablespoons extra-virgin olive oil
I medium-size onion, thinly sliced into rings and
    pulled apart
Salt and freshly ground black pepper

Bring a pot of lightly salted water to a boil. Add the potatoes and boil until just tender all the way through, 12 to 15 minutes. Remove to a colander and set aside until cool enough to handle. Peel and slice ½ inch thick.

Preheat the oven to 425°F.

In a medium-size skillet, heat 1 tablespoon of the butter and 2 tablespoons of the oil over high heat until it is hot but not smoking. Lay half of the potatoes in a single layer in the skillet. Cook until golden brown on one side, then turn the potatoes over and add half of the onions to the skillet. Sprinkle with salt and pepper to taste and continue cooking, turning occasionally, until the onions are soft and the potatoes are nicely browned. Transfer to a baking dish and place in the oven to keep warm while you cook the second batch.

PRO TIP: *To make clarified butter, slowly heat unsalted butter in a heavy skillet. When the butter is completely melted and the milk solids sink to the bottom, leaving a golden liquid on the surface, pour off the liquid. This liquid is clarified butter.*

MONTREUX RÖSTI

I'VE ALWAYS LIKED VAN GOGH'S PAINTING *THE* Potato-Eaters, *because it tells you so much about the life of the peasants it depicts. German, Swiss, and Dutch peasant cooks have invented countless recipes for potatoes over the centuries.*

Rösti, delicious pancakes of grated potato and onion mixed with cheese, are popular in Germany and Switzerland. Rösti are probably my favorite of all Swiss dishes, and I learned to make them perfectly at the Montreux Palace Hotel. Boiling the potatoes beforehand makes it easier. The secret of successful rösti *is to cook them gradually over medium heat, so they brown evenly and cook all the way through.*

MAKES 2 TO 4 SERVINGS

8 medium potatoes, peeled
1 medium onion, grated
½ cup grated Swiss appenzeller, Gruyère, or
    another hard Swiss-made cheese
1 large egg, beaten
2 teaspoons salt
Freshly ground black pepper
2 tablespoons unsalted butter
4 tablespoons extra-virgin olive oil

Bring a pot of lightly salted water to a boil. Add the potatoes and boil until just tender all the way through, about 15 minutes. Remove to a colander and set aside until cool enough to handle.

Preheat the oven to 400°F.

Using a hand grater or, preferably, a food processor, coarsely grate the potatoes and transfer to a nonreactive mixing bowl. Grate the onion and add to the potatoes. Add the cheese, egg, salt, and pepper to taste and mix well.

In a medium-size skillet, heat 1 tablespoon of the butter and 2 tablespoons of the oil over medium-high heat. Add half of the potato mixture, reduce the heat to medium, and, using the back of a spatula, spread and flatten the potatoes until they form a thick pancake.

Slowly cook until golden brown, about 10 minutes, then flip (see Pro Tip), and repeat. When both sides are golden brown and the center is hot, transfer to a baking dish and place in the oven while you repeat the process with the remaining ingredients. Serve hot. Cut into wedges or break apart at the table.

PRO TIP: *To flip any large pancake in the pan, cook it on one side until the bottom is well browned. Use a spatula to loosen it in the pan, then tilt the pan and slide the pancake out onto a serving plate. Holding the plate on the bottom with one hand, turn the empty pan upside down on top of the pancake. Quickly and gently flip the pancake so that the raw side is in the pan, then replace the pan on the heat. Use the same plate for serving.*

GREAT MASHED POTATOES

THIS IS MY FAVORITE POTATO DISH, AND A LOT *of my customers at Campagna agree. When they ask me for the secret ingredient, I tell them: butter, butter, more butter—and finish with a little butter. I also add freshly grated Parmesan cheese. You now have the perfect bed for* Osso Buco alla Fiorentina *(page 190) and almost any stew.*

MAKES 8 TO 10 SERVINGS

3 pounds potatoes, preferably Yukon Gold, peeled and quartered
½ cup whole milk or heavy cream
¼ cup (½ stick) unsalted butter, or to taste
¼ cup freshly grated Parmesan cheese
Salt
White pepper

Preheat the oven to 400°F.

Bring a pot of lightly salted water to a boil. Add the potatoes and boil until very tender all the way through, 15 to 20 minutes. Remove to a colander, place the colander on a baking sheet, and place in the oven for 4 minutes to dry the potatoes.

Meanwhile, in a small saucepan, bring the milk and butter just to a simmer. Turn off the heat.

In a large nonreactive mixing bowl, combine the potatoes and the milk mixture. Using a potato masher or hand blender, mash quickly and thoroughly until there are almost no lumps remaining. Add the cheese, season to taste with butter, salt and pepper, and serve immediately.

CAMPAGNA ROASTED POTATOES

BEING TRAINED IN EUROPE HAS PAID OFF FOR *me in more ways than I can count. European chefs are famous for their vegetables, and my knowledge of the best ways to prepare them is what helps make Campagna special. Here's a Campagna secret: You don't have to raise the temperature to get your potatoes brown and tender; just take it slow. At 350°F, small potatoes will roast nicely in under an hour.*

MAKES 6 TO 8 SERVINGS

25 small red, white, or yellow potatoes (about the size of golf balls; do not peel); see Pro Tip
Salt and freshly ground black pepper
2 cloves garlic, thinly sliced
1 tablespoon chopped fresh rosemary leaves
⅓ cup extra-virgin olive oil

Preheat the oven to 350°F.

Arrange the potatoes in a single layer in a non-stick baking dish or roasting pan. Sprinkle with salt and pepper to taste, dot with garlic and rosemary, and drizzle with oil. Bake about 45 minutes, stirring occasionally, until tender all the way through when pierced with a knife. Serve immediately or set aside to cool to room temperature.

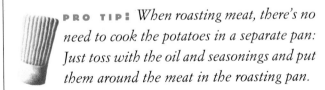 **PRO TIP:** *When roasting meat, there's no need to cook the potatoes in a separate pan: Just toss with the oil and seasonings and put them around the meat in the roasting pan.*

ONE-POT
MEALS

ONE-POT MEALS

THE SAVORY, SATISFYING ONE-POT MEALS IN THIS CHAPTER are proof that I was an Italian peasant cook in a past life. Through generations of experience, peasant cooks have learned that cooking meat, beans, vegetables, aromatics, and starches like rice or pasta together in one pot makes for incredible depth of flavor—nothing is wasted or lost. When the big harvests of the Italian countryside come around (such as grapes, olives, tobacco, tomatoes), cooks stop

cooking for six people and start cooking for sixty. According to tradition, the harvest workers must be fed a filling homemade meal in the middle of the day, to keep them going until dark. These enriched, fortified soup/stews, such as my Italian Harvest Soup, are delicious and satisfying, and true one-pot meals: You don't need to serve another thing except bread and maybe a salad.

I think that today's American families are a modern version of these peasants, with smaller kitchens and less time to cook. We work incredibly long hours—almost twice as many as our parents did. We like the idea of doing our own cooking and gardening, even if we don't have the time. Christofle is out, earthenware is in. We want to be satisfied and comforted at mealtime, not challenged. And while we don't have to

have fancy food, we want clean and wholesome food made from the best ingredients, to help us preserve our families' wellness.

Like many parents, I wish I had more time with my kids, and more time for cooking at home. Weekends are a good time to try cooking with your kids and to teach them to become careful consumers. For example, *Pasta e Fagioli* (page 113) is a great family project. The trick is to make one batch with supermarket produce, then another with organic produce. See if they can taste the difference. If they are old enough, have them add up the cost of each soup. As a family, you can decide whether the difference in health and flavor is worth the extra money. The results may surprise you. Plus, there's nothing better in the world than watching your kids try to make their spoons stand up in their thick soup, while you breathe in the pungent olive oil and know that there's only one dirty pot waiting in the kitchen.

OVERLEAF: **A FALL LUNCH OF ONE-POT MEALS: CRAZY SEAFOOD SOUP, MUSSELS IN BRODETTO, BRAISED SHORT RIBS WITH LENTILS, AND OLD-FASHIONED SAUSAGES AND PEPPERS.**

A well-made soup is one of the most tasty, most soothing, and most underrated foods there is. To me, as a chef, soup is one of the really great ways to wring the flavor out of your ingredients and into the finished dish. To me, as a home cook, soup can be a simple appetizer, a great lunch, or the perfect way to gather your family around the table on a cold night. It's too bad that some people don't think of soup as "special" enough for company. The way I see it, whenever we cook, our goal should be to make whoever is eating feel satisfied—we don't have to reinvent the wheel with every dish. A well-crafted soup is simple and sublime. Eating a bowl of homemade soup is like having your mother around taking care of you.

To me, soup is best at home. There's a huge difference between sitting in a restaurant with a single plate of soup in front of you, and collecting around a table, watching as the soup is ladled out of a steaming tureen into bowls and passed around. Sharing from a communal dish is a natural part of family life. All children love soup (why do you think there are ninety-seven varieties of Campbell's?) and the ritual of serving, and then slurping, a hot soup is fascinating to them. Children are not usually very interested in salad, and by the time you're carving up the chicken for the main course they have probably wandered off somewhere, but a steaming tureen of soup at the beginning of the meal really grabs them. Get out the tureen and the ladle just once a month, and I guarantee your kids will remember the ritual forever.

When grownups are around, make meals at your house a little more comfortable and beautiful—and make people even more

A CENTERPIECE OF McINTOSH APPLES IN A PROVENÇAL *COMPOTIER.*

impressed by the food you work hard to make—by starting a collection of serving pieces right away. If you've already started, keep going. Bowls, platters, and oversize plates in lots of colors don't have to be expensive and can be mixed and matched endlessly. A big oval soup tureen (white porcelain is nice and versatile) will be with you forever. It adds a certain drama to serving soup that really makes people appreciate it—and you. And don't put it away in a closet, or save it only for "special occasions." If you don't use your nice things, you'll forget why you bought them in the first place.

In restaurants, shallow soup plates are traditionally used for clear soups. Tiny, thin cups with two handles are considered suitable for cream soups. But for a good helping of homemade soup or stew, I like nice deep bowls—heavy enough that I don't have to worry that my kids will flip them over into their laps. The medium-size heavy bowls that the French use to drink their *café au lait* from are perfect, and they are thick enough to keep things hot. And that's the main thing about soup, right?

For appetizer soups, I don't like a big mix of flavors. These are very simple and direct—pea soup, potato soup, mushroom soup, chicken soup. Period. Of course, all of them are the absolute best they can be, but they are not fancy. Clear consommés and velouté bisques are haute cuisine, but these soups are home cooking. Soup is peasant-style cooking, however you slice it. After all, water is free! I've taken a few of my favorites (from every part of my background: Jewish, American, Italian, German, and French) and refined them into a core group that will take you through every season and every occasion.

Another thing about the soup pot: It is not a garbage can. Soup can be made without a lot of different ingredients and without anything fancy, but whatever you use has to taste good to start with; don't toss in everything hanging around in the refrigerator. A good soup has a bright, clear taste, not a murky mix of flavors. I learned this in Germany where I worked in a kitchen that produced seven completely different soups each day. Those people really loved their soup.

And what's not to love? Soup is the perfect, not-too-filling appetizer; with a piece of crusty bread and a chunk of cheese, it's lunch. Soup freezes with no problem and can be made days before you need it. When you're heading for the country on Friday evening, you can take along a container of your frozen homemade soup. Warm it up when you get there and you'll know you're in heaven. As the seasons roll around, you can use the freshest vegetables and infuse your soups with their sweetness—or you can use canned tomatoes and winter potatoes in the depths of February and still make great soup for your family and friends that is comforting, savory, and easy to eat. If you have even the slightest desire to dress up the occasion, just a few snippets of chive make everyone sit up and pay attention to your homemade soup. And if you make the easy Baked Croutons on page 18, I guarantee you will get a reputation as a great cook.

Most important, your kids will always remember the time you spent with them in the kitchen. Their senses will always respond to the smells and flavors you create. Cooking is all about sharing the tastes, smells, and traditions that you love, and making big pots of soup and stew is a wholesome way to give your kids a great meal and a great memory at the same time.

ITALIAN HARVEST SOUP

THE TUSCAN YEAR BY ELIZABETH ROMER IS, *in my opinion, the best Italian country cookbook ever written. The recipes are vague, but the writing is not. Romer describes the life of her Tuscan neighbor Silvana Cerotti, the wife of a tobacco farmer, in great detail. Tracking Silvana's daily cooking rituals and the family's seasonal preserving, cheesemaking, and meat-curing traditions through an entire year tells you all you need to know about Italian cooking.*

This recipe was inspired by Romer's account of the tobacco harvest, when Silvana goes from cooking for a household of four to a work team of forty. She does it by bringing out her huge old cauldron and cooking the old-fashioned way, over the fire. She makes thick, delicious lunchtime soups that fill everyone up—without making them too sleepy to go back to work. Sounds like a good idea, right? Whether cooked in a cauldron or your stockpot, this is a great soup to feed a family.

MAKES 8 TO 12 SERVINGS

1 cup dried white beans, such as borlotti, cannellini, navy, or Great Northern
¼ cup extra-virgin olive oil
2 cloves garlic, thinly sliced
1 onion, chopped
12 button mushrooms, thinly sliced
1 small head escarole, coarsely chopped
½ head cauliflower, coarsely chopped
1 small zucchini, sliced crosswise into 1-inch pieces
One 28-ounce can milled or crushed canned Italian plum tomatoes
¼ head red cabbage, thinly sliced
1 pound bottom or top round of beef, or beef stew meat, cut into ½-inch cubes
1 bottle (750 ml) dry red wine

5 quarts Chicken Stock (page 15), low-sodium canned broth, or water
1 tablespoon freshly chopped rosemary leaves
1 tablespoon freshly chopped sage
1 piece rind from Parmigiano-Reggiano cheese, about 2 inches square
Salt
½ cup dried tubilati or another small pasta shape
Freshly ground black pepper
1 tablespoon per serving freshly grated Parmesan cheese, for serving
Extra-virgin olive oil, for serving

The day before making the soup, cover the beans with at least 4 cups cold water. Soak 12 to 24 hours, changing the water every 8 hours or so. Drain, rinse, and drain again.

In a large soup pot, heat the olive oil over medium-high heat. Add the garlic and onion and cook, stirring, until the onion is wilted, about 3 minutes. Add the mushrooms and cook, stirring, 1 minute. Add all the vegetables, the soaked beans, beef, wine, stock, rosemary, sage, cheese rind, and a teaspoon of salt. Cover and bring to a simmer. Reduce the heat and simmer, uncovered, about 1½ hours, until the beans are tender.

Add 2 cups water and the pasta, return the soup to a simmer, and cook 20 minutes more, until the pasta and beans are both very soft. Add more water if necessary to thin the soup. Season with salt and pepper to taste. Serve sprinkled with Parmesan and drizzled with olive oil.

 PRO TIP: *In a chunky soup like this one, you can adjust the vegetables to suit your taste. Feel free to add carrots, celery, squash, and other kinds of greens.*

PAPPA AL POMODORO

THIS SOUP IS MY FAVORITE MEMBER OF THE *great Tuscan family of bread soups. It is eaten all summer long in Florence, at room temperature to bring out the flavors. I tasted a memorable one at the Cantinetta Antinori, a Florentine wine bar connected to the great Chianti estate of the Antinori family. The dish was drizzled with their Peppoli olive oil, and tasted like pure heaven.*

When cooking Pappa al Pomodoro, *you need to think like a traditional Tuscan cook, using stale bread and plentiful tomatoes and olive oil to make a satisfying dinner for your family. If your bread is white on the inside, you can use day-old bread; but brown and whole-grain breads should be at least two or three days old. The bread must be dry so that it can absorb the tomatoes and olive oil. Always garnish this soup with your most fragrant and expensive olive oil.*

MAKES **8** SERVINGS

⅓ cup extra-virgin olive oil
1 clove garlic, thinly sliced
12 very ripe tomatoes, cut into chunks
½ loaf (about 12 ounces) stale peasant bread, cut
    into 1-inch cubes
12 leaves fresh basil, torn into small pieces
Salt and freshly ground black pepper
Freshly grated Parmesan cheese, for serving
Extra-virgin olive oil, for serving

In a large soup pot, heat the olive oil over medium heat. Add the garlic and cook, stirring, until golden brown, about 5 minutes. Add the tomatoes, bring to a simmer, and simmer 5 minutes. Add the bread, basil, and salt and pepper to taste, reduce the heat, and simmer gently, uncovered, until the tomatoes are cooked and the bread has absorbed the liquid. Taste for salt and pepper. Serve hot or at room temperature, garnishing each serving with a tablespoon of Parmesan and a drizzle of olive oil.

 PRO TIP: *If your bread is not stale enough, cut into chunks and let it dry out at room temperature for a few hours before making the dish.*

MARIA'S BREAD AND ONION SOUP WITH SMOKED MOZZARELLA

MY FRIEND MARIA, BEING THE COMPLETE *Italian matriarch, has certain ideas about food and health. She always insists that anyone sick needs to* mangia bianco, *or "eat white." The ingredients in this recipe seemed to qualify, although it doesn't taste like something you have to eat when you're sick. The savory onions, soft bread, and melted cheese do make you feel well taken care of. Maybe that was Maria's point.*

This is somewhere between a soup and a casserole, making it a complete meal if you add a substantial salad. If you like smoked mozzarella, you can use it here. But there's no substitute for a good heavy crusty peasant bread, sliced thick enough to keep its shape.

MAKES 8 TO 12 SERVINGS

½ cup extra-virgin olive oil
12 medium red onions, thinly sliced
3 cloves garlic, thinly sliced
2 stalks celery, thinly sliced
2 quarts Chicken Stock (page 15), Vegetable
    Stock (page 17), or low-sodium canned broth
Salt and freshly ground black pepper
10 thick slices day-old peasant bread
8 ounces smoked or lightly salted fresh
    mozzarella cheese, thickly sliced
6 tablespoons freshly grated Parmesan cheese

In a large soup pot, heat the olive oil over medium-high heat. Add the onions, garlic, and celery, and cook, stirring, until the onions are translucent, about 8 minutes. Add the stock and a large pinch of salt, reduce the heat to a simmer, and cover. Simmer 40 minutes, until the onions are starting to melt into the broth. Working in batches in a blender, or using a hand blender, puree half of the soup until smooth. Combine with the rest of the onion mixture and mix well. Season with salt and pepper to taste.

Preheat the oven to 350°F.

Meanwhile, line a deep baking dish with half of the bread. Cover with half of the mozzarella. When the onion mixture is ready, pour half of it over the bread and cheese and let soak through. Lay the remaining bread on top, then the remaining cheese. Pour the rest of the onion mixture on top and let soak through. Sprinkle on the Parmesan cheese and cover tightly with foil or a lid. Bake 25 minutes, uncover, and bake 5 minutes more, until the top is golden brown. Serve hot or at room temperature.

PRO TIP: *When making Italian bread soups and salads, it is important to use a top-quality crusty peasant-style bread with a thick texture; other breads will become slimy.*

TUSCAN MUSHROOM SOUP

IN TUSCANY, AFTER A RAINFALL, YOU SUD-
denly see parked cars lining the roads through the
forests—with not a soul in sight. That's because
everyone is deep in the woods, hunting mushrooms.
There are up to two hundred different mushrooms in
Tuscany alone, and Tuscans learn from childhood
how to find and identify the edible ones.

Even if your mushrooms come dried from the
gourmet shop, not fresh from the woods, this soup
will fill your entire house with powerful smells of
beef, tomatoes, wine, herbs, and vegetables. You
can tell from the hefty ingredient list that this is not
a fancy soup. Thick, whole-meal soups like this are
from the peasant tradition of putting everything in
one pot and braising it all together. With salad,
bread, and cheese, it's definitely dinner.

I never discard the liquid used to reconstitute the
dried porcini mushrooms. In this dish, they're
soaked in wine and the whole mixture goes into the
soup pot.

MAKES 6 SERVINGS

½ cup dried white beans, such as borlotti,
    cannellini, navy, or Great Northern
½ cup dry red wine
3 tablespoons dried porcini mushrooms
¼ cup extra-virgin olive oil
I onion, minced
I clove garlic, minced
2 pounds assorted fresh mushrooms, such as
    cremini, shiitake, portobello, chanterelle, and
    white button, thinly sliced
8 ounces beef stewing meat, cut into ½-inch dice
    (optional)

**HERBS AND ASSORTED MUSHROOMS TO MAKE TUSCAN
MUSHROOM SOUP.**

I large carrot, diced
I leek, split lengthwise, rinsed, and coarsely
    chopped
I cup fresh or frozen peas
¼ cup minced prosciutto (optional)
2 teaspoons freshly chopped rosemary leaves
2 teaspoons freshly chopped sage
1½ cups milled or crushed canned Italian plum
    tomatoes
2 quarts Chicken Stock (page 15), Vegetable
    Stock (page 17), water, or low-sodium
    canned broth
Salt and freshly ground black pepper
8 small slices peasant bread, for serving
I clove garlic, peeled, for serving
Freshly grated Parmesan cheese, for serving

Place the beans in a bowl and cover with plenty of
cold water. Soak overnight, changing the water
every 8 hours or so. Drain, rinse, and drain again.
Set aside.

In a small nonreactive saucepan, bring the wine
to a simmer. Add the dried mushrooms and turn
off the heat. Cover and set aside for 30 minutes.

In a large soup pot, heat the olive oil over
medium-high heat. Add the onion, garlic, fresh
mushrooms, and beef, if using, and cook, stirring,
until the onion is translucent, about 5 minutes.
Add the carrot, leek, peas, and prosciutto, and
cook, stirring, 2 minutes. Add the soaked mushrooms with their liquid, the drained beans, the
rosemary, sage, tomatoes, stock, and a large pinch
of salt, mix well, cover, and reduce the heat to a
simmer. Simmer 1½ hours, or until the beans are
soft. Season with salt and pepper to taste.

When ready to serve, toast or grill the bread.
Lightly rub each slice with the garlic. To serve,
place a slice of garlic toast in the bottom of each
serving bowl. Ladle the soup over the bread and
top with Parmesan cheese.

EINTOPF SOUP

WHEN I WORKED AT THE HEISSISCHER HOF IN *Frankfurt, every Saturday morning was devoted to making* Eintopf. *The chef made it from the pieces of top-quality pork, veal, beef, and sausages that were left from a week of fine cooking, adding beans, vegetables, and of course potatoes. Everyone loved it and looked forward to it all week.* Eintopf *introduced me to the whole idea of one-pot cooking. This is my interpretation of that soup. It's still a great Saturday morning cooking project. Freeze half the batch for a cold winter day when you'd rather play in the snow than make lunch.*

MAKES 12 TO 15 SERVINGS

2 teaspoons chopped fresh rosemary leaves
6 fresh sage leaves
2 bay leaves
2 whole cloves
1 cinnamon stick
1/2 cup extra-virgin olive oil
2 onions, chopped
2 cloves garlic, thinly sliced
1 cup lentils, preferably French green
1/2 pound pork stew meat, cut into 1/2-inch dice
1/2 pound beef stew meat, cut into 1/2-inch dice
1/2 pound veal stew meat, cut into 1/2-inch dice
2 fresh sweet Italian sausages, casings removed
1 thick slice smoked bacon, diced
4 potatoes, peeled and diced
2 carrots, diced
2 celery stalks, diced
2 large leeks, split lengthwise, well rinsed, and diced
1 turnip, peeled and diced
1 cup milled or crushed canned Italian plum tomatoes
1 bottle (750 ml) dry white wine

6 quarts Chicken Stock (page 15), low-sodium canned broth, or a combination of broth and water
1 teaspoon ground white pepper
Salt and freshly ground black pepper

In a square of cheesecloth, place the rosemary, sage, bay leaves, cloves, and cinnamon stick. Tie the corners together or tie with kitchen twine to secure.

In a large soup pot, heat the oil over medium heat. Add the onions and garlic and cook, stirring, until the onions are wilted, about 3 minutes. Add the lentils and cook, stirring to coat, 1 minute. Add the remaining ingredients and a large pinch of salt, cover, and bring to a simmer. Reduce the heat and simmer, uncovered, about 1 hour, until the vegetables are soft. Skim off any scum that may rise to the surface of the soup. Remove and discard the cheesecloth bundle before serving. Season with salt and pepper to taste and serve.

 PRO TIP: *Skimming impurities from the top is a must when simmering with meat.*

PASTA E FAGIOLI

ITALIANS WILL TELL YOU THAT *PASTA E FAGIOLI* *gets thicker as you travel north. What starts as a soup down in Puglia ends up as a thick stew somewhere around Venice. The test is whether the* pasta e fagioli *is thick enough to hold the spoon standing up straight in the bowl. Some even claim that the Leaning Tower of Pisa leans at the angle of the spoon in the* pasta e fagioli *there!*

Pasta e fagioli *is one of the few Italian dishes that belongs to the entire country, not a specific region. It combines a traditional northern staple (beans) with the traditional southern staple (pasta). Only dried cranberry (borlotti) beans are traditionally used for this dish in Italy; the others are merely good substitutes. The pasta should be well cooked, but not mushy. You must add some water with the pasta, to prevent the soup from getting too thick. The longer you cook this soup, the thicker it will get.*

Don't forget the Parmesan cheese and olive oil for serving at the end; they really make the dish.

MAKES 10 TO 12 SERVINGS

2 pounds shelled fresh or 1 pound dried cranberry (borlotti) beans, or 1 pound other dried beans such as cannellini, navy, or Great Northern

3 tablespoons extra-virgin olive oil

2 cloves garlic, thinly sliced

1 large red onion, diced

1/4 pound prosciutto or smoked bacon, diced

3 rosemary sprigs

1 bay leaf

3 quarts Chicken Stock (page 15), Vegetable Stock (page 17), water, or low-sodium canned broth

2 cups crushed or milled canned Italian plum tomatoes

1 teaspoon hot red pepper flakes

Salt

1/4 pound dried tubilati or another small pasta shape, or long pasta broken up into small pieces

Freshly ground black pepper

1 tablespoon per serving freshly grated Parmesan cheese, for serving

Extra-virgin olive oil, for serving

If using dried beans, in a large bowl cover the beans with at least four times their volume of cold water. Soak 12 to 24 hours, changing the water every 8 hours or so. Drain, rinse, and drain again.

In a large soup pot, heat the olive oil over medium heat. Add the garlic, onion, and prosciutto and cook, stirring, until the onion is wilted, about 5 minutes. Add the fresh or soaked beans and cook, stirring, 1 minute. Add the rosemary, bay leaf, stock, tomatoes, red pepper flakes, and a large pinch of salt, cover, and bring to a simmer. Simmer about 1 hour, until the beans are very soft and beginning to split. Add the pasta and 1 cup cold water. Bring back to a simmer and simmer until the pasta is cooked. The finished soup should be very thick. Remove the rosemary sprigs and bay leaf. Season with salt and pepper to taste.

Serve hot or at room temperature, sprinkled with Parmesan and drizzled with extra-virgin olive oil.

PRO TIP: *Many people don't realize that cranberry beans and borlotti beans are one and the same: Either fresh or dried can be used here. You can add leftover cooked pasta instead of dried pasta at the end.*

CHICKEN POT-AU-FEU

COOKING IS ABOUT DEVELOPING SKILLS AND *techniques, but hospitality is all about caring for people. I learned a lot about both at the Montreux Palace Hotel in Switzerland. I remember watching the executive chef prepare this simple dish for a few families on Christmas Eve to eat at home after Midnight Mass. The diligence and care he put into it made as much of an impression on me as the buffets for twenty-five hundred people he used to create. He took the responsibility of cooking their holiday dinner very seriously, and I try to do that on holidays (and a little bit every day) at Campagna.*

Chicken poached in stock along with fresh vegetables and egg noodles is light but very satisfying. You'll want to begin the dish well in advance, to give the soup a chance to cool down before the final cooking. You can even complete the first half of the recipe the day before serving; cool the chicken and broth in the refrigerator overnight.

MAKES 8 SERVINGS

Two whole 4-pound chickens, preferably organic
    or free-range
2 cloves garlic, thinly sliced
1 onion, chopped
1 carrot, cut into 1-inch lengths
3 celery stalks, cut into 1-inch lengths
1 leek, halved lengthwise, well rinsed, and cut into
    1-inch lengths
1 turnip, peeled and cut into 1-inch dice
2 parsnips, peeled and cut into 1-inch dice
1 kohlrabi bulb, peeled and cut into 1-inch dice
1 cup shelled fresh or frozen peas
2 bay leaves
2 whole cloves
Pinch nutmeg
1 tablespoon freshly chopped rosemary leaves
2 teaspoons freshly chopped sage

1 teaspoon freshly chopped marjoram
4 quarts Chicken Stock (page 15) or
    low-sodium canned broth
2 cups dry white wine
Salt and freshly ground black pepper
½ pound egg noodles
4 tablespoons freshly chopped Italian parsley
2 tablespoons minced fresh chives, for serving

Reserving 2 tablespoons of the parsley, all the egg noodles, and the chives, combine all the other ingredients with a large pinch of salt in a large soup pot. Cover and bring almost to a boil over high heat, then uncover and immediately reduce the heat to a gentle simmer. Simmer as gently as possible about 2 hours, skimming as needed and adding more stock or cold water if the soup becomes too concentrated in flavor.

Turn off the heat. Carefully remove the chickens to a platter and set aside. Let the soup cool about 1 hour. A layer of golden chicken fat will have risen to the top of the soup; use a large spoon to remove as much of it as possible. Add the noodles and bring the soup back to a simmer.

Meanwhile, remove the chicken meat from the bones and cut into ½-inch chunks. Return to the soup and heat through. Season with salt and pepper to taste. When the noodles are soft, the soup is ready. Remove the bay leaves. Serve with the reserved parsley and chives.

 PRO TIP: *Even if you're not watching your weight, you'll want to remove the excess chicken fat from the top of the soup, otherwise it tastes and feels overly greasy.*

CHICKEN POT-AU-FEU SERVED IN A POT AT THE TABLE.

CRAZY SEAFOOD SOUP

THIS MIXED SEAFOOD SOUP IS FOUND UNDER *many names on the Italian coast:* Acqua pazza, *meaning "crazy water," is one.* Cacciucco, *from Livorno, is another. Legend has it that cacciucco must have at least five kinds of fish—one for each "c" in the name. Whatever you call the dish, it has become traditional for the Italian Christmas Eve dinner, when an all-seafood meal is eaten.*

This is real peasant food, not from the earth but from the sea. Fishermen sell their best catch at market and reserve the odds and ends for their own pots. When choosing your own fish, you can add and subtract from the recipe as you like. The garlic-rubbed bread adds a starchiness that makes the dish more substantial. Unlike most of the other dishes in this chapter, this seafood soup shouldn't be cooked for a long, long time. Simmer it gently just until the fish are tender and juicy and the broth is flavorful.

MAKES 6 SERVINGS

¼ cup extra-virgin olive oil, plus additional for serving

2 cloves garlic, thinly sliced

1 onion, minced

1 stalk celery, minced

1 carrot, minced

1½ pounds raw squid, cleaned and cut into 1-inch rings

1 teaspoon hot red pepper flakes

½ pound octopus, cooked as for Spicy Squid and Octopus Salad (page 70), or additional raw squid

12 mussels, rinsed

12 littleneck clams, rinsed

1 cup dry white wine

1 cup crushed canned Italian plum tomatoes

8 black brine-cured olives, such as Niçoise or Gaeta, pitted

8 capers, rinsed of salt or vinegar

2 teaspoons freshly chopped rosemary leaves

2 teaspoons freshly chopped oregano

2 teaspoons freshly chopped thyme

1 cup Fish Stock (page 17), clam juice, or additional white wine

Salt

¾ pound monkfish fillet, cut into 1-inch dice

12 sea scallops

12 medium-size shrimp, peeled and deveined

Freshly ground black pepper

1 loaf two- or three-day-old peasant bread, thickly sliced

3 cloves garlic (do not peel), halved lengthwise

2 tablespoons freshly chopped Italian parsley, for serving

In a large soup pot, heat the olive oil over medium heat. Add the thinly sliced garlic, onion, celery, carrot, squid, and red pepper flakes and cook, stirring, until the onion is translucent, 5 to 8 minutes. Add the octopus, mussels, clams, wine, tomatoes, olives, capers, herbs, stock, and a pinch of salt. Cover and bring to a boil over high heat. Uncover, reduce the heat to a simmer, and cook until the mussels and clams have opened, about 2 minutes more.

Add the monkfish and simmer 1 minute. Add the scallops and simmer 1 minute. Add the shrimp and cook 2 to 3 minutes more, just until firm. Season with salt and pepper to taste.

Meanwhile, toast or grill the bread. Rub the crusts with the cut sides of the garlic, on one or both sides of the bread. Place a slice of bread in the bottom of each serving bowl. Ladle the soup over the bread, being careful not to break up the pieces of monkfish. Drizzle with extra-virgin olive oil, sprinkle with parsley, and serve immediately, passing the remaining bread at the table.

LOBSTER AND SHRIMP FRA DIAVOLO

STRAIGHT FROM CAMPAGNA'S NOSTALGIC SUN-*day Night Supper menu, Lobster Fra Diavolo was one of the great treats of my childhood in New York City. It is spicy and tomato-rich, definitely from the old school of Italian-American cooking. It's also a great way to cook lobster, because the shells add lots of flavor to the stew and also protect the meat from drying out. This is not a pasta sauce, but a very fla-vorful stew—serve it with plenty of crusty bread and napkins. To crack the lobster claws yourself, wrap them in a kitchen towel and hit with a mallet.*

MAKES 6 SERVINGS

1/2 cup extra-virgin olive oil
6 cloves garlic, smashed and peeled
1 red onion, diced
3 to 5 dried Italian hot red peppers, halved
    lengthwise, or 1 to 3 teaspoons hot red
    pepper flakes
4 lobsters, about 1 1/2 pounds each, quartered,
    claws cracked (your fish market will do this
    for you, but cook the lobsters within 1 day)
16 jumbo shrimp in the shell, deveined
1 cup dry white wine
2 cups milled or crushed canned Italian plum
    tomatoes
3 tablespoons freshly chopped Italian parsley
2 anchovy fillets, chopped
2 teaspoons dried oregano
Salt and freshly ground black pepper

In a large soup pot, heat the olive oil over medium heat. Add the garlic and cook, stirring, until golden, about 3 minutes. Add the onion, hot pep-pers, lobsters, and shrimp and cook, stirring, until the shells begin to turn red, 5 to 10 minutes.

Add the wine and tomatoes, bring to a simmer, and add the parsley, anchovy, oregano, and a pinch of salt. Simmer about 15 minutes, until the sauce has thickened. Season with salt and pepper to taste. Serve hot.

 PRO TIP: *This is a perfect recipe for small lobsters that aren't suitable for serv-ing whole.*

POOR MAN'S CASSOULET

NO ONE WITH A STEAMING TUREEN OF THIS *dish in front of him could really feel like a poor man. But the traditional version of cassoulet, made in southwestern France, is even richer. It includes preserved goose legs (confit d'oie) as well as several cuts of pork, sausages, and creamy textured beans. This is my simplified version. The beans and meat almost melt together into a shiny stew that looks great piled up in a tureen. Cassoulet makes a great winter dinner with red wine and a big salad of crisp greens.*

MAKES 8 TO 10 SERVINGS

3 cups dried white beans, such as flageolet,
    borlotti, cannellini, navy, or Great Northern
1/4 cup plus 2 tablespoons extra-virgin olive oil
2 cloves garlic, thinly sliced
4 shallots, minced
2 pounds pork butt, in one piece
1/4 pound slab bacon, cut into 2-inch by 1-inch
    chunks
4 fresh sweet Italian sausages

8 cups Chicken Stock (page 15), Vegetable Stock
    (page 17), water, or low-sodium canned
    broth
1 piece rind from Parmesan cheese, about 2
    inches square
2 teaspoons freshly chopped rosemary leaves
Salt and freshly ground black pepper
¼ cup freshly grated Parmesan, Swiss, or
    Gruyère cheese

In a large bowl, cover the beans with at least 3 quarts of cold water. Soak 12 to 24 hours, changing the water every 8 hours or so. Drain, rinse, and drain again.

In a large soup pot, heat ¼ cup of the olive oil over medium heat. Add the garlic and shallots and cook, stirring, until golden, about 3 minutes. Add the pork butt, bacon, and sausages, and cook, stirring, 3 minutes. Add the beans and cook 2 minutes, stirring to coat. Add the stock, Parmesan rind, and rosemary, cover, and bring to a simmer. Simmer about 1½ hours, until the beans are melting into the cassoulet. Season with salt and pepper to taste.

Preheat the oven to 325°F. Transfer the cassoulet to a baking dish and sprinkle with the remaining 2 tablespoons olive oil and the grated cheese. Bake about 10 minutes, until the top is golden and crusty.

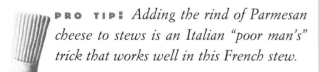

PRO TIP: *Adding the rind of Parmesan cheese to stews is an Italian "poor man's" trick that works well in this French stew.*

POOR MAN'S CASSOULET IN AN ITALIAN TERRA-COTTA OVEN CROCK.

OLD-FASHIONED SAUSAGES AND PEPPERS

SAUSAGES AND PEPPERS ARE A NATURAL *combination, and if you've never had a homemade version, you're in for a treat. This is part of Campagna's Sunday Night Supper menu, reserved for the hearty southern Italian classics of my New York childhood.*

The best way to cook sausages is not fried on a griddle but braised in a pot, so they stay plump and juicy. I learned this lesson in Germany, where they really know how to cook their sausages. For this dish, you'll sauté peppers and onions until they're sweet, then add sausages along with tomatoes and wine to braise them in. Every Italian kitchen has red and white wines on hand for cooking. Wine is cheaper than Coca-Cola in Italy, and an indispensable cooking tool. Serve this with a crusty Italian loaf.

MAKES 4 TO 6 SERVINGS

¼ cup extra-virgin olive oil
2 cloves garlic, thinly sliced
1 large red onion, cut into 2-inch chunks
2 red bell peppers, cored, seeded, and cut into
    2-inch chunks
2 green bell peppers, cored, seeded, and cut into
    2-inch chunks
4 fresh hot Italian sausages
4 fresh sweet Italian sausages
1 cup milled or crushed canned Italian plum
    tomatoes
1½ cups dry red wine
Pinch of dried oregano
Salt and freshly ground black pepper

In a large skillet with a lid, heat the olive oil over medium-high heat. Add the garlic, onion, and peppers and cook, stirring, until the onion is translucent, about 5 minutes. Add the sausages and cook about 4 minutes more, until beginning to brown. Add the tomatoes, wine, oregano, and a large pinch of salt. Cover, bring to a simmer, and simmer gently about 25 minutes, until the peppers are very soft. Season with salt and pepper to taste. Serve immediately.

PRO TIP: *This recipe can easily be doubled for a party. To please a crowd, always use a mixture of hot and sweet sausages.*

OLD-FASHIONED SAUSAGES AND PEPPERS ON CLASSICAL DERUDA POTTERY.

BRAISED SHORT RIBS WITH LENTILS

LIKE MASHED POTATOES AND MEAT LOAF, *short ribs are trendy* and *traditional right now. My Jewish ancestors knew this cut as flanken. Since the bones are cut before being added to the dish, the marrow seeps into the sauce, which becomes almost silky as it cooks slowly in the oven. You can practically walk on top of the finished dish, it's so thick and satisfying.*

Lentils and wheat berries make this into a memorable stew. Short ribs are often found in peasant cooking; they are the least expensive cut of meat. My father, like his father before him, loved his flanken.

MAKES ABOUT 6 SERVINGS

All-purpose flour, for dredging
Salt and freshly ground black pepper
8 beef short ribs
½ cup vegetable oil or pure olive oil
3 tablespoons extra-virgin olive oil
2 cloves garlic, thinly sliced
I onion, minced
I carrot, minced
I celery stalk, minced
I leek, halved lengthwise, well rinsed, and minced
½ cup lentils, preferably French green
½ cup wheat berries (or use pearl barley or spelt)
I bottle (750 ml) dry red wine
I cup milled or crushed canned Italian plum tomatoes
4 cups Chicken Stock (page 15), Veal Stock (page 16), or low-sodium canned broth
I tablespoon chopped fresh rosemary leaves
2 teaspoons chopped fresh sage

Preheat the oven to 325°F.

Spread about ½ cup of flour out on a plate. Add a large pinch of salt and pepper and mix. Dredge all the meat in the seasoned flour, shaking off any excess, adding more seasoned flour as needed.

Meanwhile, in a large casserole, heat the vegetable oil over medium-high heat. Working in batches if necessary to avoid crowding the pan, add the meat as it is dredged and cook, turning occasionally, until browned. Remove the meat to a plate as it is cooked.

Carefully wipe out the pan, add the extra-virgin olive oil, and heat over medium-high heat. Add the garlic, onion, carrot, celery, and leek and cook, stirring, until the onion is wilted, about 5 minutes. Add the remaining ingredients and a large pinch of salt and pepper and mix well. Cover and bake about 2½ hours, stirring occasionally, until the meat is very tender. Season with salt and pepper to taste. Serve hot.

JOSEPH'S FRESH PEA SOUP

THIS IS THE FIRST FOOD I EVER MADE FOR MY *baby son. Joe was born in December, so he was ready to start eating just about when spring peas came into season. To a chef, cooking for your children for the first time is like cooking for royalty or heads of state. You really want it to be good. Watching him eat that first spoonful was even more satisfying than when Jackie Onassis told me she had enjoyed her meal at Sapore di Mare.*

When your children enjoy the food you make for them, it's the highest accolade a chef can get—especially if they're only six months old.

MAKES **6** SERVINGS

1 tablespoon unsalted butter
1 medium onion, minced
3 pounds fresh peas, shelled or two 20-ounce bags frozen baby peas
4 cups Chicken Stock (page 15), Vegetable Stock (page 17), or low-sodium canned broth
Salt and freshly ground black pepper
Freshly grated Parmesan cheese, for serving
Extra-virgin olive oil, for serving

In a large soup pot, melt the butter over medium heat. Add the onion and cook, stirring, until translucent, about 5 minutes. Do not brown. Add the peas and cook, stirring, 2 minutes. Reduce the heat to low, add the stock, bring to a simmer, and simmer 15 to 20 minutes, until the peas are very tender.

Working in batches in a blender, or using a hand blender, puree the soup until smooth. If the soup is too thick to blend, add a few tablespoons of carbonated or mineral water. Season with salt and pepper to taste. Serve or set the pureed soup aside to cool. Serve hot or at room temperature, sprinkled with Parmesan cheese and drizzled with extra-virgin olive oil.

 PRO TIP: *If you reheat this or any cold soup after it has been cooled, it will thicken. Thin it with a little spring water, not stock, which will add an overpowering flavor.*

WINTER TOMATO SOUP

WE AMERICANS HAVE BEEN TRAINED TO THINK *that fresh is always best, but when we're talking about tomatoes, that's true only about three months of the year. The rest of the time, canned tomatoes from Italy are definitely the best. They have concentrated flavor, deep red color, and a sweetness that brightens up a winter day. This soup is good all year round, hot or cold. I grew up on Campbell's tomato soup, and I still like it: This is the only tomato soup that might be better.*

MAKES **6** TO **8** SERVINGS

¼ cup extra-virgin olive oil
2 cloves garlic, smashed and peeled
½ onion, minced
Two 28-ounce cans milled or crushed canned Italian plum tomatoes
2 cups Chicken Stock (page 15), Vegetable Stock (page 17), water, or low-sodium canned broth
½ cup dry, light red wine
1 teaspoon dried oregano
Salt and freshly ground black pepper
Baked Croutons, for serving (optional; page 18)
Basil Puree, for serving (optional; page 18)
Freshly grated Parmesan cheese, for serving

In a large soup pot, heat the olive oil over medium heat. Add the garlic and onion and cook, stirring, until the onion is translucent, about 5 minutes. Add the tomatoes, stock, wine, oregano, and a large pinch of salt, mix well, cover, and reduce the heat to a simmer. Simmer very gently 1 hour, stirring occasionally. Season with salt and pepper to taste. Serve hot or chilled, garnished with a handful of croutons, a swirl of basil puree, and/or a sprinkling of Parmesan cheese.

PRO TIP: *Canned tomatoes have such concentrated flavor that you can use water instead of stock when making them into soup.*

BUTTERNUT SQUASH SOUP

LIKE TOMATO SOUP IN THE SUMMER AND PEA *soup in the spring, there's something just right about a smooth, rich squash soup in the fall. The orange color really does reflect the fall foliage. Its thick warmth feels good going down and insulates you against the cold. Pureed soups are a great way to get kids to eat vegetables. You can use this method with any variety of winter squash or vegetables like turnips, parsnips, cauliflower, and broccoli. Parmesan cheese gives it an Italian zing and adds some bite to the sweet soup.*

MAKES 10 TO 12 SERVINGS

¼ cup extra-virgin olive oil
1 medium onion, minced
6 butternut squash, peeled, seeded, and cut into 2-inch chunks
2 medium potatoes, peeled and cut into eighths

3 quarts Chicken Stock (page 15), Vegetable Stock (page 17), water, or low-sodium canned broth
1 cinnamon stick
Pinch of ground cloves
Pinch of ground nutmeg
Salt and freshly ground black pepper
Baked Croutons (page 18), for serving
Freshly grated Parmesan cheese, for serving

In a large soup pot, heat the olive oil over medium-high heat. Add the onion and cook, stirring, until the onion is translucent, about 5 minutes. Add the squash and potatoes and cook, stirring, 2 minutes. Add the stock, spices, and a large pinch of salt, mix well, cover, and reduce the heat to a simmer. Simmer 1 hour, until the squash and potatoes are very soft. Remove the cinnamon stick.

Working in batches in a blender, or using a hand blender, puree the soup until smooth. Return to the pot and heat through. Season with salt and pepper to taste. Serve hot or chilled, garnished with croutons and Parmesan cheese.

PRO TIP: *Use quick strokes of a sturdy vegetable peeler, rather than a paring knife, to peel hard squash; you'll lose less of the flavorful flesh that way.*

WHITE BEAN SOUP

FROM A TUSCAN PEASANT COOK TO A THREE-*star chef, everyone loves white bean soup. It's basic, but when made correctly, it's also delicious. The fresh rosemary and sage really stand out against the creamy beans. Simple, flavorful, homey food like this is exactly what chefs like to eat. This soup deserves your finest extra-virgin olive oil as a pungent garnish. Other possible garnishes include freshly made slivers of Parmesan cheese, minced Prosciutto di Parma, or white truffle oil.*

MAKES 10 TO 12 SERVINGS

4 cups dried white beans, such as borlotti,
    cannellini, navy, or Great Northern
¼ cup extra-virgin olive oil
2 cloves garlic, minced
1 large onion, diced small
1 carrot, diced small
1 stalk celery, diced small
4 strips double-smoked bacon, diced (optional)
1 cup dry white wine
4 quarts Chicken Stock (page 15), Vegetable
    Stock (page 17), or low-sodium canned broth
1 tablespoon freshly chopped sage or marjoram
2 teaspoons freshly chopped rosemary leaves
Salt and freshly ground black pepper
Extra-virgin olive oil, for serving (optional)

Place the beans in a bowl and cover with 4 quarts cold water. Soak overnight, changing the water every 8 hours or so. Drain, rinse, and drain again. Set aside.

In a large soup pot, heat the olive oil over medium-high heat. Add the garlic, onion, carrot, celery, and bacon and cook, stirring, until the onion is translucent, about 5 minutes. Add the wine, stock, herbs, and the soaked beans. Add a large pinch of salt, mix well, cover, and bring to a boil. Reduce the heat to a simmer and simmer about 1 to 1½ hours, until the beans are very soft and melting into the soup. If desired, puree with a hand blender until smooth.

Season with salt and pepper to taste. Serve hot or at room temperature, drizzled with extra-virgin olive oil if desired.

PRO TIP: *When pureeing soups, check the consistency of the soup often, to make sure it's neither too thick nor too thin. If it becomes too thick, add a bit of chicken stock or water; if too thin, simmer gently until thickened.*

MUSSELS IN BRODETTO

EATING THIS DISH ALWAYS REMINDS ME OF *my favorite Italian seaside resort, a little town called Forte di Marmi. In Italy, seafood is usually cooked very simply; the freshness of the ingredients is the most important thing. When I was the chef at Sapore di Mare, I re-created this dish from memory, and now you can have the experience, too. Open a bottle of Pinot Grigio, close your eyes, and you're sitting by the Mediterranean.*

To make the broth bianco, *or white, leave out the tomato and swirl in a tablespoon of butter just before serving. The shiny black mussels look great in thick-rimmed soup plates. Serve with plenty of crusty bread.*

MAKES 4 SERVINGS

¼ cup extra-virgin olive oil
½ large carrot, diced small
½ large celery stalk, diced small
½ red onion, diced small
2 cloves garlic, thickly sliced
2 pounds cultivated mussels, rinsed
¼ teaspoon hot red pepper flakes
Salt
2 tablespoons freshly chopped Italian parsley
1½ cups dry white wine
⅓ cup milled or crushed canned Italian plum
    tomatoes
Freshly ground black pepper

In a large soup pot with a lid, heat the oil over medium-high heat. Add the carrot, celery, onion, and garlic, and cook, stirring, until the onion is translucent, about 5 minutes. Add the mussels, stir, and cook 1 minute. Add the red pepper flakes, a pinch of salt, parsley, wine, and tomatoes, then quickly stir and cover. Simmer without lifting the lid for 3 minutes, then check to see if all the shells have opened. If not, cover and cook 1 minute more.

Season with salt and pepper to taste. Serve immediately; or, if you prefer a thicker broth, remove the mussels to a serving bowl and simmer the broth 2 minutes more. Pour over the mussels and serve.

PRO TIP: *Make sure to use a pot with a tight-fitting lid, so that you can cover the mussels immediately after adding the liquid. That way you'll catch the first burst of steam and the mussels will cook more quickly—and stay more tender.*

PASTA,
RISOTTO, AND
POLENTA

Traditional Tomato Sauce

Quick and Fresh Summer Tomato Sauce

Penne A.O.P.

Spaghetti alla Pescatora

Penne alla Silvana

Linguine with Broccoli Rabe, Garlic, and Olive Oil

Fusilli Provençal

Pasta ai Funghi Misti

Spaghetti alle Vongole

Spaghetti with Brooklyn Clam Sauce

Spaghetti al Caruso

Pasta al Brunelleschi with Red Wine Beef Sauce

Tagliatelle alle Bolognese

Risotto alla Milanese

Spinach Risotto

Springtime Risotto with Mushrooms, Asparagus, and Peas

Risotto al Barolo

Classic Soft Polenta

Polenta with Fontina, Arugula, and Tomato

Polenta al Sugo di Agnello

PASTA, RISOTTO, AND POLENTA

PASTA DOES NOT WAIT FOR PEOPLE—PEOPLE WAIT for pasta." That's the key piece of knowledge I picked up when learning to cook pasta in Italy.

The cooking and saucing of pasta are more important to Italians than anything else that happens in the kitchen, which probably explains why it is so good there. Italians have strong emotional feelings about pasta. Many Italians eat pasta every single day of their lives. And when you make these

recipes, I think you'll understand why. "People wait for pasta" means that everyone except the cook should be already sitting at the table when the pasta comes out of the pot, so that its warmth, aromas, and flavors can be experienced at their peak.

When I was growing up, Americans ate egg noodles all the time, as a side dish. Today Italian-style dried pasta is the American family staple, and it's usually served as a main dish. But for special meals, you might want to serve the more elegant pastas as a first course, or *primo piatto,* to experience the dishes as Italians do. My goal in this chapter is to give you the experience of eating pasta in Italy, top to bottom.

Italian menus are divided between fresh pasta dishes and dried pasta dishes. Fresh pasta is a traditional product that is time-consuming to make but wonderful to eat. Even in Italy, the real thing—flour and eggs worked together by hand and rolled out very, very thin—is getting

hard to find. Grandmothers in Emilia-Romagna, the capital of fresh pasta, say that if you can't read a newspaper through a sheet of pasta, it isn't thin enough.

Fresh pasta is more of a special-occasion treat than an everyday *primo.* It is often served as a main course, or as an appetizer with seasonal or luxurious ingredients. White truffles, wild mushrooms, and the ripest summer tomatoes are often served in very simple sauces for fresh pasta. Lasagne is always made with fresh pasta, and you see whole families eating it for Sunday lunch in Rome's trattorias. Sauces based on butter rather than olive oil generally suit fresh pasta well. And of course stuffed fresh pastas like tortellini and ravioli are classics of northern Italy, where egg yolks and butter are plentiful and the cooks are very patient.

Since really good fresh pasta is so hard to obtain in this country, I haven't included many recipes that require it. But there are many sauces that work equally well with dried or fresh pasta. For fresh pasta dishes, whenever possible buy imported frozen Italian fresh pasta and cook it directly from the frozen state—or go to a good gourmet store to buy it.

The good news: Dried pasta is more than just a substitute for the fresh product. It's a great thing in its own right. And the fact that it is so easy to keep on hand is a bonus. Dried pasta, made from only water and flour, is what most Italians eat day in and day out. The imported Italian pasta we get here is exactly the same as you would find in Italy. And since we grow garlic, tomatoes, onions, and other produce here that is just as good as what they use in Italy, it is possible to cook totally authentic and excellent sauces for dried pasta anywhere in America. I'll take dried pasta over fresh as a home kitchen staple any day of the week.

A bowl of cooked pasta with sauce on the top is something you'll never see in Italy. To complete a pasta dish, you have to put the sauce and pasta together and let them simmer for a few minutes, so that the pasta can soak up the sauce. Dried pasta is an absorbent and porous product. That is the whole reason for cooking it al dente. If your pasta still has a bit of firmness to it when it goes into the sauce, it will be able to absorb the liquid from the sauce and absorb its flavor at the same time. If your sauce isn't liquid enough to do this, thin it with a little pasta cooking water, which contains some starch that will help bind the dish together.

"Always put olive oil in the pasta water" and "Never put olive oil in the pasta water" are old wives' tales. After years of experience, I can confidently say that it doesn't make any difference at all. Oil won't keep it from sticking together (you need to stir it to do that, and boil it in a lot of water) and it won't prevent your pasta from absorbing the sauce.

I like to serve pasta family style at home, from a big platter in the center of the table. You can serve it in individual shallow bowls, of course, as we do in the restaurant—but it looks so beautiful piled up in a mass that I pour it onto a platter whenever I can. This is the time to bring out your Italian pottery serving pieces. Traditionally, fresh and stuffed pastas are served on flat plates to show off their shape and texture (they are also served in smaller portions than dried pastas, as they are richer). Dried pasta piles higher and is more slippery to eat. It's easier to chase it down when you serve it in a shallow bowl. When appropriate, sprinkle each serving individually with cheese and/or parsley.

Pasta has assumed staple status almost everywhere in Italy, but around Milan people are still fiercely proud of their rice and especially their risottos. Risotto is a dish, not an ingredient. It's all about the cooking method. Arborio rice is usually used for risotto (although vialone rice is another option) and it is simply a particularly starchy variety of short-grain rice. It can be cooked like any other rice. But the method of slowly adding boiling liquid to sautéed rice, stirring frequently, and letting the rice absorb all the liquid before adding more, is what makes a risotto. Risotto makes a wonderful first course, or, if it is especially delicious, a good main course. I like it best in small portions as a smooth, savory, comforting prelude to something with more texture.

Risotto is an elegant dish with an aristocratic heritage. The Duke of Milan gave precious arborio rice to visiting dignitaries as a mark of respect. (Thomas Jefferson came away with a kilo, which he planted at Monticello.) Like many Italian dishes made with butter and Parmesan, it is considered luxurious and is associated with ingredients like saffron and white truffles. But even without those additions, the dishes in this chapter really show off the creaminess of risotto.

As you're cooking your risotto, keep in mind that it should be creamy and a little runny when it's finished. The rice grains should have just the slightest firmness at the center, and the risotto should move and settle when you shake the serving plate. The best way to learn to make risotto is to cook it a few times. When you get it right, you'll know—it will taste light but rich, creamy but savory, and it will be gone before you know it.

Polenta is a peasant staple in the northeastern regions of Italy. Corn came to Italy from the Americas in the seventeenth century. It took a very long time for Italians to eat corn instead of feeding it to their animals, and even now polenta is the only popular corn dish. But I understand why they make the exception for polenta. Although it's just cornmeal and water, the slow cooking really brings out the bright corn taste. Mixing it with butter and Parmesan cheese, of course, only makes it better. The finished product is soft, smooth, aromatic, and comforting. It's like the best baby food, but incredibly flavorful and delicious with meat sauces and stews or a topping of melted fontina, fresh arugula, and tomato. I've only rarely seen grilled polenta in Italy (and I don't think the charcoal flavor does much for it), but it is sometimes fried in squares after it's cooled, and served under little roast birds or game sauces. My recipe for Tuscan Quail with Crispy Polenta on page 187 treats polenta in this way.

Both risotto and polenta look wonderful spread on platters, and that's how they are always served in Italy—never in bowls. Both dishes should be thin enough to pour onto the platter, then served right away so they don't get cold.

The dishes in this chapter are a big part of what makes Italian cooking unique. Even though they're based on unglamorous grains like corn, rice, and wheat, they're some of the most typical and beloved dishes in the whole country. I have such good memories of eating pasta in Italy and I try to put that feeling into the recipes. My customers rarely eat a meal that doesn't include one of these dishes. These authentic, classic recipes are all you need to build up a great repertoire. Keeping pasta, arborio rice, and polenta on hand, plus a few pantry ingredients or frozen homemade sauces, means that a great dinner is never more than twenty minutes away.

TRADITIONAL TOMATO SAUCE

THE BEST RECIPE FOR TOMATO SAUCE IS IN A *scene from* The Godfather, Part I. *Frankie Pantangelo is cooking for a family "meeting" as they get ready for another battle. He takes the time to go through every detail of the sauce, so you can see the love and care he has for his "brothers." You can almost smell the garlic and taste the sauce as he cooks, and if you follow his directions you'll have this perfect old-fashioned Sicilian-style tomato sauce from Brooklyn in the 1930s.*

This basic sauce is always made with canned plum tomatoes, which are better than fresh for sauce—already peeled, low in moisture, and ripened on the vine. The idea is to make a huge batch and freeze most of it, then use it to create other dishes. Sauté peppers, mushrooms, and carrots—then add this sauce for a vegetarian pasta sauce. You can sauté onions, garlic, and shrimp—then add this sauce for a quick shrimp stew. Or use it to top Sicilian Peppers Stuffed with Rice (page 41) or in Real Eggplant Parmigiana (page 185).

MAKES ENOUGH SAUCE FOR ABOUT 4 POUNDS OF PASTA

½ cup extra-virgin olive oil
4 cloves garlic, smashed and peeled
Four 28-ounce cans milled or crushed Italian
    plum tomatoes
1 cup dry red wine
1 teaspoon hot red pepper flakes
2 tablespoons dried oregano
Salt

In a large soup pot, heat the olive oil over medium-high heat. Add the garlic and cook, stirring, until golden, about 3 minutes. Add the tomatoes, wine, red pepper flakes, oregano, and salt to taste. Cover and bring to a simmer, then uncover and simmer gently about 1½ hours, stirring occasionally. The sauce is done when it has a rich flavor but does not taste overcooked.

 PRO TIP: *For a rich, tangy sauce, add along with the canned tomatoes 12 whole oil-packed sundried tomatoes, wiped of excess oil and cut into quarters.*

QUICK AND FRESH SUMMER TOMATO SAUCE IN A CHEF'S
FAVORITE COPPER POT.

QUICK AND FRESH SUMMER TOMATO SAUCE

RIPE SUMMER TOMATOES, OF COURSE, ARE THE
*key here. Canned tomatoes are great and I use them
all the time (see Traditional Tomato Sauce, page
133), but not for this sauce. You want to just warm
the flesh of the ripe tomatoes, without cooking it.
The longer you cook the tomatoes, the more liquid
they will release. Red tomatoes have the most sweetness and acidity, but adding a few yellow tomatoes
cuts down on the liquid and looks beautiful.*

MAKES **6** APPETIZER SERVINGS OR
4 MAIN-COURSE SERVINGS

1 tablespoon salt, plus additional for seasoning
1 pound fresh or dried pasta, such as spaghetti,
    penne, or rigatoni
⅓ cup extra-virgin olive oil
1 clove garlic, thickly sliced
12 large ripe tomatoes or 24 ripe plum
    tomatoes, coarsely diced, with their juices
1 teaspoon hot red pepper flakes, or to taste
8 fresh basil leaves, torn into small pieces

In a large covered pot, heat a gallon of water with
a tablespoon of salt to a boil. When it boils, add
the pasta, stir well, and cover until it returns to the
boil. Uncover and boil until just tender to the bite
all the way through.

Meanwhile, make the sauce. In a skillet (with a
cover) large enough to hold the pasta later on,
heat the oil over medium heat. Add the garlic and
cook, stirring, until golden. Add the tomatoes, red
pepper flakes, and salt to taste, bring to a simmer,
and cook about 4 minutes, until the tomatoes are
just cooked through. Remove from the heat and
stir in the basil.

Reserving ½ cup of cooking water, drain the
pasta in a colander. Add the drained pasta to the
sauce and mix well, adding a few tablespoons of
pasta cooking water, if needed, to coat the pasta
evenly. Cover and cook 1 minute. Taste for salt.
Serve immediately.

PRO TIP: *To preserve the color and flavor of fresh basil when adding it to a dish,
tear it with your fingers instead of cutting it
with a knife.*

PENNE A.O.P.

OKAY FOLKS, HERE IT IS: THE NUMBER-ONE *recipe requested at Campagna. After my customers eat it, they always want to know how to make it. Somewhere between an* arrabiata *spicy tomato sauce and a garlic and oil sauce, this is a true classic.*

We make this so often that we finally had to shorten the name in the kitchen. We call it "A.O.P." for the aglio *(garlic),* olio *(oil), and* pomodoro *(tomato) in the sauce. The trick is to slowly heat the garlic and cook it until golden brown. The garlic will give off a nutty, toasted smell that will let you (and anyone else in your kitchen) know that it's correctly cooked. You do have to watch it carefully and stir it often, because if the garlic gets too brown, the dish will be bitter.*

MAKES 6 APPETIZER SERVINGS OR 4 MAIN-COURSE SERVINGS

1 tablespoon salt, plus additional for seasoning
1 pound dried penne pasta
¼ cup extra-virgin olive oil
3 cloves garlic, thickly sliced
½ teaspoon hot red pepper flakes
1 cup milled or crushed canned Italian plum tomatoes
2 tablespoons freshly chopped Italian parsley

In a large covered pot, heat a gallon of water with a tablespoon of salt to a boil. When it boils, add the pasta, stir well, and cover until it returns to the boil. Uncover and boil until just tender to the bite all the way through.

Meanwhile, make the sauce. In a skillet (with a lid) large enough to hold the pasta later on, heat the oil over medium-high heat. Add the garlic and cook, stirring, until golden, about 3 minutes. Add

THE INGREDIENTS FOR CAMPAGNA'S SIGNATURE DISH, PENNE A.O.P.

the red pepper flakes and cook, stirring, 30 seconds. Add the tomatoes and salt to taste. Simmer just until the sauce thickens and darkens slightly.

Reserving ½ cup cooking water, drain the pasta in a colander. Add the drained pasta to the sauce and mix well, adding a few tablespoons of pasta cooking water if needed to coat the pasta evenly. Cover and cook 1 minute. Taste for salt. Add the parsley, and toss until evenly coated. Serve immediately.

SPAGHETTI ALLA PESCATORA

SOME OF MY FAVORITE DISHES COME FROM *the Mediterranean coast. Spaghetti alla pescatora is a classic from the toe to the top of the Italian "boot." I think I've had it at every restaurant in between, so this dish feels like an old friend who reminds me of all my trips to Italy.*

Spaghetti alla pescatora can seem festive and fancy, with its combination of clams, mussels, shrimp, and scallops, but it comes from a tradition of peasant cooking. Fishermen's families have traditionally eaten whatever they couldn't sell, inventing dishes that include a lot of different kinds of seafood like Crazy Seafood Soup (page 117). The name means "fisherman's wife's spaghetti," which frees you up to use any kind of seafood you like. This combination is my personal favorite.

MAKES 6 APPETIZER SERVINGS OR 4 MAIN-COURSE SERVINGS

1 tablespoon salt, plus additional for seasoning

1 pound dried spaghetti

½ cup extra-virgin olive oil

2 cloves garlic, thickly sliced

1 pound octopus, cooked as for Classic Italian Seafood Salad (page 27), and cut into 1-inch pieces

½ pound raw squid (calamari), cut into ½-inch rings

8 littleneck clams, rinsed

8 mussels, rinsed

½ cup milled or crushed canned Italian plum tomatoes

½ cup dry white wine

½ teaspoon dried oregano

Pinch of hot red pepper flakes

Freshly ground black pepper

6 medium-size shrimp, peeled and deveined

8 sea scallops

In a large covered pot, heat a gallon of water with a tablespoon of salt to a boil. When it boils, add the pasta, stir well, and cover until it returns to the boil. Uncover and boil until just tender to the bite all the way through.

Meanwhile, make the sauce. In a skillet large enough to hold the pasta later on, heat the oil over medium-high heat. Add the garlic and cook, stirring, until golden. Add the octopus and squid and cook, stirring, until the calamari starts to turn opaque, about 3 minutes. Add the clams and mussels and cook 1 minute. Add the tomatoes, wine, oregano, red pepper flakes, and salt and pepper to taste. Mix well, bring to a simmer, and simmer about 4 minutes, until the shellfish start to open and the sauce has thickened slightly.

Add the shrimp and scallops to the sauce, mix well, and simmer about 2 minutes, until the shrimp and scallops are just cooked through. If the sauce seems too thick, add a few tablespoons of pasta cooking water.

Reserving ½ cup cooking water, drain the pasta in a colander. Add the drained pasta to the sauce and mix well, adding a few tablespoons of pasta cooking water if needed to coat the pasta evenly. Cover and cook 1 minute. Taste for salt.

Toss well and serve immediately. If desired, arrange on a serving platter with the mussels and clams around the rim.

SPAGHETTI ALLA PESCATORA SERVED IN AN IRREGULAR-SHAPED ALETHA SOULÉ BOWL.

PENNE ALLA SILVANA

THE FIRST TIME I VISITED MY OLIVE OIL PRO-*ducer in Tuscany, I was invited to dinner at the* frantoio, *or farmhouse. They had told me that they had a wonderful cook,* signora *Silvana, and I was expecting the usual matriarch in black. So I was pretty surprised when the real Silvana, a stunning woman in Dolce & Gabbana leopard pants, brought out the pasta. She was sexy, but her pasta was sexier. This rich dish is a wonderful first course for a special occasion, and anyone who likes creamed spinach will love it.*

MAKES 4 APPETIZER SERVINGS

1 tablespoon salt, plus additional for seasoning
¾ pound dried penne pasta
¼ cup extra-virgin olive oil
2 cloves garlic, thickly sliced
One 10-ounce box frozen spinach, thawed and finely chopped
1 cup heavy cream
4 tablespoons butter, cut into pieces
6 tablespoons freshly grated Parmesan cheese
Freshly ground black pepper

In a large covered pot, heat a gallon of water with a tablespoon of salt to a boil. When it boils, add the pasta, stir well, and cover until it returns to the boil. Uncover and boil until just tender to the bite all the way through.

Meanwhile, make the sauce. In a skillet (with a lid) large enough to hold the pasta later on, heat the oil over medium-high heat. Add the garlic and cook, stirring, until golden, about 3 minutes. Add the spinach and mix well. Add the heavy cream, mix, and simmer until slightly thickened.

Reserving ½ cup cooking water, drain the pasta in a colander. Add the drained pasta to the sauce and mix well, adding a few tablespoons of pasta cooking water if needed to coat the pasta evenly. Cover and cook 1 minute. Taste for salt. Mixing with a wooden spoon, add the butter, cheese, and salt and pepper to taste. Serve immediately.

LINGUINE WITH BROCCOLI RABE, GARLIC, AND OLIVE OIL

HERE'S ONE THING I'VE LEARNED IN MY *cooking life: Women love broccoli rabe. I'd recommend that all single men learn how to make this dish—when they're ready to stop being single. It's the expressway to a woman's heart. Every guy knows how to make spaghetti with tomato sauce these days, but broccoli rabe will make you look like a true Renaissance man.*

This pasta is extremely easy to make, because you just cook the broccoli rabe in the pasta water: The key to its success is plenty of freshly grated real Parmesan cheese. The bitter green and nutty cheese are great together.

MAKES 6 APPETIZER SERVINGS OR 4 MAIN-COURSE SERVINGS

1 tablespoon plus ½ teaspoon salt
1 pound dried linguine pasta
½ cup extra-virgin olive oil
4 cloves garlic, thickly sliced
½ to 1 teaspoon hot red pepper flakes
2 bunches broccoli rabe, cut into 2-inch lengths
⅓ cup freshly grated Parmesan cheese

PENNE ALLA SILVANA IN AN EMMA BRIDGEWATER BOWL.

CONTINUED

In a large covered pot, heat a gallon of water with a tablespoon of salt to a boil. When it boils, add the pasta, stir well, and cover until it returns to the boil. Uncover and boil until just tender to the bite all the way through.

Meanwhile, make the sauce. In a skillet (with a lid) large enough to hold the pasta later on, heat the oil over medium-high heat. Add the garlic and cook, stirring, until golden, about 3 minutes. Add the red pepper flakes and cook, stirring, 30 seconds. Add the broccoli rabe and ½ teaspoon salt and stir until evenly coated with oil. Add ½ cup of the pasta cooking water, cover, and simmer, stirring occasionally, until the broccoli rabe is tender, about 5 minutes.

Reserving ½ cup cooking water, drain the pasta in a colander. Add the drained pasta to the sauce and mix well, adding a few tablespoons of pasta cooking water if needed to coat the pasta evenly. Cover and cook 1 minute. Taste for salt. Serve immediately, generously sprinkled with Parmesan.

 PRO TIP: *Always use pasta cooking water when adding water to a pasta dish; the starch will help bind the sauce and pasta together.*

FUSILLI PROVENÇAL

THIS IS MY FAVORITE SUMMER VEGETABLE *pasta. If you have vegetarians in your life, this is a very handy recipe to know. Zucchini and string beans cook down soft and sweet and blend with tomato into a punchy but light pasta sauce. Pasta is very common in southern Provence, right near the Italian border. Tomatoes, zucchini, and garlic are the classic ingredients of Provençal cooking. You can also serve this at room temperature, as part of a summer buffet.*

MAKES **6** APPETIZER SERVINGS OR **4** MAIN-COURSE SERVINGS

Salt
1 cup trimmed and chopped string beans (2-inch lengths)
1 pound dried or fresh fusilli or another short, chunky pasta shape
¼ cup extra-virgin olive oil
1 onion, diced
2 cloves garlic, thickly sliced
2 small zucchini, halved lengthwise and cut crosswise into ½-inch pieces
12 oil-packed sundried tomatoes, drained of excess oil and cut into ¼-inch strips
2 cups milled or crushed canned Italian plum tomatoes
1 tablespoon dried oregano
¼ cup freshly grated Parmesan cheese

Bring a large covered pot of salted water to a boil. Prepare a large bowl of ice water. When the water boils, add the green beans and cook about 8 minutes, until tender all the way through. With a slotted spoon, transfer to the ice water to stop the cooking.

Return the water to the boil. Add the pasta, stir well, and cover until it returns to the boil.

Uncover and boil until just tender to the bite all the way through.

Meanwhile, make the sauce. In a skillet (with a lid) large enough to hold the pasta later on, heat the oil over medium-high heat. Add the onion and garlic and cook, stirring, until the garlic is golden, about 3 minutes. Add the zucchini, stir, cover, and cook 4 minutes. Add the cooked green beans, both kinds of tomatoes, oregano, and salt to taste, and cook, uncovered, 2 minutes more.

Reserving ½ cup cooking water, drain the pasta in a colander. Add the drained pasta to the sauce and mix well, adding a few tablespoons of pasta cooking water if needed to coat the pasta evenly. Cover and cook 1 minute. Taste for salt. Serve immediately, generously sprinkled with Parmesan.

PASTA AI FUNGHI MISTI

WILD MUSHROOMS, LIKE ASPARAGUS AND WILD *boar, are strictly seasonal ingredients in Italy. They get very special treatment in my kitchen. The autumn rains produce an enormous crop of mushrooms after a summer of living and breathing tomatoes. Suddenly the rich, earthy taste of mushrooms is just what you want. This is not a mushroom cream sauce, but mushrooms simply sautéed with olive oil and garlic and bound with a little stock and water. Woodsy rosemary is my favorite herb for mushrooms.*

Vegetarian customers at Campagna love this recipe. It does taste incredibly meaty for a fungus dish.

MAKES 6 APPETIZER SERVINGS OR 4 MAIN-COURSE SERVINGS

1 tablespoon salt, plus additional for seasoning
1 pound fresh or dried pasta, any shape
¼ cup extra-virgin olive oil
1 clove garlic, thickly sliced
½ red onion, minced
1 pound mixed mushrooms, such as shiitake, cremini, porcini, chanterelle, oyster, and hen-of-the-woods, very thinly sliced
½ cup Chicken Stock (page 15), Vegetable Stock (page 17), low-sodium canned broth, or water
1 teaspoon freshly chopped rosemary leaves
2 tablespoons cold unsalted butter
¼ cup freshly grated Parmesan cheese
Freshly ground black pepper

In a large covered pot, heat a gallon of water with a tablespoon of salt to a boil. When it boils, add the pasta, stir well, and cover until it returns to the boil. Uncover and boil until just tender to the bite all the way through.

Meanwhile, make the sauce. In a skillet (with a lid) large enough to hold the pasta later on, heat the oil over medium-high heat. Add the garlic and cook, stirring, until golden, about 3 minutes. Add the onion and mushrooms and cook, stirring, until wilted, about 2 minutes. Add the stock and simmer, uncovered, 5 minutes.

Reserving ½ cup cooking water, drain the pasta in a colander. Add the drained pasta to the sauce and mix well, adding a few tablespoons of pasta cooking water if needed to coat the pasta evenly. Cover and cook 1 minute. Sprinkle over the rosemary and add the butter and cheese. Stir for a moment to melt the butter and cheese. Taste for pepper and salt. Serve immediately.

 PRO TIP: *To make sure that different size mushrooms cook evenly, slice them into uniform pieces.*

SPAGHETTI ALLE VONGOLE

THIS IS THE DISH ITALIANS GO TO THE BEACH *for. At oceanside restaurants all over Italy, you'll see people eating spaghetti* alle vongole, *made with nothing but olive oil, garlic, and the dime-size clams they call* vongole veraci. *When cooking at Sapore di Mare, I decided to experiment until I found a way to make a perfect reproduction of that dish. Cockles have a different shape, but the same sweetness as* vongole veraci. *Now spaghetti* alle vongole *is a Campagna classic.*

A little tomato adds just a touch of sweetness and acidity, and helps to bind the sauce.

MAKES 6 APPETIZER SERVINGS OR 4 MAIN-COURSE SERVINGS

1 tablespoon salt, plus additional for seasoning
1 pound dried spaghetti
⅓ cup extra-virgin olive oil
2 cloves garlic, thickly sliced
48 very small clams in the shell, such as cockles or baby clams (not littlenecks)
½ cup dry white wine
⅓ cup crushed or milled canned Italian plum tomatoes
½ teaspoon hot red pepper flakes
¼ cup freshly chopped Italian parsley
Freshly ground black pepper

In a large covered pot, heat a gallon of water with a tablespoon of salt to a boil. When it boils, add the pasta, stir well, and cover until it returns to the boil. Uncover and boil until just tender to the bite all the way through.

Meanwhile, make the sauce. In a skillet (with a lid) large enough to hold the pasta later on, heat the oil over medium-high heat. Add the garlic and cook, stirring, until golden, about 3 minutes. Add the clams and cook, stirring, 1 minute. Add the wine, tomatoes, and red pepper flakes, stir, cover, reduce the heat to a simmer, and simmer until the clams open, about 5 minutes.

Reserving ½ cup cooking water, drain the pasta in a colander. Add the drained pasta, parsley, and salt and pepper to taste to the sauce and mix well, adding a few tablespoons of pasta cooking water if needed to coat the pasta evenly. Cover and cook 1 minute. Serve immediately.

NEW ZEALAND COCKLES ON SEA SALT FOR SPAGHETTI ALLE VONGOLE.

SPAGHETTI WITH BROOKLYN CLAM SAUCE

SUNDAY NIGHT AT CAMPAGNA IS THE TIME *for chicken cacciatore, spumoni, and the "white clam sauce" of my childhood. This dish reminds me of New York Italian restaurants in the 1950s. It's a true Italian-American classic and everyone loves it.*

Please don't try to make this recipe with fresh clams—it is best with canned clams.

MAKES 6 APPETIZER SERVINGS OR 4 MAIN-COURSE SERVINGS

1 tablespoon salt, plus additional for seasoning
1 pound dried spaghetti or linguine
¼ cup extra-virgin olive oil
2 cloves garlic, smashed and peeled
Two 6-ounce cans chopped clams, with their juice
¼ cup dry white wine
1 cup milled or crushed canned Italian plum tomatoes
¼ teaspoon hot red pepper flakes
Freshly ground black pepper
¼ cup freshly chopped Italian parsley
1 tablespoon cold unsalted butter

In a large covered pot, heat a gallon of water with a tablespoon of salt to a boil. When it boils, add the pasta, stir well, and cover until it returns to the boil. Uncover and boil until just tender to the bite all the way through.

Meanwhile, make the sauce. In a skillet (with a lid) large enough to hold the pasta later on, heat the oil over medium-low heat. Add the garlic and slowly cook, stirring, until golden, about 5 minutes. Add the clams with their juice, wine, tomatoes, red pepper flakes, and salt and pepper to taste, keeping in mind that the clams are quite salty. Stir, reduce the heat to a simmer, and simmer

until slightly thickened, about 5 minutes.

Reserving ½ cup cooking water, drain the pasta in a colander. Add the drained pasta, parsley, butter, and salt and pepper to taste to the sauce and mix well, adding a few tablespoons of pasta cooking water if needed to coat the pasta evenly. Cover and cook 1 minute. Serve immediately.

 PRO TIP: *Italian cooks always use pasta water to thin out a pasta sauce. The starch in the water helps to add body to the sauce.*

ITALIAN PASTA-COOKING UTENSILS.

SPAGHETTI AL CARUSO

ALL AMERICANS SEEM TO HAVE GROWN UP *with their own version of Italian food. My friend Allen Grubman used to eat this pasta in Brooklyn, but he hadn't had it for years—until he asked me to make it for him. To Allen, it's one of those childhood recipes that you carry the taste of in your mind for years.*

Chicken livers are what make the meat sauces of the Piedmont region so good, but they also work well for two nice Jewish boys in New York.

MAKES 6 APPETIZER SERVINGS OR 4 MAIN-COURSE SERVINGS

1 tablespoon salt, plus additional for seasoning
1 pound dried spaghetti
¼ cup extra-virgin olive oil
½ onion, minced
2 pounds whole fresh chicken livers, cleaned of
  membranes and bile
3 cups milled or crushed canned Italian plum
  tomatoes
1 teaspoon cold unsalted butter
½ teaspoon hot red pepper flakes
Freshly ground black pepper
2 tablespoons freshly chopped Italian parsley

In a large covered pot, heat a gallon of water with a tablespoon of salt to a boil. When it boils, add the pasta, stir well, and cover until it returns to the boil. Uncover and boil until just tender to the bite all the way through.

Meanwhile, make the sauce. In a skillet (with a lid) large enough to hold the pasta later on, heat the oil over medium-high heat. Add the onion and livers and cook, stirring, until the onion is translucent, about 5 minutes. Add the tomatoes, butter, and red pepper flakes. Stir, reduce the heat, and simmer, uncovered, until the sauce thickens and darkens slightly, about 10 minutes. Add salt and pepper to taste.

Reserving ½ cup cooking water, drain the pasta in a colander. Add the drained pasta to the sauce and mix well, adding a few tablespoons of pasta cooking water if needed to coat the pasta evenly. Cover and cook 1 minute. Taste for salt and pepper and serve immediately, garnished with parsley.

 PRO TIP: *Chicken livers are an easy, inexpensive way to add rich, meaty flavor to a sauce.*

PASTA AL BRUNELLESCHI WITH RED WINE BEEF SAUCE

WHEN I'M IN ITALY, I ALWAYS TAKE THE ADVICE *of my wine and olive oil suppliers about where to eat. That's how I found myself on a twisting road in southern Tuscany, looking for the highly recommended Osteria Vecchio Castello. After an hour we were sure we were lost. Then out of nowhere, we spotted a parking lot filled with Alfa Romeos and BMWs from as far away as Zurich and Milan. "I think this is the place," I said.*

This dish, which I ate that day, is named for Renaissance architect Brunelleschi, who collected recipes from Italy's pre-Roman history. Dishes like this were eaten by the Etruscans, who had wine and pepper to flavor their food, but hadn't yet learned to make olive oil. This is a very peppery, warming stew with no added fat, which becomes a sauce as the beef falls apart in the pot. The tomatoes are my modern addition.

MAKES 6 MAIN-COURSE SERVINGS

2 pounds top round of beef or beef stew meat,
  cut into 1-inch cubes
1 bottle (750 ml) dry, full-bodied red wine
2 tablespoons coarsely ground black pepper
1 tablespoon plus 1 teaspoon salt
½ cup milled or crushed canned Italian plum
  tomatoes
2 tablespoons chopped fresh rosemary leaves
2 bay leaves
2 cloves garlic, smashed and peeled
1 red onion, minced
1 pound dried rigatoni or penne
3 tablespoons freshly chopped Italian parsley

Place the meat in a heavy pot and pour the wine over it. The wine should cover the meat by at least 2 inches. If it doesn't, add more wine or water. Add the pepper, 1 teaspoon salt, tomatoes, rosemary, bay leaves, garlic, and onion. Cover and bring to a simmer; do not boil. Simmer gently, partly covered, about 2 hours, until the meat is very tender and the sauce is thick enough to coat a spoon.

In a large covered pot, heat a gallon of water with a tablespoon of salt to a boil. When it boils, add the pasta, stir well, and cover until it returns to the boil. Uncover and boil until just tender to the bite all the way through.

Reserving ½ cup cooking water, drain the pasta in a colander. Add the drained pasta to the sauce and mix well, adding a few tablespoons of pasta cooking water if needed to coat the pasta evenly. Cover and cook 1 minute. Taste for salt. Remove the bay leaves. Serve immediately, sprinkled with parsley.

PASTA AL BRUNELLESCHI IN AN ITALIAN MAJOLICA PLATE.

TAGLIATELLE ALLA BOLOGNESE

WHEN YOU CAN GET YOUR HANDS ON SOME *good fresh pasta, this is the way to use it. The sauce for* Tagliatelle alla Bolognese, *a classic dish of Emilia-Romagna, is meat, vegetables, herbs, and wine simmered long and slow until they melt into a smooth sauce. There's a whole can of tomatoes in the sauce, but it isn't a tomato sauce—the tomatoes become part of the mix. You'll want to take this sauce all the way, cooking it for hours until it turns a dark, rich color.*

Bologna is the capital of Emilia-Romagna, home to Italy's most luxurious cooking—and the cheese of nearby Parmigiano-Reggiano. Many pasta sauces and soups of the region have a piece of Parmigiano rind in the pot, to add its rich flavor.

MAKES 8 APPETIZER SERVINGS OR 6 MAIN-COURSE SERVINGS

¼ cup vegetable oil (omit if using a nonstick skillet)
4 ounces lean ground beef
4 ounces ground veal
4 ounces ground pork, or 2 ounces ground pork plus 2 ounces fresh pork sausage
½ cup extra-virgin olive oil
2 cloves garlic, minced
1 large onion, minced
2 small carrots, minced
2 stalks celery, minced
One 28-ounce can milled or crushed canned Italian plum tomatoes
2 cups dry red wine
1 teaspoon hot red pepper flakes
2 teaspoons dried oregano
3 tablespoons chopped fresh rosemary leaves
1 piece rind from Parmesan cheese (about 2 inches square)
1 tablespoon salt, plus additional for seasoning
1½ pounds fresh tagliatelle or tagliolini, or dried linguine
Freshly grated Parmesan cheese, for serving

In a large skillet, heat the vegetable oil over medium-high heat. Gradually add all the meat and cook, stirring to break up any chunks, just until browned, about 5 minutes. With a slotted spoon, remove the meat to a colander to drain.

In a large soup pot, heat the olive oil over medium-high heat. Add the garlic and cook, stirring, until golden, about 3 minutes. Add the onion, carrots, celery, and cooked meat. Cook, stirring, until the onion is translucent, about 5 minutes. Add the tomatoes, wine, red pepper flakes, 1 teaspoon of the oregano, 1½ tablespoons of the rosemary, the Parmesan cheese rind, and salt to taste. Mix well and bring to a simmer. Simmer slowly, uncovered, about 1½ hours, stirring occasionally. If the liquid is evaporating too quickly, add water or water mixed with additional milled tomatoes. Add the remaining 1 teaspoon oregano and 1½ tablespoons rosemary at the end of the cooking.

In a large covered pot, heat a gallon of water with a tablespoon of salt to a boil. When it boils, add the pasta, stir well, and cover until it returns to the boil. Uncover and boil until just tender to the bite all the way through.

Reserving ½ cup cooking water, drain the pasta in a colander. Add the drained pasta to the sauce and mix well, adding a few tablespoons of pasta cooking water if needed to coat the pasta evenly. Cover and cook 1 minute. Taste for salt. Serve immediately, sprinkled with Parmesan cheese.

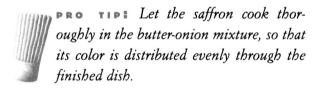

PRO TIP: *Adding the rind from a piece of Parmigiano-Reggiano to soups and pasta sauces is a great way to get the most flavor and value out of your investment in this expensive, high-quality cheese. The stamp is completely edible and nontoxic.*

RISOTTO ALLA MILANESE

MILAN IS THE FASHION CAPITAL OF ITALY, AND *this subtle risotto is the city's signature dish. You can think of it as the culinary equivalent of an Armani suit. It is refined and elegant, can be dressed up or down, and never goes out of fashion. The aristocrats of northern Italy have been eating risotto since the sixteenth century. The combination of golden saffron, Parmigiano-Reggiano cheese, and creamy arborio rice is a classic.*

As the risotto cooks, stir it up from the center of the pot, where it is most likely to burn first. Stir it often, but not constantly, using a wooden spoon so it doesn't break up.

MAKES 6 APPETIZER SERVINGS

3 tablespoons unsalted butter
1 medium red onion, minced
1 large pinch saffron threads
1½ cups arborio rice (do not rinse)
⅛ teaspoon salt
⅛ teaspoon freshly ground black pepper
1 cup dry white wine
3 to 4 cups hot Chicken Stock (page 15),
    Vegetable Stock (page 17), or low-sodium
    canned broth
¼ cup freshly grated Parmesan cheese
1 tablespoon freshly chopped Italian parsley
    (optional)

In a medium-size heavy soup po[...] spoons of the butter over [...] When it foams, add the [...] cook, stirring, until th[...] the saffron is "melted, [...] ce the heat to medium, add th[...] pper and cook, stirring with a wooden [...] til well coated, about 1 minute.

Add the wine and simmer gently until the liquid is absorbed, 3 to 5 minutes. Add ½ cup of the chicken stock, stir, and simmer, stirring occasionally, until the liquid is absorbed. Repeat, adding ½ cup stock at a time, until the rice is cooked through but still firm, about 25 minutes total.

Add the remaining tablespoon of butter and the Parmesan cheese. Mix well, taste for salt, and serve immediately, sprinkled with parsley, if desired.

PRO TIP: *Let the saffron cook thoroughly in the butter-onion mixture, so that its color is distributed evenly through the finished dish.*

SPINACH RISOTTO

PUREED SPINACH IS THE EASIEST AND PRETTI-
*est thing you can add to a risotto for a little variety
in flavor. The texture will stay smooth and creamy.
The rice grains should be just firm on the inside,
and the dish should be runny enough to move
around when you shake the plate.*

*This dish reminds me of the best steakhouse
creamed spinach: light, flavorful, and a great shade
of green.*

MAKES 6 APPETIZER SERVINGS

2 pounds fresh spinach, well washed and rolled in
    a towel to dry or one 10-ounce box frozen
    spinach, thawed
3 tablespoons unsalted butter
1/2 medium onion, minced
1 clove garlic, minced
1 1/2 cups arborio rice (do not rinse)
1/8 teaspoon salt
1/8 teaspoon freshly ground black pepper
1 cup dry white wine
3 to 4 cups hot Chicken Stock (page 15),
    Vegetable Stock (page 17), or low-sodium
    canned broth
1/3 cup freshly grated Parmesan cheese

In a food processor, puree the fresh or thawed
spinach.

In a medium-size heavy soup pot, melt 2 tablespoons of the butter over medium-high heat.
When it foams, add the onion and garlic and
cook, stirring, until the onion is translucent, about
5 minutes. Reduce the heat to medium, add the
rice, salt, and pepper, and cook, stirring with a
wooden spoon, until well coated, about 1 minute.

Add the wine and simmer gently until the liquid is absorbed, 3 to 5 minutes. Add 1/2 cup
chicken stock, stir, and simmer, stirring occasionally, until the liquid is absorbed. Repeat, adding 1/2
cup stock at a time, until the rice is cooked
through but still firm, about 25 minutes total.
When the rice is almost cooked, stir in the spinach
and continue cooking, stirring constantly, until
done. The spinach should not cook for more than
4 minutes, or it will turn brown.

Add the remaining tablespoon butter and the
Parmesan cheese. Mix well, taste for salt and pepper, and serve immediately.

SPRINGTIME RISOTTO WITH MUSHROOMS, ASPARAGUS, AND PEAS

EVERY SPRING, I CAN'T WAIT UNTIL ASPARA-*gus, fava beans, and peas come into season so I can put them on the menu. These tender green vegetables are the signs of spring, and I like to combine them with earthy mushrooms in a delicate risotto. Fava beans, a Tuscan favorite, are sometimes called broad beans or faba beans. You can find them raw at farmer's markets. Fresh sweet peas are also excellent in risotto, or you can use fresh lima beans.*

MAKES 6 APPETIZER SERVINGS OR 4 MAIN-COURSE SERVINGS

¼ cup extra-virgin olive oil
1 medium onion, minced
1 clove garlic, minced
1½ cups arborio rice (do not rinse)
8 ounces mixed mushrooms, such as shiitake, oyster, cremini, chanterelle, morel, porcini, and button, sliced or torn into ½-inch pieces
1 cup fresh or frozen peas, or shelled and peeled fava beans (page 68)
1 pound asparagus, bottoms cut off and bottom 3 inches peeled, cut into ½-inch lengths
1 teaspoon freshly chopped rosemary leaves
⅛ teaspoon salt
⅛ teaspoon freshly ground black pepper
1 cup dry white wine
3 to 4 cups hot Chicken Stock (page 15), Vegetable Stock (page 17), or low-sodium canned broth
2 tablespoons unsalted butter
¼ cup freshly grated Parmesan cheese

In a medium-size heavy soup pot, heat the olive oil over medium-high heat. Add the onion and garlic and cook, stirring, until the onion is translucent, about 5 minutes. Reduce the heat to medium, add the rice, mushrooms, peas, asparagus, rosemary, salt, and pepper and cook, stirring with a wooden spoon, until well coated in oil, about 1 minute.

Add the wine and simmer gently until the liquid is absorbed, 3 to 5 minutes. Add ½ cup chicken stock, stir, and simmer, stirring occasionally, until the liquid is absorbed. Repeat, adding ½ cup stock at a time, until the rice is cooked through but still firm, about 25 minutes total.

Add the butter and the Parmesan cheese. Mix well, taste for salt and pepper, and serve immediately.

PRO TIP: *Risotto should be stirred frequently to prevent burning, but constant stirring is unnecessary and may break up the rice grains, resulting in a gummy risotto.*

RISOTTO AL BAROLO

THE ROBUST CUISINE OF PIEDMONT IS FAMOUS, *so I was full of anticipation when Bruno Ceretto, a famous local maker of Barolo wine, took me to his favorite Piemontese restaurant. After a wonderful* agnolotti Piemontese *(little pasta envelopes of rabbit, chicken, butter, and sage), a strange lavender-colored dish appeared. Bruno and the chef wanted me to guess what it was, but I couldn't imagine. As soon as I tasted it, I realized that I was eating a risotto made with red wine instead of the usual white. I've made the dish with Tuscan Chianti, with excellent results. The red wine and juicy grapes balance out the salty Parmesan.*

MAKES 6 APPETIZER SERVINGS

3 tablespoons unsalted butter
1 red onion, minced
1 small clove garlic, minced
1½ cups arborio rice (do not rinse)
⅛ teaspoon salt
⅛ teaspoon freshly ground black pepper
2 cups Barolo, Chianti, or another dry, full-bodied red wine
2 to 3 cups hot Chicken Stock (page 15), Vegetable Stock (page 17), or low-sodium canned broth
¼ cup freshly grated Parmesan cheese
1 tablespoon freshly chopped Italian parsley
16 to 20 seedless red grapes, halved

In a medium-size heavy soup pot, melt 2 tablespoons of the butter over medium-high heat. When it foams, add the onion and garlic and cook, stirring, until the onion is translucent, about 5 minutes. Reduce the heat to medium, add the rice, salt, and pepper, and cook, stirring with a wooden spoon, until well coated, about 1 minute.

Add enough red wine to cover the rice and simmer gently until the liquid is absorbed, 3 to 5 minutes. Repeat until no more wine remains. Add ½ cup chicken stock, stir, and simmer, stirring occasionally, until the liquid is absorbed. Repeat, adding ½ cup stock at a time, until the rice is cooked through but still firm, about 25 minutes total.

Add the remaining tablespoon butter and the Parmesan cheese. Mix well, taste for salt and pepper, and serve immediately, sprinkled with parsley and grape halves.

CLASSIC SOFT POLENTA

IN 1992, I WAS INVITED TO REPRESENT THE *United States at a dinner at the legendary Italian restaurant San Domenico to commemorate the five hundredth anniversary of Columbus's voyage. The theme was Old World and New World ingredients.*

Knowing that Italians eat corn (New World) only in the form of polenta, I decided to introduce them to fresh sweet corn in a salad. When I came rolling through customs with a big Styrofoam cooler full of corn on the cob, I was immediately surrounded by agents and dogs. But when I explained that it was corn (grana di Turco in Italian), the officials just looked at me like I was out of my mind and waved me through. They never even opened the cooler.

Polenta is deeply rustic Italian comfort food, especially in the North. I love it with rich stews and roasted game birds. It is also a wonderful medium for thin shavings of truffles. In most supermarkets, polenta is sold as cornmeal, and the coarse variety is most traditional. You can also use fine cornmeal, but the cooking time will be reduced.

MAKES ABOUT 4 CUPS

6 cups water
1 tablespoon salt
2 cups polenta (cornmeal)
2 tablespoons cold unsalted butter
1/2 cup freshly grated Parmesan cheese

In a heavy-bottomed soup pot, bring the water and salt to a rolling boil over high heat. Reduce the heat to medium and gradually pour in the polenta, 1/4 cup at a time, whisking constantly so the polenta doesn't clump or stick. When all the polenta has been added, reduce the heat to medium-low.

Cover and cook about 25 minutes, stirring occasionally. Taste the polenta occasionally to check for doneness; it should be creamy, with no hardness at the center of the grain. Stir constantly toward the end of the cooking to make sure it does not stick to the pot. When the polenta is done, turn off the heat and stir in the butter and cheese with a wooden spoon. Taste for salt and set aside 1 to 2 minutes before serving to let the flavors develop.

 PRO TIP: *You don't have to stir polenta constantly; just whisk it up from the bottom fairly often, to make sure it doesn't scorch.*

POLENTA WITH FONTINA, ARUGULA, AND TOMATO

IF YOU WERE REALLY DETERMINED, YOU COULD *ski from Switzerland into Italy simply by scaling the Matterhorn. On your way down from the peak, you would ski right through the Italian alpine village of Cervina, where I first had this dish. The sun is so warm, even in the winter, that skiers can often eat lunch at outdoor terrace restaurants, then head back to the slopes. (I usually prefer a nap, but to each his own.)*

You don't have to look hard to find the Swiss influence here: The polenta is topped with a creamy cheese fondue, then topped with bits of fresh tomato and arugula. The combination of hot and cool, smooth and peppery, soft and crisp is incredible.

MAKES ABOUT 6 SERVINGS

1 pound Italian fontina cheese, coarsely grated
¼ cup whole or low-fat milk
¼ cup dry white wine
½ teaspoon salt
¼ teaspoon freshly ground black pepper
1 recipe Classic Soft Polenta (page 153)
2 ripe plum tomatoes, diced
½ cup freshly chopped arugula
1 tablespoon freshly chopped Italian parsley

In the top of an empty double boiler, combine the cheese, milk, wine, salt, and pepper. Stir and set aside to come to room temperature, about 20 minutes. Bring a kettle of water to the boil.

Meanwhile, cook the polenta as directed. When the polenta is almost cooked, pour boiling water into the base of the double boiler. Set the cheese mixture on top and cook, stirring, over low heat, until thick and smooth.

Ladle the polenta into individual serving bowls. Top with 1 or 2 generous spoonfuls of the fondue. Sprinkle with tomatoes, arugula, and parsley, and serve immediately.

 PRO TIP: *When you're using a fine cheese like fontina, always melt it carefully in a double boiler to avoid waste.*

POLENTA AL SUGO DI AGNELLO

IT WAS ON A ROMANTICALLY GLOOMY AUTUMN *day in Umbria that I understood why polenta is so beloved in northern Italy. At lunch in the hill town of Todi, I perked up when the waiter brought a first course of sunny yellow polenta with a deep red* ragù *of lamb and freshly grated Parmesan cheese.*

When serving polenta at home, pass the polenta first, then the ragù, *letting your guests serve themselves. If you combine the polenta and sauce on one platter, things get pretty messy by the time the last guest is served. Polenta with tomato sauce, meat sauce, or mushroom sauce is ideal winter comfort food; see the pasta recipes for more ideas. For smaller groups, make less polenta and freeze half the sauce for another time.*

MAKES 8 TO 10 SERVINGS

2 tablespoons extra-virgin olive oil, plus
   additional for serving (optional)
3 cloves garlic, thinly sliced
2 pounds lamb stew meat, cubed
1 onion, minced
1 tablespoon freshly chopped rosemary leaves
1 tablespoon freshly chopped thyme
1 bottle (750 ml) dry red wine
1 cup milled or crushed canned Italian plum
   tomatoes
Pinch of ground nutmeg
Pinch of ground cloves
Salt and freshly ground black pepper
1½ recipes Classic Soft Polenta (page 153)
6 tablespoons freshly grated Parmesan cheese

In a large soup pot, heat the olive oil over medium-high heat. Add the garlic and cook, stirring, until golden, about 3 minutes. Add the lamb and cook, stirring, until the meat starts to brown.

Add the onion, rosemary, and thyme and cook, stirring, 1 minute. Add the wine, tomatoes, nutmeg, cloves, and salt and pepper to taste. Reduce the heat and simmer, uncovered, until the meat is tender and the sauce has thickened, about 45 minutes.

Cook the polenta as directed. Ladle the polenta into individual serving bowls. Top with 1 or 2 generous ladles of lamb sauce. Sprinkle with Parmesan and, if desired, drizzle with olive oil. Serve immediately.

QUICK-COOK MAIN DISHES

Roasted Sole with Sicilian Peperonata

Thyme-Roasted Halibut on a Bed of Roasted Vegetables

Roasted Red Snapper with Olives and Oregano

Roasted Cod with Rosemary-Shallot Potatoes

Salmon in Cartoccio

Braised Striped Bass with Fennel, Pernod, and Saffron

Sautéed Shrimp with Lemon and Garlic

Sea Scallops with Orange and Fennel

Chicken Breasts alla Romana

Sautéed Chicken Breasts with Zucchini and Balsamic Glaze

Sliced Breast of Duck with Vin Santo and Herb Sauce

Italian Sausage with Broccoli Rabe

Roast Loin of Pork with Port Wine and Figs

Rosemary-Balsamic Pork Chops

Veal Scaloppine with Tomatoes and Onions

Emincé de Veau

Veal Cutlets with Chianti Sauce

QUICK-COOK MAIN DISHES

ERE'S A STATISTIC THAT WILL SHOCK YOU. ON ANY given day, by 4:00 P.M., 80 percent of Americans haven't decided what they're having for dinner.

When I heard that, my first thought was: What can I do to help these people? I really believe that professional chefs take a kind of Hippocratic oath of hospitality. As chefs, we have to use our knowledge to comfort and entertain and generally make life better. And we have to do it with a certain

integrity, in the ingredients, flavors, and the methods of the food we cook.

In this chapter, my job is to help you put dinner on the table faster, easier, and better than you think you can. And to do it with real food and real flavor. My customers at Campagna think I have mysterious "chef tricks" up my sleeve. In this book I keep nothing hidden. All my tricks are here for you to see. I don't do anything that you can't learn. There's no secret handshake you learn at culinary school, and the only secret ingredients in my spice rack are passion and TLC.

Cooking isn't magic—it's more like sex. It's about caring, passion, and having fun. And, of course, timing is everything.

Every kind of cooking has its time and place.

OVERLEAF: **A QUICK-COOK ITALIAN FAMILY DINNER WITH FRESH DAFFODILS FROM THE GARDEN AND INVOLTINI DI POLLO AL TAORMINA AND CAMPAGNA ROASTED POTATOES.**

That's why we have separate chapters for the two kinds of main dishes you need in your life: one for days when you have a little extra time for cooking, the other for days when you have none at all, but you still want to eat real food with your family. When you have no time, the worst thing you can do for yourself is embark on some gourmet experiment. It will be 9:00 P.M., you'll have used every pot in the kitchen, and your kids still won't be fed! When you have forty-five minutes, do a forty-five-minute recipe. When you have three hours, then you can do a three-hour recipe. You'll find them in our chapter on Slow-Cook Main Dishes.

Quick cooking is what this chapter is all about. It's also what most restaurant food is all about. Except for the traditional trattorias and bistros that slow-braise the customary stews every morning and serve them all day, most restaurants today cook their food to order, just like you have to. Italian ingredients, with their strong, direct flavors, are particularly good for cooking "à la minute" or quickly, to order. The light roasted fish-and-vegetable recipes and the chicken and veal sautés in this chapter were developed at Campagna as recipes that can be quickly assembled, then cooked in just the time it takes people to eat their appetizers. As a home cook, you can use that time to go change your clothes, pour a glass of wine, get your kids to wash up for dinner—whatever you want.

I always say that purchasing and menu planning are just as important as cooking for any chef, and that includes home cooks, too. Keeping a variety of seasonal vegetables, plus garlic, onions, potatoes, and of course extra-virgin olive oil on hand helps speed things up. It's really hard to cook quickly when you have to build in a nightly trip to the grocery store, or stop at four different shops to get the fish, vegetables, white wine, and olive oil you need for a recipe. Restaurant chefs have it easy—we get everything delivered!

Restaurant chefs have another advantage over home cooks. We cook for a different crowd every night. We don't have to change the menu for every meal, and we don't have to come home from work and then make dinner. I know how hard that is. But using these recipes as a starting-point can make it easier. You can adapt the methods for your taste, or your family's, using different vegetables, herbs, fish, and seasonings. You can change the vegetables with the season. You can use a salmon recipe even if your twelve-year-old hates salmon—make it with flounder or scallops.

Remember nouvelle cuisine? It's so easy to make fun of those tiny portions now. But we've all pulled a lot of good things out of that move-ment. Real nouvelle cuisine is a way of eating that's both light and full of flavor. The method of cooking a simple sauté and serving it with a quick pan sauce came out of nouvelle cuisine. Saucing with strong ingredients like herbs, citrus juices, vinegars, olives, and mustard is from nouvelle cuisine, too. Both of those methods are used in this chapter.

Right along with nouvelle cuisine came the rediscovery of rustic Provençal, Italian, and Mediterranean cooking. Italian cooking had to come to America twice: the first time with the immigrants, the second time with the new breed of Italian restaurants. The Italian ingredients that are my quick-cooking standbys—tomatoes, rosemary, onions, olive oil, balsamic vinegar—are the best things that ever happened to American home cooks. Making good-tasting food with them is so easy. Peasant cooks in Italy have used them for centuries. The difference is that peasants had time to cook at night! We don't. So I've adapted their slow-cooking ingredients to quicker dishes, using the easiest professional techniques.

I hope you'll use these recipes to learn techniques that can be used with many ingredients, creating your own dishes and your own cooking style. They are really intended to inspire you, not to pin you down to a certain vegetable or a certain type of fish fillet. Roasting fish, making vinaigrettes as sauces, and cooking fish and vegetables together in aluminum foil are supposed to make it easy for you to feed your family real food. My point is: Don't drive yourself crazy. If the store is out of snapper, use char or halibut. If the zucchini looks bruised, use summer squash or red peppers. You can take ownership of these recipes. It's for you to decide.

I know how easy it is to choose not to cook, to have pizza one more time or order Chinese food again—especially when you get home at 7:00 P.M. and soccer practice, homework, and all the other business of life means that the family will spend only half an hour at the table, no matter how good the food is. But just because it's optional doesn't mean it's not worthwhile, or that your kids won't remember your cooking all the rest of their lives. Knowing what to cook when is half the battle, and we've fought that fight for you. These recipes can become your weeknight staples. Do what you can handle. Do what you can in the time you have. And just like sex, cooking will be fun and satisfying.

ROASTED SOLE WITH SICILIAN PEPERONATA

NEW YORK CITY IS PRETTY FAR FROM A SICILIAN *fishing village, but the city actually has a terrific variety of seafood. Fish from all over the world come through New York's markets; I think that's why New York is probably the best place in the world to be a chef. It's a pleasure to choose from among the sole, salmon, scallops, calamari, shrimp, and snapper, to name just a few. And the freshness and quality of fish all over America is definitely improving.*

Peperonata—an intense, slow-cooked dish of peppers, onions, and olive oil—is one of my favorite side dishes, and a great shortcut in cooking. It's a vegetable and a sauce at the same time. The bright colors and sweet flavors make it great for a snowy-white fish like sole, but any mild fish can be used here. This recipe will yield more peperonata *than*

you need, but it freezes extremely well and can also be used as an antipasto, a pasta sauce, or a side dish.

MAKES 6 SERVINGS

FOR THE *PEPERONATA*
    ¼ cup extra-virgin olive oil
    ½ onion, minced
    1 clove garlic, thickly sliced
    1 anchovy fillet, chopped
    2 red bell peppers, cored, seeded, and cut into 1-inch dice
    1 yellow pepper, cored, seeded, and cut into 1-inch dice
    1 green pepper, cored, seeded, and cut into 1-inch dice
    1 cup milled or crushed canned Italian plum tomatoes
    ½ teaspoon dried oregano
    Pinch of hot red pepper flakes
    Salt and freshly ground black pepper

FOR THE FISH
    Six 8-ounce sole or lemon sole fillets
    Salt and freshly ground black pepper
    Flour for dredging
    1 cup pure olive oil

To make the *peperonata,* heat the olive oil in a large skillet over medium heat. Add the onion and garlic and cook, stirring, until the onion begins to wilt, about 3 minutes. Add the anchovy, peppers, tomatoes, oregano, red pepper flakes, and salt and pepper to taste. Cook, stirring to break up the anchovies. Reduce the heat to a simmer, and cook for about 35 minutes, until the peppers are very soft.

To make the fish, season the fillets on both sides with salt and pepper. Dredge lightly with

SOLE FILLETS WITH SICILIAN PEPERONATA ON A PUMPKIN ALETHA SOULÉ DINNER PLATE.

flour. Heat the oil in a deep skillet until hot but not smoking. Slip the fillets into the hot oil and cook, turning once, until golden on both sides.

To serve, spoon the *peperonata* onto six serving plates. Place a fillet on top of each, grind black pepper on top, and serve immediately.

PRO TIP: *When adding garlic and anchovy together to a dish, you'll get the best flavor if you make them into a paste on the cutting board beforehand. Chop finely, sprinkle on some coarse salt, and use the flat side of the knife to rub them all together.*

THYME-ROASTED HALIBUT ON A BED OF ROASTED VEGETABLES

I LOVE IT WHEN MY CUSTOMERS ASK ME FOR *cooking advice. Over the years, I've noticed that most of them have a fear of cooking fish. I'd like to cure them of it with this technique, because for quick-cook dinners, fish fillets are a cook's dream. Roasting fish at a high temperature saves you from having to stand at the stove to sauté it, and you can cook the vegetables in the same pan. This is about the healthiest and quickest one-pot meal you can make.*

Here's the technique that will make this dish come out well: Cut all the vegetables into uniform sizes, and in small enough pieces so they will cook quickly. When buying your fish fillets, look for fillets with a smooth surface. A choppy surface may mean that the fish market had trouble removing the flesh from the bones because the fish was old.

MAKES 4 SERVINGS

1 zucchini, cut into ¼-inch dice
1 small fennel bulb, cut into ¼-inch dice
1 beet, boiled until tender, peeled and cut into ¼-inch dice
1 turnip, peeled and cut into ¼-inch dice
1 onion, thinly sliced
2 cloves garlic, thinly sliced
¼ cup plus 2 tablespoons extra-virgin olive oil
Salt and freshly ground black pepper
Four 8-ounce halibut fillets, at least 1 inch thick
1 tablespoon freshly chopped thyme

Preheat the oven to 450°F.

In a large roasting pan, toss the vegetables and garlic with ¼ cup of the olive oil and salt and pepper to taste.

Rub the fillets with the remaining 2 tablespoons olive oil and season on both sides with salt and pepper. Arrange the fillets in a single layer on top of the vegetables. Sprinkle with thyme. Bake 18 to 22 minutes, until cooked to your liking. Check the dish after 10 minutes; if the vegetables seem to be browning too quickly, reduce the heat to 400°F.

ROASTED RED SNAPPER WITH OLIVES AND OREGANO

ONCE YOU FEEL AT HOME AT THE FISH *counter, quick cooking on weeknights is no problem. A fish fillet is just as easy to cook as a chicken breast, and I love to contrast smooth white fish like snapper, grouper, halibut, and cod with intense ingredients like black olives. When roasted correctly, fish fillets develop a crispy top that protects the tender meat underneath. Children seem to like roasted fish because of that crispness.*

This aromatic entrée includes the intense ingredients of the Sicilian kitchen. Oregano grows wild all over the island and turns up in almost every dish. Sicilian cooks use it dried rather than fresh— it's one of the few dried herbs that really works well in cooking. To make this dish even lower in fat, substitute capers for some or all of the rich olives.

MAKES **4** SERVINGS

Four 8-ounce fillets red snapper, grouper, tilefish,
    or striped bass, at least I inch thick
6 tablespoons extra-virgin olive oil
Salt and freshly ground black pepper
I clove garlic, thinly sliced
I tablespoon dried oregano
½ cup dry white wine
12 black brine-cured olives such as Niçoise or
    Gaeta, pitted and chopped
3 tablespoons water

Preheat the oven to 350°F.

Rub each fillet with 1 tablespoon olive oil, season on both sides with salt and pepper, and arrange in a single layer in a roasting pan.

In a small bowl, mix the remaining 2 tablespoons olive oil, garlic, and oregano. Drizzle this mixture over the fish and bake 12 to 18 minutes, until cooked to your liking. Immediately transfer the fillets to serving plates and put the pan on the stove. Add the wine, olives, and water and boil 1 minute, until slightly thickened. Spoon over the fish and serve immediately.

PRO TIP: *Because of their high fat content, olives can burn and become bitter if cooked at high temperatures. Cooking them with plenty of liquid protects the olives from burning.*

ROASTED COD WITH ROSEMARY-SHALLOT POTATOES

COD AND POTATOES JUST SEEM TO GO *together in New England fish chowder or French* brandade, *a garlicky puree of salt cod and mashed potatoes. And in Tuscany, roasted potatoes and white fish is a classic combination on the coast. The juices of the fish flavor the whole dish, including the crispy potatoes.*

To test roasted fish for doneness, press it with your finger; it should feel firm, like a tire full of air. Or test to make sure the center is heated through by inserting a trussing needle or thin, sharp knife tip into the thickest part, then checking the needle with your fingers. If it feels very hot, the fish is cooked.

JOHN DORY STILL LIFE.

MAKES **4** SERVINGS

¼ cup plus 2 tablespoons extra-virgin olive oil
8 medium potatoes, sliced ½ thick
2 cloves garlic, halved
Salt and freshly ground black pepper
2 teaspoons fresh chopped rosemary leaves
4 shallots, coarsely chopped
Four 8-ounce codfish fillets, at least 1 inch thick
2 tablespoons freshly chopped Italian parsley

Preheat the oven to 350°F.

In a large ovenproof skillet, heat ¼ cup of the olive oil over medium-high heat. Add the potatoes, garlic, and salt and pepper to taste. Cook, stirring, until lightly browned, about 4 minutes. Bake 8 minutes, then remove from the oven and place on top of the stove. Sprinkle with the rosemary and shallots.

Rub the fish with the remaining 2 tablespoons olive oil and season on both sides with salt and pepper. Lay the fish on top of the potatoes and bake 12 to 15 minutes, until cooked to your liking.

Serve immediately, sprinkled with chopped parsley.

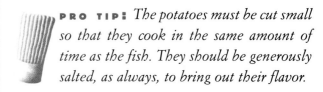

PRO TIP: *The potatoes must be cut small so that they cook in the same amount of time as the fish. They should be generously salted, as always, to bring out their flavor.*

SALMON IN CARTOCCIO

YOU CAN'T BEAT THIS COOKING METHOD FOR *high drama at the table. Fish wrapped and baked with aromatics release incredible smells when you slash open the foil package at the table. The method combines the best of braising, steaming, and roasting—with not even one pot to wash. Fish really takes well to this moist cooking method, and it's a great way to cook rich fish like salmon without making it even richer, but most any fish will do. To vary the flavors, add seasonings of fresh herbs, thinly sliced lemon or orange peel, or butter.*

In cartoccio is the same as the French method called en papillote. *But I've never found a difference in the end result when I use aluminum foil for the wrapping. Just wrap each fillet in a foil envelope with the shiny side in (to provide slightly more heat in the cooking). I've actually had spaghetti and clams cooked by this method in Italy.*

MAKES 4 SERVINGS

2 lemons, sliced ¼ inch thick
Four 8-ounce salmon, striped bass, or snapper
    fillets, at least 1 inch thick
Salt and freshly ground black pepper
½ cup dry white wine
¼ cup extra-virgin olive oil
2 cloves garlic, thickly sliced
8 small sprigs fresh rosemary
2 small sprigs fresh oregano

Preheat the oven to 400°F.

Cut four 12 x 12-inch squares of aluminum foil and arrange them on a baking sheet. Divide the lemon slices on the foil squares. Lay the fillets on the lemon slices and sprinkle both sides with salt and pepper. Fold up the sides of each foil square to make boxes around the fillets. Pour 2 table-spoons wine and 1 tablespoon olive oil into each box. Divide the garlic and herbs among the boxes. Tightly close the boxes by folding the sides together as if you are wrapping a present.

Bake 10 to 15 minutes, until done to your liking. (Be careful of escaping steam when you open a packet to check the doneness.) Bring the packets to the table on a platter. Standing back from the steam, slash open each package and quickly scoop the contents onto serving plates. Serve immediately.

PRO TIP: *Whenever I'm asked which kind of salmon is the best, I have to say "the freshest." Salmon is a very oily fish, and it's the oils in fish that deteriorate quickly. Whenever it's available, I choose fresh sockeye salmon from the Pacific Northwest.*

BRAISED STRIPED BASS WITH FENNEL, PERNOD, AND SAFFRON

IF YOU LIKE BOUILLABAISSE AS MUCH AS I DO, *and if you hate washing dishes as much as I do, this simplified fish entrée will change your life. It gives you all the flavors of the Provençal classic—fennel, garlic, saffron, and golden olive oil—with only a little of the fuss. Striped bass is a good substitute for the Mediterranean fish known as* loup de mer *in France and* branzino *in Italy. Oven-braising at a moderate temperature is an excellent technique for many white fish; it really picks up flavor from the cooking liquid, which also keeps the fish moist.*

MAKES **4** SERVINGS

4 tablespoons extra-virgin olive oil
Pinch of saffron threads
I clove garlic, thickly sliced
I fennel bulb, thinly sliced lengthwise
Four 8-ounce striped bass, char, or snapper
    fillets, with the skin on
Salt
½ cup dry white wine
¼ cup Pernod or Ricard (French anise-flavored
    aperitif, available at liquor stores)
I cup Fish Stock (page 17), or ½ cup additional
    dry white wine mixed with ½ cup water

Preheat the oven to 350°F.

In a large ovenproof pot with a lid, heat 2 tablespoons of the olive oil over medium-high heat. Add the saffron, garlic, and fennel and cook, stirring, until the fennel is lightly browned, about 5 minutes.

Season the fillets on both sides with salt and arrange them skin side down on top of the fennel.

Pour the wine, Pernod, and stock around the fillets, cover, and bake 12 to 18 minutes, until cooked to your liking. Transfer the fillets to a plate and set aside. Put the pot on top of the stove over medium heat. Add the remaining 2 tablespoons olive oil and simmer about 1 minute, until slightly reduced. Taste for salt.

Spread the fennel on a serving platter, arrange the fillets on top, and pour the sauce over the fish. Serve immediately.

 PRO TIP: *Skin-on fillets will hold together in braising liquid better than skinned ones.*

SAUTÉED SHRIMP WITH LEMON AND GARLIC

LEMON AND GARLIC ARE A MAGICAL COMBINA-*tion. This is a more Italian-American than Italian dish, and brings back great memories for those of us who grew up with Italian neighbors. Sometimes customers ask for this dish at Campagna, for nostalgic reasons, and I'm always happy to oblige.*

There's just nothing easier or better than a simple sauté of shrimp, garlic, and parsley. A little white wine binds it together just enough to make a sauce. You can serve it with sautéed spinach or a white bean salad on the side (you can also serve it with pasta). Have all the ingredients ready to go, and you'll be sitting down to dinner five minutes later.

MAKES **4** SERVINGS

¼ cup extra-virgin olive oil
2 cloves garlic, smashed and peeled
24 large shrimp, peeled and deveined
¼ cup dry white wine

Freshly squeezed juice of 1 lemon
Salt and freshly ground black pepper
¼ cup freshly chopped Italian parsley

In a large skillet, heat the olive oil over high heat. Add the garlic and shrimp and cook, tossing occasionally, just until pink and lightly browned, about 3 minutes. Add the wine, lemon juice, and salt and pepper to taste, and cook, stirring, 1 minute more. Add the parsley, toss, and serve immediately.

 PRO TIP: *Using whole, smashed garlic cloves instead of minced garlic allows you to remove, or your dinner guests to push aside, the indigestible chunks of garlic.*

SEA SCALLOPS WITH ORANGE AND FENNEL

have everything ready!

THIS DISH WILL TAKE YOU TO THE SOUTH OF *France in just a few minutes. The Côte d'Azur is the land of pastis, an anise-flavored aperitif. The Pernod used in this recipe is a good brand of pastis. Pastis and orange juice are often used to flavor seafood dishes on the French Mediterranean.*

Scallops are great for quick cooking. They're soft and sweet and look nice on the plate. The technique of adding liquid to the sauté pan after the cooking is called deglazing. The liquid (which can be wine, stock, vinegar, cream, or juice) combines with the cooking juices and browned bits into a simple "pan sauce." It takes about twenty seconds to make, can be done with fish, poultry, or meat, and gives your cooking extra style and flavor.

MAKES 4 SERVINGS

16 sea scallops
Salt and freshly ground black pepper

All-purpose flour, for dredging
¼ cup extra-virgin olive oil or grapeseed oil
1 clove garlic, thickly sliced
2 shallots, minced
½ fennel bulb, thinly sliced
1 pinch saffron
¼ cup Pernod or Ricard (French anise-flavored aperitif, available at liquor stores)
1½ teaspoons freshly grated orange zest
Fresh-squeezed juice of 1 orange
½ cup Fish Stock (page 17), or ¼ cup dry white wine mixed with ¼ cup water
1 tablespoon cold unsalted butter, cut into pieces
2 tablespoons freshly chopped chives

Sprinkle the scallops with salt and pepper. Spread about ½ cup flour in a shallow bowl and, working in batches, dredge the scallops, shaking off any excess flour. Add more flour as needed.

In a large skillet, heat the olive oil over medium-high heat. Add the dredged scallops and cook, turning once, until golden brown on both sides. As they are cooked, remove and set aside. Turn off the heat and, using paper towels, carefully wipe out the excess oil from the pan.

Add the garlic, shallots, and fennel and cook over medium heat 1 minute. Remove the pan from the heat and, tilting the pan away from you, add the saffron and Pernod. Once the liquid has settled, return the pan to the heat and add the orange zest, juice, and stock. Simmer until slightly thickened, about 3 minutes. Whisk in the butter and chives and add the scallops, turning them over in the sauce just until heated through. Taste for salt and pepper, and serve immediately.

 PRO TIP: *Lightly dusting the scallops in flour gives them a crust that seals the juices in and prevents the scallops from sticking to the pan.*

CHICKEN BREASTS ALLA ROMANA

WHENEVER YOU SEE ARTICHOKES, MINT, AND *pecorino Romano cheese in the same recipe, that's the tip-off that it comes from Rome. Artichokes and mint have long grown wild on the hills around Rome, and the trattoria classic* carciofi alla Romana *is a dish of baby spring artichokes braised in olive oil, garlic, and mint. This flavor-packed combination makes a great pan sauce for chicken.*

Pecorino Romano is southern Italy's equivalent of the North's Parmigiano-Reggiano. It is made entirely from sheep's milk, which makes it much sharper than Parmesan, but in some dishes the acidity really wakes up the dish. Whenever possible, I buy organic chickens, which are fed only organic chicken feed. The taste really is much better.

MAKES **4** SERVINGS

- 1 lemon, halved
- 4 baby artichokes
- 2 tablespoons extra-virgin olive oil
- 1 onion, minced
- 1 clove garlic, thickly sliced
- 4 large boneless, skinless chicken breast halves
- Salt and freshly ground black pepper
- 1 cup Chicken Stock (page 15), low-sodium canned broth, or a mixture of white wine and water
- 3 tablespoons freshly grated pecorino Romano cheese
- 6 fresh mint leaves, chopped

To prepare the artichokes, fill a large bowl with cold water and squeeze the lemon into it. Pull or cut the outer leaves off the artichokes until you get to the pale greenish yellow inner leaves. Place in the water. When ready to cook, drain the artichokes and slice very thinly.

In a nonstick skillet, heat the olive oil over medium-high heat. Add the onion and garlic and cook, stirring, until the onion is wilted, about 3 minutes. Season the chicken on both sides with salt and pepper and cook 2 minutes on one side, until lightly browned. Turn and cook 2 minutes more.

Reduce the heat to medium and add the artichokes, stock, and salt and pepper to taste. Simmer about 10 minutes, until the chicken is cooked through. Add the cheese and mint, stir, and cook 2 minutes more. Taste for salt and pepper. Transfer the chicken to serving plates and spoon the sauce over the top. Serve immediately.

SAUTÉED CHICKEN BREASTS WITH ZUCCHINI AND BALSAMIC GLAZE

SIMPLE, WHOLESOME DISHES WITH CLEAN *flavors and only a little added fat are what we're all looking for these days. Chicken breasts, of course, are a popular solution. Like a lot of people, I can eat chicken every day and never get tired of it. I like to cook chicken breasts with vegetables, fresh herbs, and intense seasonings like mustard and balsamic vinegar. Quickly cooking good-quality balsamic vinegar tames the acid and turns the vinegar into a sweet-sour glaze, great for coating the tender zucchini and chicken with color and flavor.*

Using this technique, you could substitute yellow squash or green beans for the zucchini, and fresh marjoram or sage for the thyme. Zucchini and thyme are a classic combination.

MAKES 4 SERVINGS

4 large tablespoons extra-virgin olive oil
4 boneless, skinless chicken breast halves
Salt and freshly ground black pepper
1 clove garlic, thickly sliced
½ onion, minced
2 cups thinly sliced zucchini, cut into half-moons (about 2 small zucchini)
2 teaspoons dried thyme or 4 teaspoons chopped fresh thyme
¼ cup top-quality balsamic vinegar, preferably aged
½ cup Chicken Stock (page 15), low-sodium canned broth, or water

In a large nonstick skillet, heat 2 tablespoons of the olive oil over medium-high heat. Season the chicken on both sides with salt and pepper. Add the chicken to the oil and cook 2 minutes on one side. Turn and cook 2 minutes more. Transfer to a plate and set aside. Using paper towels, carefully wipe out the fat from the pan.

Add the remaining 2 tablespoons olive oil to the skillet and heat over medium-high heat. Add the garlic and onion and cook, stirring, until the onion is wilted, about 3 minutes. Add the zucchini and cook, stirring, 1 minute. Add the chicken breasts, thyme, vinegar, stock, and salt and pepper to taste. Cover, reduce the heat to low, and simmer about 12 minutes, until the chicken is cooked through. Serve immediately.

PRO TIP: *If you are really determined to cut fat from your diet, you can eliminate half of the olive oil, as long as you are using a nonstick pan for the cooking.*

Excellent!
Easy!

SLICED BREAST OF DUCK WITH VIN SANTO AND HERB SAUCE

I'VE LOVED DUCK EVER SINCE I SPENT THREE *years cooking in the Hamptons, close enough to the duck farms of Long Island that I could drive over and pick out my own birds! Preparing duck doesn't have to be scary for home cooks. Unlike whole ducks, duck breasts are lean and easy to cook. And unlike chicken breasts, duck breasts have a satisfying game-bird flavor. I love them in the fall, with side dishes like Campagna Roasted Potatoes (page 100).*

A little sweetness is good with the richness of duck. I like to get it from vin santo *or marsala wine, instead of the traditional orange and cherry sauces.*

MAKES 4 SERVINGS

4 mallard or Muscovy duck breast halves, with
    the skin, trimmed of excess fat
Salt and freshly ground black pepper
2 tablespoons vegetable oil
2 tablespoons extra-virgin olive oil
½ red onion, minced
6 button mushrooms, thinly sliced
1 cup Tuscan *vin santo* or another rich dessert
    wine, such as marsala, sauternes, or port
1 tablespoon chopped fresh thyme
2 teaspoons chopped fresh rosemary leaves
½ cup Chicken Stock (page 15), or
    low-sodium canned broth

Preheat the oven to 450°F.

Using a small sharp knife, cut a large X in the skin of each duck breast. Season on both sides with salt and pepper.

In a large ovenproof skillet, heat the vegetable oil over medium-high heat. Reduce the heat to medium, add the duck breasts skin side down, and cook until browned and the fat has begun to melt, about 10 minutes. Turn the breasts over and place in the oven for 10 to 15 minutes, until the duck feels firm but springy to the touch (medium rare). Transfer the breasts to a plate and set aside.

Using paper towels, carefully wipe out the skillet. Add the olive oil and heat over medium-high heat. Add the onion and mushrooms and cook, stirring, until the onion is wilted, about 3 minutes. Add the *vin santo*, simmer 1 minute, and add the thyme, rosemary, and stock. Simmer gently until thickened. Taste for salt and pepper.

When the sauce is almost cooked, use a sharp knife to slice the duck breasts into even slices. Spoon some of the sauce onto serving plates. Fan a duck breast on each plate and drizzle with remaining sauce. Serve immediately.

 PRO TIP: *Mallard and Muscovy duck breasts are much leaner than the Peking and Long Island varieties, making them a better choice for this recipe.*

ITALIAN SAUSAGE WITH BROCCOLI RABE

THIS IS AN OLD RECIPE FROM GARGANO IN *southern Italy. Bitter greens with pork sausage is a simple dish from peasant kitchens. Thin parsley-and-cheese sausages called* luganica *are available at good Italian delis and butcher shops; or you can use fresh Italian sweet or hot sausages.*

This quick dish is especially good for weeknight cooking. Serve it with grilled or toasted bruschetta to make it more substantial.

MAKES 4 SERVINGS

¼ cup plus 2 tablespoons extra-virgin olive oil
1 clove garlic, thickly sliced
1 bunch broccoli rabe, cut into 2-inch lengths
4 *luganica* or another thin fresh sausage, such as parsley-cheese, about 1½ pounds
1 cup water
Salt and freshly ground black pepper
4 thick slices peasant bread

In a large heavy pot, heat ¼ cup of the olive oil over medium-high heat. Add the garlic and cook, stirring, until golden, about 3 minutes. Add the broccoli rabe and cook, stirring occasionally, just until wilted. Add the sausage, cover, and cook 3 minutes, stirring occasionally. Add the water and simmer uncovered 5 minutes, until the sausage is cooked through and the liquid is almost gone. Add the remaining 2 tablespoons olive oil, cover, and cook 1 minute. Taste for salt and pepper.

Meanwhile, toast or grill the bread. Place the bread in serving bowls and ladle the stew on top. Serve immediately.

ROAST LOIN OF PORK WITH PORT WINE AND FIGS

FRESH FIGS AND SWEET WINE ARE A SEXY *combination that Italians adore, and this is my favorite way to use them together—straight from the autumn menu at Campagna. Port and other sweet wines are good to have on hand for making savory-sweet pan sauces on the spur of the moment.*

Slow-roasting pork is the best way to keep the juices in the meat, especially when you're cooking a delicate cut like the tenderloin. Serve it with Spinach Sautéed with Olive Oil and Garlic (page 95) or an oniony dish like Leek Gratin (page 93).

MAKES 4 TO 6 SERVINGS

One 2-pound pork tenderloin
Salt and freshly ground black pepper
½ cup ruby port, plus extra for basting
½ cup extra-virgin olive oil
1 shallot, minced
8 fresh Black Mission figs, cut into ½-inch dice or dried figs, coarsely chopped
½ cup chicken stock
2 teaspoons cold unsalted butter, cut into pieces (optional)

Preheat the oven to 300°F. Season the pork all over with salt and pepper and place in a roasting pan. Roast 20 to 30 minutes, basting with port every 10 minutes, until a meat thermometer registers 165°F. Set the pork aside, covered with foil, while you make the sauce.

Set the roasting pan on the stove. Add the oil and heat over medium-high heat. Add the shallot, figs, ½ cup port, and chicken stock, and simmer 1 to 2 minutes, until lightly thickened. If desired, swirl in the butter at the last minute.

ROSEMARY-BALSAMIC PORK CHOPS

PORK CHOPS ARE THE ULTIMATE AMERICAN *weeknight dinner, and pork with rosemary gives it an Italian twist. This super-easy dish brings them together with the sweetness of balsamic vinegar. Aged balsamic vinegar is the best; it comes only from the town of Modena in Emilia-Romagna and is so dense and complex that it makes rich sauces almost by itself. The vinegar's acidity is smoothed out when you cook it.*

I like to roast pork chops instead of pan-frying them. The lower cooking temperature keeps the juices in the meat, so they don't dry out. The fresh rosemary in this recipe is heated for just a few minutes to release its incredible fragrance.

MAKES 4 SERVINGS

4 pork chops, at least 1 inch thick
Salt and freshly ground black pepper
¼ cup extra-virgin olive oil
4 teaspoons chopped fresh rosemary leaves
¼ cup top-quality balsamic vinegar, preferably aged

Preheat the oven to 300°F.

Season the pork chops on both sides with salt and pepper. Rub each chop with 1 tablespoon of the olive oil. Arrange in a baking dish and bake 15 to 20 minutes, until firm but springy to the touch. Remove the chops from the oven (leaving the oven on) and sprinkle with rosemary and vinegar. Return to the oven and bake 5 minutes more to caramelize the vinegar. Serve immediately.

PRO TIP: *To give the sauce a creamy texture with no added fat, mix a tablespoon of mustard with the vinegar before adding it to the pan.*

VEAL SCALOPPINE WITH TOMATOES AND ONIONS

WHEN YOU'RE BRAINSTORMING A QUICK DIN-*ner, think about the foods that cook in no time at all. Veal scaloppine is the perfect cut of meat (chicken breasts are the equivalent), and tomatoes, onions, and zucchini, the ideal vegetables.*

This is the time to bring out that nonstick skillet. Veal scaloppine will cook with no trouble when they don't stick to the pan. They should be protected during the cooking with a thin coating of flour to prevent them from toughening and to give them a little crispness. The pan must be very hot when you add the scaloppine; quickly cooking them is the key to the dish.

MAKES 2 TO 4 SERVINGS

8 thin veal scaloppine, about 2 ounces each
    (you can get these at a butcher shop)
Salt and freshly ground black pepper
All-purpose flour, for dredging
¼ cup vegetable oil
2 tablespoons unsalted butter
¼ cup extra-virgin olive oil
1 clove garlic, peeled and smashed
1 onion, minced
2 zucchini, halved lengthwise and sliced crosswise
    ½ inch thick
4 plum tomatoes, diced, or 1 cup milled or
    crushed canned Italian tomatoes
1 teaspoon dried oregano
Pinch of hot red pepper flakes
Freshly grated Parmesan cheese
4 fresh basil sprigs (optional)

Season the veal on both sides with salt and pepper. Lightly dredge the veal on both sides in flour.

In a large skillet, heat the vegetable oil and butter over medium-high heat until very hot. Working in 2 batches if necessary to avoid crowding the pan, add the veal and cook just until lightly browned on both sides, about 1 minute per side. As it is cooked, set the veal aside. Carefully wipe out the skillet with paper towels.

Add the extra-virgin olive oil to the pan and heat over medium-high heat. Add the garlic, onion, zucchini, tomatoes, oregano, red pepper flakes, and salt to taste. If necessary, add a little water or wine to get the browned bits up from the bottom of the pan. Cook, stirring occasionally, until slightly thickened.

To serve, transfer the scaloppine to serving plates and mound the vegetables on top. Garnish each plate with Parmesan cheese and a fresh basil sprig and serve immediately.

PRO TIP: *Scaloppine of chicken, turkey, or beef can be cooked in the same manner.*

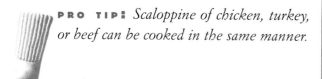

EMINCÉ DE VEAU

HOW CAN YOU GO WRONG WITH SHALLOTS, *mushrooms, herbs, and cream? Served on a Montreux Rösti (page 99), this easy sauté is the Swiss national dish. It's simple, quick, comforting, and even a little bit sexy with its creamy texture. Just a small amount of cream can thicken a sauce and carry its flavors, making your whole dish feel rich.*

To sauté correctly, it's important to have the pan very hot before adding the veal. The sauce is made right in the pan with the meat. (You can easily make this dish with chicken instead of veal.) And if you like the technique but not the richness of

cream, use milled or crushed canned Italian plum tomatoes to bind the sauce instead, adding them along with the wine.

MAKES 4 SERVINGS

1½ pounds veal cutlets (preferably top round), cut into finger-size strips
Salt and freshly ground black pepper
All-purpose flour, for dredging
½ cup clarified butter (page 98), or vegetable oil
3 shallots, thinly sliced
1 tablespoon freshly chopped rosemary leaves
1 tablespoon freshly chopped chives
1 tablespoon freshly chopped Italian parsley
1 cup thinly sliced button mushrooms
1 cup dry white wine
½ cup heavy cream or 3 tablespoons crème fraîche

Sprinkle the veal with salt and pepper and toss to coat. Lightly dredge the veal with flour, shaking off any excess.

In a large skillet, heat ¼ cup of the clarified butter over medium-high heat until very hot. Gradually add the veal and cook, stirring occasionally, until lightly browned. Transfer to a plate and turn off the heat.

Using paper towels, carefully wipe out the skillet. Add the remaining ¼ cup butter and heat over medium-high heat. Add the shallots and almost all of the herbs, reserving a quarter of each. Add the mushrooms and cook, stirring, until the shallots are translucent, about 5 minutes. Return the veal to the pan and toss. Add the wine and simmer 2 minutes. Add the cream and remaining herbs and cook until heated through and creamy. Serve immediately.

VEAL CUTLETS WITH CHIANTI SAUCE

WINE IS A KEY INGREDIENT IN EVERY KITCHEN *I've cooked in. For the rural peasants of the Italian countryside, wine has never been a luxury or a special-occasion drink; it's part of their lives and part of their cuisine. Sauces made with Chianti are a famous Tuscan specialty.*

This recipe is a simple way to bring wine into your kitchen. Chianti has lots of flavor, and the cooking removes any alcohol. You may like to add a handful of sliced mushrooms with the onion and garlic to vary the recipe.

MAKES 4 SERVINGS

4 veal cutlets or veal chops, about 1 inch thick
Salt and freshly ground black pepper
All-purpose flour, for dredging
¼ cup extra-virgin olive oil or vegetable oil
1 onion, minced
1 clove garlic, peeled and smashed
4 teaspoons freshly chopped rosemary leaves
2 cups Chianti or another dry, full-bodied red wine
½ cup chicken stock
1 teaspoon tomato paste
1 tablespoon cold unsalted butter, cut into pieces

Season the veal on both sides with salt and pepper. Lightly dredge the veal on both sides in flour.

In a large skillet, heat the oil over medium-high heat. Add the cutlets and cook until lightly browned, turning once. Transfer to a plate and turn off the heat.

Using paper towels, carefully wipe out the skillet. Add the onion and garlic to the pan and cook, stirring, 2 minutes. Add the rosemary, wine, chicken stock, and tomato paste and bring to a simmer. Stir, scraping up the browned bits from the bottom of the pan, return the veal to the pan, and simmer gently about 20 minutes, until the veal is firm and cooked through. If the veal is cooked before the sauce is thick, transfer the cutlets to serving plates and simmer the sauce until lightly thickened. Just before serving, swirl in the butter to give the sauce a silky finish.

PRO TIP: *Always keep a few bottles of inexpensive dry wine on hand for cooking. If you have to make an extra stop every time you're shopping for dinner, you're less likely to want to cook!*

SLOW-COOK MAIN DISHES

Lasagne della Nonna

Italian Roast Chicken with Vegetables

Real Eggplant Parmigiana

Tuscan Red Wine Chicken Stew

Tuscan Quail with Crispy Polenta

Trattoria-style Braised Veal with
Tomatoes and White Beans

Franz's Roasted Veal

Osso Buco alla Fiorentina

Lamb and Pepper Stew

Tagliata alla Fiorentina

SLOW-COOK MAIN DISHES

THE QUICK-COOK CHAPTER COVERS THE NIGHTS WHEN you eat to live, but this chapter is for the times when you live to eat. It's for family dinners, winter weekends, Sunday lunches—whenever you have time to cook, but also time to gather at the table, eat slowly, and really appreciate the food you cook.

If quick cooking is like sex (because it includes timing, passion, and fun), then slow cooking is like an all-night lovemaking session. Having

time on our hands has become a rare event, but it does happen. And by then we're so harried we don't even know what to do with it! It can be hard to slow down, but it's worth it.

Cooking is more fun when you have time to do it, and it's also therapeutic because it involves tasks outside our workaday world. Try these recipes when you don't feel rushed. Clear off your counters, free up some space in your kitchen and your head, and use these recipes to escape for a while. That way you can enjoy the process *and* the product. And at the end of it all, you'll have wonderful leftovers to freeze for when you have less time.

Slowing down the cooking process isn't the only way to relax; it's also nice to slow down when eating the meal, and take time over dinner

OVERLEAF: **A LATE-WINTER SLOW-COOK COUNTRY TABLE WITH MIMOSAS, FRANZ'S ROASTED VEAL, BROCCOLI RABE, AND REAL EGGPLANT PARMIGIANA.**

with family and friends. The Italians and the French are the best at this. Spending two or three hours at the table eating, drinking, and talking is par for the course. Europeans seem to understand that breaking bread together and slowing down for meals is important and spiritually rewarding, as well as being very healthy. Nutritionists say that eating slowly is better for the digestion, and you also eat less because your body gets a chance to tell you that you're full.

We have really become an eat-and-run society, and I am as guilty of this as anyone else. When I was a kid and my mother would call me in for dinner, all I ever wanted was to eat as fast as I could and get back out to the playground for another game. I'm not preaching that you should glue your kids to their seats, but every so often my parents kept me at the table and I'm glad they did. It was painful to have to sit still, but the memories of those weekend and holiday dinners with family and friends still linger. I always remember the anticipation of a big roast beef or leg of lamb and the excitement of finally sitting down to eat.

As a parent I've found that letting my kids invite their friends over for dinner makes them more interested in the cooking and the meal. They are really proud of the food we make (although we know there will be a stage when they will be embarrassed to be with the family). You can even go so far as to let them help you with the menu planning, so that their favorite foods are on the table and they can start young with the great feeling of entertaining their friends. The meals will leave lasting memories. Special food has a special effect, because it's set apart from the everyday meals all families rely on week in and week out. I'm not saying this can't happen with quick-cooking recipes, but there is something different about a slower, more formal dining experience.

The good thing is that these recipes really show the work you've put into them. They feel and taste impressive and luxurious, even the homey ones that reflect peasant-cooking traditions. They show the luxury of time, not money. Italian family classics like Osso Buco and Lasagne della Nonna didn't get that way by accident. People love the ceremony of serving them, the deep flavors that come from the slow cooking, and the fact that you care enough to cook it for them. Cook from this chapter only when you know you have an appreciative audience coming. If you go to the trouble of making Osso Buco and no one comes to the table to eat it because they're watching the game or on a diet, there's no fun in it.

These dishes are mostly from the rustic Italian home-cooking tradition. Some, like Tuscan

Red Wine Chicken Stew and Trattoria-style Braised Veal, are cooked long at low temperatures to let the flavors develop. Others, like *Tagliata alla Fiorentina*, a mighty grilled steak, or Tuscan Quail with Crispy Polenta, are already packed with flavor and tradition and need only a little time on the stove. With these simple methods, roasts of chicken and veal take minutes to prepare, then cook slowly until tender and juicy. The stews are good for cold nights when you want the oven to warm your kitchen and the cooking aromas to fill your house. (And you'll find even more stews in One-Pot Meals, page 102.) These recipes are not at all difficult to make, but each step must be done with care and patience. They just require a little more "mothering" than other dishes in this book.

For a sense of occasion, it's also important to serve with a little drama. Presenting a roast on a platter, carving a chicken at the table, bringing out a steaming platter of veal shanks and a bright bowl of saffron risotto are all guaranteed to get you those "mmm"s from around the table—music to any cook's ears. These are robust dinners that call for colorful, traditional side dishes, like String Beans with Brown Butter and Almonds (page 87), Campagna Roasted Potatoes (page 100), or a Winter Vegetable Roast (page 97), Spiced Beet Puree (page 96), and Asparagus with Butter and Parmesan (page 215). Bring out your best china and most elegant serving pieces—they'll make the food seem even more impressive. Everyone, down to the smallest child, is excited to see an elegant, candlelit table set with china and crystal—more proof that you really care about their pleasure.

With all of today's emphasis on getting the food on the table as fast as possible, so that families can snatch a few minutes together having dinner, we forget that there's togetherness to be had in the kitchen as well. We don't have to be full-time food snobs; there are times when only McDonald's French fries will fit the bill, and giving your kids what they want will save you a lot of time and grief. But there are also times when participating in the process of cooking a special-occasion meal can make children feel involved and useful, as well as teaching them valuable skills. Outfit your children with aprons. Give them spoons for stirring, or have them help you make meatballs. Make sure you and they remember that the kitchen can be a dangerous place, so don't leave them there alone. Teach them that the kitchen is a place for togetherness, where the whole family enjoys their time together. And they'll also learn that there is a time and a place for good, homemade food.

LASAGNE DELLA NONNA

IN ITALY, WHEN THEY DON'T KNOW WHAT TO *call a dish, they tend to dub it "della nonna," or "Grandma's." There's no particular grandmother in mind but the collective grandmother of all Italian cooks, who teaches the value of making good food from the best quality ingredients.*

Grandma's lasagne is very different from the version I grew up with. This recipe comes from a small restaurant in Rome where families come to eat lasagne every Sunday. It's made in big pans on Saturday, then heated through for Sunday lunch.

MAKES 12 TO 15 SERVINGS

½ cup extra-virgin olive oil
I pound lean ground beef
I pound ground veal
I pound ground pork
3 cloves garlic, minced
I red onion, minced
I carrot, minced
3 stalks celery, minced
I tablespoon chopped fresh rosemary leaves
2 teaspoons dried thyme
2 bay leaves
One 28-ounce can milled or crushed Italian plum
    tomatoes
I cup dry red wine
Salt and freshly ground black pepper
I quart whole or 2 percent milk
I medium onion, peeled, left whole, studded with
    6 cloves
I tablespoon ground nutmeg
White pepper
I cup (2 sticks) unsalted butter
2¼ cups all-purpose flour
2 pounds dried lasagne pasta
¼ cup freshly grated Parmesan cheese
2 tablespoons freshly chopped Italian parsley

CONTINUED

In a large skillet, heat ¼ cup of the olive oil over medium-high heat. Add the beef, veal, and pork and cook, stirring to break up any chunks, just until browned, about 5 minutes. With a slotted spoon, remove the meats to a colander to drain.

Wipe out the skillet with paper towels, then heat the remaining ¼ cup olive oil over medium-high heat. Add the garlic, minced onion, carrot, celery, rosemary, thyme, and 1 bay leaf and cook, stirring, until the onion is wilted, about 3 minutes. Add the cooked meat, tomatoes, and wine, mix well, and bring to a gentle boil. Reduce the heat to a simmer and simmer gently until thickened, about 1 hour. Remove and discard the bay leaf. Taste for salt and black pepper.

Meanwhile, make the béchamel. In a saucepan, heat the milk, whole onion, remaining bay leaf, nutmeg, and salt and white pepper to taste over low heat until hot but not boiling. Melt the butter in a large pot over medium heat, being careful not to let the butter brown. Working in a few tablespoons at a time, sprinkle the flour over the butter and whisk together. Repeat until all the flour is incorporated. Whisking, gradually add the hot milk mixture and whisk together. Simmer very gently until thickened, about 20 minutes. Do not let the sauce boil or become brown; lower the heat if necessary. Remove and discard the onion, cloves, and bay leaf. Taste for salt and pepper.

Bring a large pot of salted water to a boil. Add half of the pasta, stir, and cover until it returns to a boil. Uncover and boil, stirring occasionally, until tender but still firm to the tooth, about 10 minutes. Lift the whole pasta sheets out of the boiling water, drain well in a colander and run cool water over them. Repeat with the remaining pasta. Pat dry and set aside.

Preheat the oven to 350°F. Mix the meat sauce and béchamel together. Line the bottom and sides of a large, deep baking dish with pasta sheets. Spread with a thin layer of sauce, cover with a layer of pasta, and repeat until the dish is full or you have run out of ingredients. The top layer should be sauce. Sprinkle evenly with cheese and bake, uncovered, 45 minutes, until heated through. Check the lasagne after 30 minutes; if the top is browning, cover with aluminum foil.

Serve immediately, sprinkled with parsley.

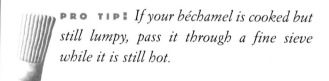 **PRO TIP:** *If your béchamel is cooked but still lumpy, pass it through a fine sieve while it is still hot.*

ITALIAN ROAST CHICKEN WITH VEGETABLES

IT'S FUNNY HOW EVERYONE KNOWS HOW TO *roast a chicken, but nobody knows how to roast a chicken. There's a simple rule about roasting: Roast red meat at high temperatures, pale meat like veal, poultry, and pork at low temperatures. Cooking them sloooowly keeps those juices right where you want them—in the roast. To complete your meal, potatoes roast right alongside the bird. The vegetables in the cavity add flavor, but aren't meant to be eaten.*

To test for doneness, prick the chicken under its "arm," then lift it up with tongs or a big fork, and check for clear juices to run from the hole. Sprinkling hot food as it comes out of the oven with a bit of top-quality balsamic vinegar is the easiest way I know to add fantastic flavor to your food in under two seconds.

MAKES 4 SERVINGS

One whole 3½- to 4-pound chicken
Salt and freshly ground black pepper
2 teaspoons dried oregano
3 sprigs fresh thyme
2 sprigs fresh rosemary
1 clove garlic, smashed and peeled
1 lemon, scrubbed and quartered
½ carrot, diced
½ celery stalk, diced
½ onion, diced
1 tablespoon extra-virgin olive oil
12 small potatoes, halved
1 to 2 tablespoons balsamic vinegar

Preheat the oven to 350°F.

Season the cavity of the chicken with salt and pepper. In a bowl, toss together the oregano, thyme, rosemary, garlic, lemon, carrot, celery, and onion and use this mixture to stuff the cavity,

packing tightly. Tie the legs of the chicken together. Rub the skin of the chicken with the olive oil and sprinkle with salt and pepper.

Place the chicken in a roasting pan. Surround it with the potatoes and sprinkle them with salt. Roast about 1¼ hours, until the juices are clear and show no signs of blood. Sprinkle the chicken and potatoes with balsamic vinegar to taste, cover, and set aside 10 minutes before carving.

PRO TIP: *When seasoning a whole bird, always rub it with oil or butter before sprinkling on the salt and pepper to help the seasonings stay on the skin.*

REAL EGGPLANT PARMIGIANA

THIS IS ONE OF THE MOST REQUESTED RECIPES *at Campagna. The classic dish is different from the eggplant Parmigiana of our childhood, and people are always surprised when it arrives. "Where's the mozzarella cheese?" I see them wondering. "Where's the ricotta?" Then they taste it, and they stop thinking about what's missing. Plenty of freshly grated Parmesan and real tomato sauce layered with perfectly cooked eggplant slices and just a few seasonings make it a true taste of Italy.*

Making Eggplant Parmigiana requires a lot of room, so spread out and work carefully when constructing this classic. I always leave the skin on eggplant because it holds the slices together and because I like the slight texture it adds.

MAKES 8 SERVINGS

3 large eggplant (do not peel)
Salt
Vegetable oil, for frying
All-purpose flour, for dredging
4 cups Traditional Tomato Sauce (page 133)
1 cup freshly grated Parmesan cheese
2 teaspoons dried oregano
3 tablespoons freshly chopped Italian parsley

Cut off the top and bottom of each eggplant. Slice ½ inch thick and lay a single layer of slices on a baking sheet. Sprinkle generously with salt (about ¼ teaspoon per slice), then turn and salt the other side. Repeat with the remaining eggplant, putting a sheet of wax paper between each layer. Rest another baking sheet on the very top and weigh it down with full cans (or anything heavy). Set aside

to drain for 2 to 4 hours. Rinse under running water and drain on paper or kitchen towels.

In a large, deep skillet, heat 2 inches of oil until very hot but not smoking. Spread about ½ cup flour out on a plate. Working in batches to avoid crowding the pan, dredge the eggplant slices on both sides in flour. Shake off any excess and immediately slip into the oil. Cook until golden brown on both sides. Drain on paper towels.

Preheat the oven to 350°F. In a 9- by 13-inch baking dish, arrange half of the eggplant slices in overlapping rows. Spread with half the tomato sauce and sprinkle on half the cheese, half the oregano, and half the parsley. Repeat with remaining ingredients. Bake 40 minutes, until heated through and the cheese is golden.

PRO TIP: *When frying eggplant, the oil must be very hot to ensure that the surface sears immediately, preventing the spongy eggplant flesh from soaking up the oil.*

REAL EGGPLANT PARMIGIANA IN A COPPER *LÉGUMIER.*

TUSCAN RED WINE CHICKEN STEW

THERE'S A TINY VILLAGE CALLED BEFA HID-
*den in the Tuscan forest that stretches between
Montalcino and Siena. One brilliant autumn day, I
went looking for it on the recommendation of the
winemakers at Fattoria di Barbi. When we left the
paved road for a dirt one I knew it was going to be
an experience. Forty minutes later, the car was covered with dust and we arrived in Befa.*

*It was an unpretentious place—just a food shop,
or* alimentari, *with a few tables. Boar braised
slowly in Chianti until tender was the only dish
they made, so I ate boar and ice cream for lunch that
day. I still wonder how the gelato truck could make
it up that dirt road.*

*I've adapted the recipe for chicken, infusing it
with flavor through the long cooking.*

MAKES 4 SERVINGS

One 3½-pound chicken, cut into 8 serving pieces
Salt and freshly ground black pepper
¼ cup plus 1 tablespoon extra-virgin olive oil
1 red onion, minced
2 cloves garlic, smashed and peeled
1 tablespoon chopped fresh rosemary leaves
2 teaspoons chopped fresh sage
2 cups dry red wine
1 cup Chicken Stock (page 15) or low-sodium
   canned broth
1 cup milled or crushed canned Italian plum
   tomatoes

Season the chicken with salt and pepper.

In a large, heavy pot, heat ¼ cup of the olive oil
over medium-high heat. Working in 2 batches if
necessary to avoid crowding the pot, add the
chicken pieces and brown on both sides. Remove
the browned chicken from the pot, turn off the
heat, and carefully wipe out the pot with paper
towels.

Add the remaining 1 tablespoon olive oil to the
pot and heat over medium heat. Add the onion,
garlic, rosemary, and sage and cook until the
onion is wilted, about 5 minutes. Return the
chicken to the pot, add the wine, and mix well,
scraping up any brown bits from the bottom of
the pot with a wooden spoon. Bring to a simmer
and simmer 1 minute. Add the stock, tomatoes,
and salt and pepper to taste. Reduce the heat to a
bare simmer, cover, and simmer about 1 hour,
until the chicken is tender and falling off the bone.
If the chicken is tender before the sauce is thick
enough, remove the chicken to a platter and simmer the sauce until it is slightly thickened.

Taste for salt and pepper. Pour the sauce over
the chicken and serve hot.

PRO TIP: *To give the sauce an even
darker red color and a stronger wine flavor,
marinate the chicken overnight in red
wine. Drain and pat the chicken dry before
browning, but reserve the wine and use it to cook
the chicken.*

TUSCAN QUAIL WITH CRISPY POLENTA

AUTUMN IS GAME SEASON ALL OVER EUROPE. *Once the leaves turn colors, the hunters come out and the menus are full of quail, pigeon, duck, and other birds. One afternoon in the town of Todi, I was having lunch when a man came into the restaurant carrying the birds for the dinner service, with their beautiful feathers still on. This was quite an exciting experience for a chef.*

Some game birds are available from good butchers here, and quail, which is sold slightly flattened and with some of the bones removed, is easy to cook and very tasty. You can also make this dish with halved game hens or even pieces of chicken. They are simply browned whole, then simmered in a light tomato-herb mixture. It's the crisp, hot squares of golden polenta that complete the dish.

MAKES 4 SERVINGS

1 recipe Classic Soft Polenta (page 153)
4 semi-deboned quail, quartered (your butcher
    will do this for you)
Salt and freshly ground black pepper
4 tablespoons extra-virgin olive oil
6 plum tomatoes, diced
½ onion, minced
1 clove garlic, thinly sliced
1 teaspoon freshly chopped rosemary leaves
2 teaspoons freshly chopped thyme

The day before you plan to serve the dish, make the polenta. While still hot, spread the polenta about 1 inch thick on a baking sheet. Let cool, cover and refrigerate overnight, until cold and firm. With a pizza cutter or the tip of a sharp knife, cut into 2-inch squares. Cut each square into 2 triangles.

Season the quail quarters with salt and pepper. In a large skillet, heat 2 tablespoons of the olive oil over medium-high heat. Add the quail and cook, turning once, until just browned on both sides, about 5 minutes. Transfer to a plate and set aside.

Add the remaining 2 tablespoons olive oil to the skillet and heat over medium-high heat. Working in batches if necessary, add the polenta and cook, turning occasionally, until browned and crispy on both sides. Remove from the pan and set aside.

Add the tomatoes, onion, garlic, rosemary, and thyme to the skillet and cook until the onion is just wilting and the tomatoes have started to cook, about 2 minutes. Arrange the quail on top of the mixture, cover, and cook 2 minutes just to reheat. Taste for salt and pepper and serve immediately, over the polenta triangles.

PRO TIP: *When sautéing, keep in mind that quail are tiny and delicate; just brown them on the outside but don't cook them through, as they will cook more later in the recipe.*

TRATTORIA-STYLE BRAISED VEAL WITH TOMATOES AND WHITE BEANS

THIS IS A MEMORABLE DISH THAT I HAD RIGHT *after arriving in Italy. I don't know if it's just that I'm so excited to be there, or if I go to the best restaurants as soon as possible after landing, but my most memorable meals have often been my first. I had this at one of the oldest and least inviting trattorias in Florence, which happens to have great food! Il Latini serves classic Tuscan home cooking with incredible flavor and a healthy pinch of attitude, but it's worth it.*

When I got this plate of tender, falling-apart veal in a fragrant tomato sauce made slightly creamy from Tuscan white beans, I couldn't wish for anything more to know I was in Italy—except the recipe.

MAKES ABOUT 8 SERVINGS

2 cups dried white beans, such as borlotti, cannellini, navy, or Great Northern
4 pounds veal breast, rolled and tied (your butcher will do this for you)
Salt and freshly ground black pepper
¼ cup vegetable oil
¼ cup extra-virgin olive oil
2 cloves garlic, thinly sliced
1 onion, minced
1 carrot, minced
1 stalk celery, minced
1 leek, halved lengthwise, well rinsed, and chopped
1 bottle (750 ml) dry white wine
1½ cups milled or crushed canned Italian plum tomatoes
2 cups Veal Stock (page 16), Chicken Stock (page 15), or low-sodium canned broth
1 tablespoon freshly chopped rosemary leaves
1 tablespoon freshly chopped sage

In a large bowl, cover the beans with at least four times their volume of cold water. Soak 12 to 24 hours, changing the water every 8 hours or so. Drain, rinse, and drain again.

Preheat the oven to 325°F. Season the veal with salt and pepper.

In a large pot or casserole dish, heat the vegetable oil over medium-high heat. Add the veal and brown on all sides. Remove from the pot and set aside. Carefully wipe out the pot with paper towels.

Add the extra-virgin olive oil to the pot and heat over medium-high heat. Add the garlic and onion and cook, stirring, until the onion is wilted, about 5 minutes. Add the carrot, celery, and leek and cook, stirring, 3 minutes. Rest the veal on top of the vegetables, cover, and cook 2 minutes. Add the beans and wine and bring to a simmer. Add the tomatoes, stock, rosemary, sage, and salt and pepper to taste, bring to a simmer, cover, and place in the oven. Cook 2½ to 3 hours, turning the meat every 30 minutes, until the meat is tender. If the mixture becomes too thick, add water as needed.

When the meat is cooked, remove the meat from the pot and let rest 20 minutes. Remove the twine.

To serve, reheat the bean mixture. Taste for salt and pepper. Slice the veal, arrange on a platter, and spoon the bean mixture over it. Serve immediately.

FRANZ'S ROASTED VEAL

MORE THAN ANY AWARD OR THREE-STAR *review or diploma, this dish represents a turning point in my cooking life. When I think about my long career (which I don't like to do that much because it makes me feel old!), I see that the whole thing is built on great methods. The connection might be indirect, but if I hadn't learned to make perfect roast veal in Switzerland, I wouldn't have been the first chef to earn three stars for an Italian restaurant from the* New York Times. *Franz was the chef at the Montreux Palace in Switzerland, and he could make this dish in his sleep. He would make it for twenty-five hundred people without even breaking a sweat.*

Learning from a Swiss chef is something I would recommend to anyone just starting out. Swiss cooking is like Swiss watchmaking: a combination of luxury and precision. Franz had bricks of foie gras, bushels of white asparagus, and out-of-season raspberries at his fingertips, but none of this was as necessary to his cooking as this perfect method.

If you like, you can cut this recipe in half. Just make sure that the cooking liquid comes a third of the way up the meat.

MAKES 12 TO 15 SERVINGS

1 whole loin of veal (about 6 pounds) cut in 2 pieces and tied for roasting (your butcher will do this for you)
Salt and freshly ground black pepper
2 carrots, cut into ½-inch dice
1 onion, cut into ½-inch dice
2 stalks celery, diced
2 leeks, split lengthwise, well rinsed, and thinly sliced crosswise
1 parsnip, cut into ½-inch dice
1 turnip, cut into ½-inch dice
12 assorted herb sprigs such as rosemary, thyme, oregano, and sage
1 bottle (750 ml) dry white wine

Preheat the oven to 325°F.

Season the veal with salt and pepper. In a large, heavy roasting pan, combine the carrots, onion, celery, leeks, parsnip, turnip, and herbs and toss. Rest the roast on top of the vegetables. Roast 5 minutes, then pour over ½ of the bottle of wine. Roast 10 minutes more, then pour over the rest of the wine. Roast 1½ to 2 hours in total, basting every 5 minutes with the liquid in the bottom of the pan. Cook until the roast reaches an internal temperature of 140°F. Remove from the oven, transfer to a carving surface, cover with foil and let rest 20 minutes before slicing.

 PRO TIP: *This method can be used with any large, lean roast, and red wine can be substituted for white if cooking beef or lamb.*

OSSO BUCO ALLA FIORENTINA

OSSO BUCO, BRAISED VEAL SHANKS, IS A CLAS- *sic I've had all over northern Italy. But I especially remember the one at Coco Lezzone, a Florentine trattoria whose name means "dirty chef" in Tuscan dialect. Everyone sits together at plank tables and eats whatever is served to them. It's a simple place with a simple menu—one antipasto, two pastas, and on this occasion, two main courses.*

Once they heard us speaking English, they came over to help with the menu. A waiter who clearly spoke little English, but still wanted to be helpful, asked us: "Osso Buco. Roast beef. What you like?" I've always remembered that sentence and I still laugh when I think about it. Of course, we ordered the osso buco. Once we tasted it, we knew why Coco Lezzone is a Tuscan institution.

MAKES **4** SERVINGS

4 veal shanks, cut 1½ to 2 inches thick
Kosher salt and freshly ground black pepper
All-purpose flour, for dredging
¼ cup vegetable oil
3 tablespoons extra-virgin olive oil
4 1 small carrot, cut into ¼-inch dice
3 1 stalk celery, cut into ¼-inch dice
shallots 1 small red onion, cut into ¼-inch dice
1 cup milled or crushed canned Italian plum tomatoes
1 bottle (750 ml) dry red wine *(stock)*
2 cups Veal Stock (page 16), Chicken Stock (page 15), or low-sodium canned broth
1 teaspoon chopped fresh thyme *Rosemary Bay leaves*
1 teaspoon chopped fresh sage
1 teaspoon chopped fresh oregano
½ teaspoon freshly grated lemon zest

Preheat the oven to 325°F.

Sprinkle the veal shanks with salt and pepper. Spread about ½ cup of flour on a plate and dredge the shanks in flour, shaking off any excess.

In a heavy ovenproof pot with a lid, heat the vegetable oil over medium heat. Add the shanks and cook until lightly browned on both sides, turning once. Transfer to a plate and turn off the heat. Using paper towels, carefully wipe out the pot.

Add the olive oil to the pot and heat over medium heat. Add the carrot, celery, and onion and cook until the onion is wilted, about 3 minutes. Add the shanks and all the tomatoes, wine, stock, herbs, zest, and salt and pepper to taste, and bring to a simmer. Cover and bake about 2½ hours, until the veal is very tender.

Taste for salt and pepper and serve immediately.

PRO TIP: *Have your butcher tie the shanks so that they cook evenly and hold together during the cooking.*

*Hartford Courant
#4. fresh lemon juice 1 a 2Tbl
Did not make Gremolata
Anchovies - put in w/veggies
Broth - used veal broth
Used 2 shanks; 4 chic legs
    split into drumsticks / thighs*

LAMB AND PEPPER STEW

RIGHT OUT OF COOKING SCHOOL, EVERY *young chef wants to work the sauté line. But I like to hand them a whole leg of lamb and see how they do. Sautéing is good for a few cuts of meat, but not all of them. To be a good cook, it's just as important to know how to make a great stew.*

Lamb and peppers, like sausage and peppers, are a classic combination for stew, because they are both so full of flavor. The sweetness of the peppers in this recipe gets picked up by the sweetness of the vinegar, which in turn has the acidity to brighten up all the flavors. This is a very flexible recipe, which can be made with beef or veal rather than lamb, fennel or turnips rather than peppers, and white wine rather than red.

MAKES 8 TO 10 SERVINGS

3 pounds lamb stew meat, cut into 2-inch chunks
Salt and freshly ground black pepper
All-purpose flour, for dredging
¼ cup vegetable oil
3 tablespoons extra-virgin olive oil
3 cloves garlic, thinly sliced
1 red onion, diced
4 red bell peppers, cored, seeded, and cut into
    2-inch chunks
1 bottle (750 ml) dry red wine
1 cup Chicken Stock (page 15) or low-sodium
    canned broth
2 cups milled or crushed canned Italian plum
    tomatoes
1 to 2 tablespoons red wine vinegar
1 tablespoon freshly chopped thyme
1 teaspoon dried oregano

Sprinkle the lamb with salt and pepper. Spread about ½ cup flour on a plate and lightly dredge the lamb, shaking off any excess.

In a large ovenproof pot with a lid, heat the vegetable oil over high heat until just smoking. Working in batches if necessary to avoid crowding the pot, add the lamb and cook, stirring occasionally, until browned on all sides. As the meat is browned, remove from the pot and set aside.

When all the meat is browned, pour off any fat in the pot. Add the olive oil and heat over medium heat. Add the garlic, onion, and peppers and cook, stirring, until the onion is translucent, about 5 minutes. Add the cooked lamb and cook, stirring, 2 minutes. Add the wine, bring to a simmer, and simmer uncovered 15 minutes. Add the stock, tomatoes, vinegar, thyme, oregano, and salt and pepper to taste. Cover and cook at a bare simmer (or bake in a 350°F oven) until the meat is fork-tender, about 1½ hours. If necessary, thicken the sauce by raising the heat at the end of the cooking time.

PRO TIP: *A good cook, among other things, is someone who knows a good butcher. Find a butcher who knows his way around the kitchen, and he'll always be able to tell you the best cut of meat he has in stock for a particular dish.*

TAGLIATA ALLA FIORENTINA

THIS IS THE MOST FAMOUS STEAK DISH IN ALL *of Italy. It is always served the same way: Each person gets a few slices of very rare, crusty meat, plenty of spinach and roasted potatoes, and wedges of lemon. I've always liked the Italian habit of squeezing lemon juice over grilled steak, cutting the richness and adding to the flavor. The cut is a very large porterhouse, but at Campagna we make it with a rib-eye of Certified Angus Beef. It's possible to make an authentic* Tagliata alla Fiorentina *at home, using a hot grill or broiler. You want the coals to be on their way down from the hottest point, gray on the outside with only a little red in the center—but there should be a lot of them.*

MAKES 8 SERVINGS

Two 24-ounce rib-eye or T-bone steaks
Salt and freshly ground black pepper
12 ounces large mushrooms, such as cremini, shiitake, portobello, oyster, or hen-of-the-woods (optional)
¼ cup extra-virgin olive oil
6 sprigs fresh rosemary
6 sprigs fresh sage
2 lemons, quartered

Preheat a grill to very, very hot; or preheat the broiler to high for at least 20 minutes; or preheat the oven to 550°F for at least 30 minutes.

Meanwhile, liberally season the steaks on both sides with salt and pepper, pressing into the meat with your hands. When the grill is hot, grill the steak on the hottest part of the grill until charred outside and blood-rare within, turning once, about 5 minutes per side. When the steak goes on the grill, sprinkle the mushrooms (if using) with

TAGLIATA ALLA FIORENTINA ON AN ALETHA SOULÉ LEAF PLATTER.

olive oil, salt, and pepper. Arrange cap side down on a medium-hot area of the grill and cook until lightly charred on the outside and soft within.

Heat the olive oil in a skillet over medium heat just until it begins to smoke, watching carefully. Remove from the heat and immediately add the herbs, letting them fry for a moment in the oil.

When the steak is cooked, let rest 5 minutes. Slice ½ inch thick and arrange on a platter with the mushrooms. Season with salt and pepper and squeeze the lemons over the steak. Pour the herb oil over the steak, including the herb sprigs. Serve immediately.

193

HOLIDAYS

PASSOVER MENU

EASTER MENU

THANKSGIVING MENU

CHANUKAH MENU

ITALIAN CHRISTMAS EVE MENU

CHRISTMAS DAY MENU

HOLIDAYS

BY NOW YOU KNOW MY VIEWS ON FAMILY, COOKING, LIFE, dining, and many other subjects. But holidays are the time to focus on hospitality. When I was in my apprenticeship stage as a chef, holidays were an opportunity to test my new cooking skills and let family and friends see and taste the results. You can always tell a young chef: He's the one with the dirtiest apron and the most scars on his hands. He also has the most stars in his eyes: The passion and love for cooking shine through.

Like most young chefs, I interpreted the holidays as my chance to try out all my new methods and ideas. Except for the fact that the kitchen looked like a tornado had been through by the time I was finished, the results were usually great, and my family was happy that I picked cooking as a profession. (I was certainly better at cooking than cleaning.)

Holiday meals are still special for me, partly because I remember those early days. It brings back the first Thanksgiving dinner I ever made and the first Chanukah latkes I cooked for my son. I also have great memories of the year Campagna opened, when we did our first big Easter Sunday dinner. Passover is one of my favorite holidays, because it combines food and ritual, and I am proud of the care I've taken over the years in getting all the recipes just right.

Holidays are a natural time to share and show off your cooking skills. Unfortunately, the holidays can also become a high-pressure situation where you are attempting new recipes and methods for the first time. For those who didn't go to cooking school, hosting a holiday dinner for the first time can be a recipe for trouble. So whether you're starting from the beginning, or you're interested in tips and recipes to do something a little different this year, this chapter is for you.

Planning is the key to an easy but high-quality holiday experience. Planning the menu at least one week ahead of time (more for Thanksgiving, when you'll need to order your turkey well in advance) is a necessity. Always write down your ideas as you go along. It's even a good idea to start a cooking journal in a nice bound book, so that you can keep track of what you cooked from year to year. There will always be someone who remembers those amazing potato pancakes or the asparagus you made and will be hoping to see them again.

In planning the menu, a professional trick is

to choose at least one dish that can be made ahead for every dish that will be made on the day of the holiday. I find that cooking the main attraction (pot roast, roast turkey, leg of lamb) on the day itself is enough to do, along with setting the table and dealing with the guests. I like to make most of the side dishes in advance. After choosing the menu, make out a shopping list and a separate list for the *mise en place,* or what you'll need to take out of the cabinets and have ready for each dish. Map out the days leading up to the holiday, assign tasks for each day, and cooking for twelve will suddenly be a lot simpler. If you need stock for a recipe, you can make it a week or two in advance and freeze it. Sauces also freeze extremely well.

Cooking for family and friends on the holidays is the true essence of hospitality. One lesson from school has always stuck in my head: We were taught that we were learning not the restaurant business or the hotel business but the hospitality business. Hospitality is a word with real meaning. Holidays are very important to people, and a good host will try to meet or surpass the guests' expectations. It is your job as a chef to blend your own ideas and traditions with those of your guests. You don't want to disappoint anyone on his or her favorite holiday.

That's why relying on the classics is the best guide for the holidays. And that's how a Jewish chef like me can make a Passover dinner on a Thursday and Friday night and Easter lunch on the following Sunday, which happened one year at Campagna. They may not be your own traditions, but as a chef you can learn them and respect them. Following the classics is the only way to pull this off. When setting your holiday table, use your serving pieces, good linens, china, candlesticks, and best wineglasses.

My inspiration for holiday cooking is the chef at the Montreux Palace Hotel, where I worked in Switzerland. He would carefully create a simple boiled chicken dinner for families to eat after Midnight Mass on Christmas Eve. It was a traditional dish and the integrity and respect he put into it has really stayed with me throughout my cooking career. That idea is what also sent me to Italy to interview families about their Passover, Easter, and Chanukah traditions, and to develop these recipes. All they need is your passion, TLC, and holiday spirit to make them perfect. And then they will make you a star!

PASSOVER MENU

Sephardic Haroset

Italian-Jewish Chicken Soup

Tuscan Chicken Liver Crostini

Turkey Polpette with Leek Sauce

Sephardic Rack and Shoulder of Lamb

Baby Artichokes Baked with Mint and Garlic, page 86

Pizzarelle

PASSOVER AT CAMPAGNA IS AN IMPORTANT TIME FOR all of us. It is a major Jewish holiday and now that I have kids, it's an especially interesting and important event on the calendar. Children have a tendency to change your priorities and your role in life. Suddenly, as a parent, you have to be the one to establish and maintain the traditions, memories, and meanings. Since Campagna is a country Italian restaurant, I decided to learn about the traditions of Italian Jews. The modern community is small but both Venice and Rome had thriving Jewish ghettos for centuries. Only a few people returned after the Second World War, but most survivors immigrated to Israel and the United States. While researching the traditions I was introduced to a magical woman of Italian-Jewish descent who had settled in New Jersey. Not knowing what to expect, I went to visit her and stumbled on a wealth of information and tradition. We sat in her kitchen and as she told me stories about Passovers in Rome

THE PASSOVER TABLE WITH MULTICOLORED RANUNCULUS.

when she was young, we were laughing together and eventually crying together. It was a nostalgic kind of weeping, not a painful kind. It made a lasting impression on me, and makes me even more determined to make holidays special for my children while they are young. She and I agreed that children always grow up too fast, and that passing the traditions from generation to generation is a duty that we all share.

Through this fascinating woman, I made arrangements to visit two Roman Jewish families. The trip was informative but also fun and colorful. All the interviews seemed to take place in kitchens and were packed with heartwarming stories about recipes and childhood. Two of my best teachers were the mother and daughter who gave me the recipe for *pizzarelle*. The mother told me the story of how her mother invented a special dessert for her children, because they couldn't eat pizza during the

Passover holiday (pizza, of course, is the universal food for kids). All the children in the family would wait impatiently in the kitchen for the *pizzarelle* to be finished, but of course they couldn't wait long enough and would burn their tongues on the hot dough year after year.

She told me how to make the *pizzarelle*, but the daughter (who had heard the story a thousand times) interrupted and disagreed with one part of the method. The mother made an appointment with me the next day to taste the family recipe. I showed up to find that both women had made a batch of *pizzarelle*, and neither would be satisfied until I had picked the best one. I am lucky that one of the hats a restaurateur wears is that of a diplomat, so I was able to wiggle out of the question. Only they will know whose recipe I picked for this book. I am grateful for all the recipes they shared with me, especially the ones I have included in this chapter.

SEPHARDIC HAROSET

MAKES ABOUT 5 CUPS

24 dried figs
24 pitted dried dates
8 prunes
4 oranges, peeled and sectioned
Fresh juice of 1 lemon
1 cup walnut halves
1 cup almonds
¼ cup sugar
Pinch of nutmeg
Pinch of cinnamon

In a food processor or on a large cutting board, coarsely chop the figs. Working in order, add the remaining ingredients one at a time, pulsing or chopping after each addition. The mixture will be almost smooth and pasty, like mortar. Refrigerate until ready to serve, up to 1 week. Bring to room temperature before serving.

PARROT TULIPS IN ANCIENT OLIVE JUGS CONNOTE SPRING AND MAKE A WONDERFUL ARRANGEMENT FOR PASSOVER OR EASTER.

ITALIAN-JEWISH CHICKEN SOUP

THIS SOUP ATTRACTED MY ATTENTION WHEN I *was researching the Passover food traditions of the Jews of Rome. It has all the potency of American-Jewish chicken soup, with delicious Italian additions of artichokes and arborio rice. (Italian Jews, unlike most observant American Jews, eat rice during Passover. During Passover, bits of matzoh are floated on top.) It also has the great flavor and texture of lightly cooked vegetables, making it satisfying and comforting. If you don't have a Jewish grandmother or an Italian one, this soup is the next best thing.*

MAKES 8 SERVINGS

3 quarts Chicken Stock (page 15)
1 large whole (double) boneless, skinless chicken
    breast, finely diced
2 small carrots, thinly sliced
1 stalk celery, thinly sliced
2 scallions, trimmed and thinly sliced
1 leek, halved lengthwise, well rinsed, and thinly
    sliced
1 cup fresh or frozen peas
1 cup thinly sliced baby artichokes (in season;
    see page 85 for trimming instructions)
1 cup raw arborio rice
Salt and freshly ground black pepper
3 large sprigs fresh Italian parsley, leaves only,
    coarsely chopped, for serving

In a large soup pot, heat the stock to a simmer over medium-high heat. Add all the remaining ingredients except the parsley and simmer gently, stirring occasionally, about 30 minutes, until the vegetables are cooked. Season with salt and pepper to taste. Serve immediately, garnished with parsley.

PRO TIP: *Make sure the vegetables are thinly and evenly sliced, so that they cook quickly in the stock. They also look more elegant this way! Make sure not to boil the soup; simmer it instead.*

TUSCAN CHICKEN LIVER CROSTINI

MAKES ABOUT **8** SERVINGS

1 tablespoon unsalted butter
2 tablespoons extra-virgin olive oil
½ onion, minced
1 clove garlic, thickly sliced
1 pound chicken livers, cleaned of fat and bile
¼ cup Cognac or other brandy
2 capers
Salt and freshly ground black pepper
Matzoh, for serving

In a large skillet, heat the butter and olive oil over high heat until the butter solids are just starting to brown. Add the onion, garlic, and chicken livers and toss together in the pan. Tilting the pan away from you, carefully pour in the Cognac. Lower the heat to medium-high and cook, stirring occasionally, just until the livers are cooked through but still pink at the center.

Remove from the heat and stir in the capers and salt and pepper to taste. Refrigerate until cool. Transfer the mixture to a food processor and process until smooth. Taste for salt and pepper.

Serve with thin strips of matzoh or, if not serving at Passover, with toasted or grilled peasant bread rubbed with garlic (crostini).

PRO TIP: *If you are going to store the chicken livers, clean them as soon as you get home from the market. Place them in a bowl and cover with milk. Keep refrigerated and drain just before using.*

TUSCAN CHICKEN LIVER CROSTINI WITH CAMPAGNA'S HOMEMADE MATZOH.

TURKEY POLPETTE WITH LEEK SAUCE

THIS DELICATE DISH OF PLUMP, SOFT MEAT-*balls and a subtle leek sauce is traditionally served at Passover by Roman Jews. If you like to eat meatballs but want a leaner meal, you will love this dish. I know my family does.*

Meatballs (called polpette, polpettine, *or* polpettone, *depending on the size) are popular in Italy, but they aren't served with pasta. They are a main course that follows the pasta, served with vegetable side dishes like roasted potatoes and sautéed spinach. Italian* polpette *are usually made with a combination of beef, veal, and pork. Ground turkey, which is made from the dark leg and thigh meat, is an excellent substitute. Browning the* polpette *gives them a nice crust, but isn't absolutely necessary if you're in a hurry. Children love this dish, and you can make it with a tomato sauce instead of the leeks. Serve it with rice, mashed potatoes, or even pasta!*

MAKES **6** TO **8** SERVINGS

FOR THE MEATBALLS
2 pounds ground turkey, chicken, or veal
½ teaspoon salt
½ teaspoon freshly ground black pepper
2 teaspoons extra-virgin olive oil
½ onion, minced
1 clove garlic, minced
½ cup plain dried bread crumbs or matzoh meal
2 large eggs, beaten
3 tablespoons freshly grated Parmesan cheese (optional; do not add during Passover)
2 teaspoons chopped fresh rosemary, sage, or thyme or a combination of the three
Pinch of nutmeg
¼ cup vegetable oil
½ cup all-purpose flour or matzoh cake meal

CONTINUED

FOR THE SAUCE

1 large leek, split lengthwise, well rinsed, and
    thinly sliced crosswise

¼ cup dry white wine

1 cup Chicken Stock (page 15) or low-sodium
    canned broth

2 teaspoons chopped fresh rosemary, sage, or
    thyme or a combination of the three

1 tablespoon cold unsalted butter, cut into pieces
    (optional; do not add during Passover)

To make the meatballs, combine the ground meat, salt, and pepper in a large mixing bowl. Mix lightly and set aside.

In a small skillet, heat the olive oil over medium-high heat. Add the onion and garlic and cook, stirring, until the onion is wilted, about 3 minutes. Let cool 10 minutes and add to the meat. Add the bread crumbs, eggs, Parmesan (if using), herbs, and nutmeg, and mix well. If possible, refrigerate 1 hour to let the mixture firm up. Using your hands, shape the mixture into balls almost, but not quite, as big as a golf ball.

In a large skillet, heat the vegetable oil over medium-high heat. Spread the flour out on a plate. Working in batches if necessary to avoid crowding the pan, dredge the balls in flour, shake off any excess, and add to the pan. Cook until browned. As the balls brown, set aside to drain on paper towels. When all the balls are browned and removed from the skillet, turn off the heat. Using paper towels, carefully wipe out the skillet.

To make the sauce, add the leek and wine to the skillet. Bring to a simmer and simmer 1 minute. Add the stock, herbs, and meatballs and simmer gently until the sauce is slightly thickened and the meatballs are cooked through, about 10 minutes. Add the butter (if using), mix well, taste for salt and pepper, and serve immediately.

PRO TIP: *Chill the meat mixture before shaping it into balls to make it easier to work with. Wet your hands lightly as you work to prevent the mixture from sticking to your hands.*

SEPHARDIC RACK AND SHOULDER OF LAMB

MAKES ABOUT 8 SERVINGS

FOR THE SHOULDER
    2 tablespoons extra-virgin olive oil
    2 cloves garlic, minced
    I whole lamb shoulder roast, boned and tied
        (about 2½ pounds; your butcher will do this
        for you)
    I onion, minced
    I tablespoon freshly chopped rosemary leaves
    I tablespoon freshly chopped thyme
    I bottle (750 ml) dry red wine
    I cup milled or crushed canned Italian plum
        tomatoes
    Pinch of ground nutmeg
    Pinch of ground cloves
    Salt and freshly ground black pepper

FOR THE RACKS
    2 racks of lamb, frenched (your butcher will do
        this for you)
    2 tablespoons Dijon mustard
    ¼ cup matzoh meal
    I clove garlic, peeled
    2 teaspoons freshly chopped rosemary leaves
    Freshly grated zest of 2 lemons
    Salt

To make the shoulder, preheat the oven to 325°F. Heat the oil in a large casserole with a tight-fitting lid over high heat. Add the garlic and the lamb and cook, turning occasionally, until the meat is lightly browned on all sides. Add the onion and herbs, toss well, and cook 1 minute. Add the wine, tomatoes, nutmeg, cloves, and salt and pepper to taste. Bring to a boil, cover, and bake in the oven until the meat is fork-tender, about 1½ hours. (The shoulder can be cooked up to 48 hours in advance and refrigerated, then reheated before serving.) When the meat is cooked, remove it from the pot, set aside covered, and simmer the pan juices on the stove until thick enough to use as a sauce. Taste for salt and pepper.

To make the rack, preheat the oven to 500°F. Wrap the bones in aluminum foil so they do not burn. Mix the mustard and matzoh meal together. Chop or pound the garlic, rosemary, lemon zest, and salt to taste together until they form a paste. Spread the mustard mixture all over the meat. Then spread the garlic paste over the mustard. Place on a rack in a roasting pan and roast until the lamb feels firm but still springy to the touch, like a bicycle tire filled with air, about 12 minutes for medium-rare meat. The firmer the meat, the more cooked it is. Remove from the oven and let rest 5 minutes.

To serve, reheat the sauce if necessary. Slice the shoulder meat and put the sauce in a gravy boat. Slice the racks into individual chops. Serve each person a chop and some sliced shoulder, with hot sauce on top. Serve very hot.

PIZZARELLE

MAKES ABOUT 10 SERVINGS

FOR THE BATTER

One 12-ounce box matzoh
4 cups milk
3 large eggs
2 large egg yolks
1/4 cup granulated sugar
3 tablespoons dried currants
1/4 cup honey
1/4 cup ground almonds
Pinch of salt
1 teaspoon extra-virgin olive oil
1/4 teaspoon ground cinnamon
1/4 teaspoon ground nutmeg
1 tablespoon dark brown sugar
1/2 teaspoon pure vanilla extract
Fresh-squeezed juice of 1 orange
Matzoh meal or additional matzoh, for thickening

FOR THE FRYING

3 to 4 cups pure olive oil
Powdered sugar

To make the batter, using your hands, crumble the matzoh into about 1-inch pieces and place in a large bowl. Add the milk, mix well, and refrigerate 1 hour.

In a separate bowl, whisk the eggs, egg yolks, and granulated sugar together until smooth. Add to the soaked matzoh, mix, add the remaining batter ingredients, and mix well. If the mixture is too loose to hold together in patties, add the matzoh meal a few tablespoons at a time, or use additional crumbled matzoh.

When ready to serve, heat 1 cup of olive oil in a skillet over medium-low heat until smoking. To shape each *pizzarella,* roll the batter into a lump the size of a golf ball. Flatten into a pancake and slip it into the hot oil. The oil should sizzle and dance around each pancake, and the pancakes should be slowly browned on both sides until the center is completely cooked. The *pizzarelle* should look like potato latkes. Drain on paper bags or paper towels. Repeat with remaining batter, changing the oil if it becomes very brown.

Sprinkle with powdered sugar and serve hot.

EASTER MENU

Mixed Greens with Garlic-Anchovy Dressing

Springtime Risotto with Mushrooms, Asparagus, and Peas, page 151

Asparagus with Butter and Parmesan

Rosemary-Garlic Leg of Lamb

Campagna Roasted Potatoes, page 100

Peas and Prosciutto, page 86

N ITALY EASTER IS ONE OF THE MOST SACRED DAYS OF the year. It has the double significance of being a major religious holiday and the day that signifies the coming of spring in everyone's mind and in the agricultural season.

In America, Easter is an important holiday for restaurants (after Mother's Day, which you could also cook this menu for). The year Campagna opened, I made a point of researching the recipes of the Italian Easter. At Campagna and in Italy, whole spring lambs are roasted and served all day long. Since your home oven probably isn't big enough to cook a whole lamb, I'd advise a whole leg of lamb, with the bone left in for extra flavor. The seasonings of garlic and rosemary are the same.

The rest of the menu is designed around all the vegetables of spring. If you want to change it, just remember to include asparagus, peas, fava beans, artichokes, and of course the little new potatoes that really are new this time of year.

A PROVENÇAL EASTER TABLE WITH LAVENDER IN A WOODEN WINE BOX, SPRINGTIME RISOTTO WITH MUSHROOMS, ASPARAGUS, AND PEAS; PEAS AND PROSCIUTTO; AND ASPARAGUS WITH BUTTER AND PARMESAN.

MIXED GREENS WITH GARLIC-ANCHOVY DRESSING

MAKES ⅔ CUP

2 cloves garlic, thickly sliced
1 anchovy fillet, rinsed of salt or oil, or more to
    taste (optional)
2 lemons, halved
2 tablespoons finely chopped Italian parsley
Salt and freshly ground black pepper
⅓ to ½ cup extra-virgin olive oil
Dandelion greens, arugula, or other mixed greens

In a mortar or a food processor, mash or process the garlic and anchovy into a smooth paste. Transfer to a large mixing bowl and squeeze the lemons over the mixture. Add the parsley and a pinch of salt and pepper and mix well. While whisking, drizzle in the olive oil. Season to taste with salt and pepper and set aside to marinate at room temperature at least 2 hours. Whisk before using; or keep refrigerated and shake well before using.

Toss with the greens or serve the dressing on the side.

ASPARAGUS WITH BUTTER AND PARMESAN

ASPARAGUS IN SEASON IS WORSHIPED IN *Europe. In Switzerland, we served it as a separate course, with a little cooking liquid spooned over to keep it moist. Spring asparagus is still the best. Don't be seduced by those bundles of pencil-sized asparagus; the thicker ones actually have more flavor. I always peel the bottoms of the spears. A graceful stalk of fresh asparagus is as naturally beautiful as any tree, but you don't want it to taste like one. I love the effect of light green shading into dark, especially when the asparagus is arranged on a platter with all the tips facing the same way.*

Glazing tender asparagus with a little butter and Parmesan is the classic Italian preparation, and it's really easy to do, especially if you boil the asparagus beforehand. Use a vegetable peeler to make thin sheets of cheese. As it comes out of the oven, you can even drizzle a little aged balsamic vinegar on top, to bring back memories of Emilia-Romagna (or just because you like it). This is a perfect dish for spring holiday dinners.

MAKES 8 SERVINGS

2 pounds asparagus
2 tablespoons unsalted butter, cut into pieces
Salt and freshly ground black pepper
10 large shavings Parmesan cheese

Bring a large pot of lightly salted water to a boil. Meanwhile, cut off the woody ends of the asparagus. Peel the bottom 3 inches of each stalk with a vegetable peeler. Tie in bundles of up to 12 spears, using cooking twine.

Add the asparagus to the pot and boil uncovered until bright green and cooked through but not soft, 7 to 10 minutes. Prepare a large bowl of ice water. When the asparagus are cooked, transfer them to the ice water. When cool, drain and pat dry. Set aside.

When ready to serve, preheat the oven to 500°F. Arrange the asparagus spears in one or two layers on a sheet pan or in a baking dish. Dot with butter and sprinkle with salt and pepper. Top with Parmesan and bake 3 minutes, until the butter and cheese have melted and are starting to brown. Serve immediately.

ROSEMARY-GARLIC LEG OF LAMB

MAKES **8** SERVINGS

1 bone-in leg of lamb, about 7 pounds
Salt and freshly ground black pepper
3 cloves garlic, thickly sliced
12 small sprigs fresh rosemary, plus additional for
    garnish
2 carrots, diced
2 stalks celery, diced
1 onion, diced
Extra-virgin olive oil
1½ cups dry red wine
½ cup water

Preheat the oven to 425°F for 30 minutes.

Season the meat with salt and pepper. Make about 12 small incisions in the meat with the point of a sharp knife. Reserving a little garlic and rosemary to toss with the vegetables, insert a piece of garlic and a sprig of rosemary into each incision, pressing them into the flesh. In a roasting pan, toss the carrots, celery, and onion with the remaining garlic and rosemary, a little olive oil, and salt and pepper to taste.

Place the leg on top of the vegetables and roast for 20 minutes. Pour the wine and water into the roasting pan and continue roasting until the meat reaches an internal temperature of 120°F for rare meat, 130°F for medium rare, about 45 minutes more. (The internal temperature will continue to rise as the meat rests.) Let rest 15 minutes.

While the meat rests, strain the juices in the pan. Simmer the sauce until thick, or thin it if necessary with additional wine and water. Season with salt and pepper to taste and serve, garnishing the lamb with rosemary sprigs.

THANKSGIVING MENU

Butternut Squash Soup, page 125

Olive Oil–Roasted Turkey

Spiced Beet Puree, page 96

Great Mashed Potatoes, page 100

Leek Gratin, page 93

Winter Vegetable Roast, page 97

THANKSGIVING IS A BIG DAY FOR HOTEL RESTAURANTS, and when I worked in them I had to be there every Thanksgiving. But I always hated it because Thanksgiving is my favorite holiday. That's why Campagna is closed on Thanksgiving, even though it's open for Christmas and Passover. That way everyone including me can have a holiday dinner at home. I have always made our Thanksgiving dinner myself at the restaurant (our home kitchen is tiny), but now that my sons are old enough to understand the holiday I will be making it at home, so they can watch and learn. I remember from my own childhood waking up early to watch my mother put the turkey in and watching the parade on television while the aromas of her cooking filled the house. I want my kids to have that, too. (The only difference is that we are lucky enough to live near the parade. While my children are still small enough to sit on my shoulders and watch Road Runner go by, we'll go every year.)

Organic turkeys and vegetables really make a difference on Thanksgiving. Basting the turkey with olive oil gives it a wonderful finish and flavor. I haven't included a recipe for cranberry sauce because I know that every family has its own favorite!

OLIVE OIL–ROASTED TURKEY

MAKES 8 TO 12 SERVINGS

One 12- to 14-pound turkey, preferably fresh and
    organically raised
Salt and freshly ground black pepper
2 heads garlic (do not peel), cut in half
2 carrots, cut into chunks
1 onion, cut into chunks
4 large sprigs fresh rosemary
2 cups white wine or water
1 cup extra-virgin olive oil

Preheat the oven to 375°F.

Rub the turkey skin and inside the cavity with
plenty of salt and pepper. Place half the vegetables
and rosemary inside the cavity. Tie the legs
together. Place the remaining vegetables and rosemary in the bottom of the roasting pan. Place the
turkey on top, breast side up. Pour the wine into
the roasting pan. Pour ¼ cup of the oil into the
cavity (use a turkey baster if necessary). Slowly
pour the remaining oil over the turkey, rubbing it
all over and into the skin with your hands.

Roast 4 to 5 hours, about 22 minutes per
pound, basting every 20 minutes with the liquid in
the pan. Roast until the internal temperature of
the breast meat is 160°F. Remove from the oven
and let sit 15 minutes (do not turn the oven off).

Meanwhile, strain the pan juices and simmer
until thick to make a gravy.

To present the bird, bring it to the table intact.
Carve off the legs and return them to the oven to
roast until the temperature is 165°F at the joint.
Meanwhile, carve and serve the white meat.

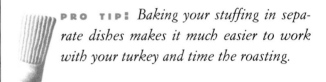 **PRO TIP:** *Baking your stuffing in sepa-
rate dishes makes it much easier to work
with your turkey and time the roasting.*

CHANUKAH MENU

Tuscan Mushroom Soup, page 111

Tuscan-Jewish Pot Roast

Pearl Onions Baked in Red Wine, page 93

Potato Latkes

Winter Vegetable Roast, page 97

CHANUKAH IS A HOLIDAY THAT WE STARTED TO CELEbrate at Campagna almost by accident, but now it's a tradition we love. The first year the restaurant was open, all we did was light a menorah. But one of my regular customers saw it and told me it reminded him of when his children were young, even though they were now all grown and spread across the country. Almost as though he knew the answer would be no, he asked: "Do you possibly have potato latkes on the menu?" I was about to shake my head and say no, but then something about his wistful expression set off a voice in my brain. It was the voice of my teachers at school, reminding me of the meaning of hospitality. So instead of no, I said, "Give me fifteen minutes." I went into the kitchen and made them for him by hand. Someone else in the dining room saw them and asked for them, then another, and another. The rest is history, and now Campagna is famous for its latkes. Our customers even burn their tongues on them because they can't wait for them to cool, just like my brother and I used to!

Mushroom soup is a traditional Jewish dish, and my recipe gives it an Italian twist. The same goes for my pot roast, which is braised in Tuscan red wine.

TUSCAN-JEWISH POT ROAST

MAKES **8** SERVINGS

2 tablespoons extra-virgin olive oil
1 carrot, diced
1 celery stalk, diced
1 onion, diced
1 bay leaf
3 tablespoons freshly chopped rosemary leaves
¼ cup freshly chopped Italian parsley
2 cloves garlic, minced
Salt and freshly ground black pepper
3 chicken livers, cleaned of membranes and bile
One brisket of beef (5 to 6 pounds), trimmed of
    excess fat (eye round of beef or short ribs
    can also be used)
1 bottle (750 ml) dry red wine
1½ cups Chicken Stock (page 15) or low-sodium
    canned broth
1½ cups milled or crushed canned Italian plum
    tomatoes

Preheat the oven to 325°F.

In a large, heavy pot with a lid, heat the olive oil over medium-high heat. Add the carrot, celery, and onion and cook, stirring, until the onion is wilted, about 3 minutes. Add the bay leaf, rosemary, parsley, garlic, and salt and pepper to taste. Add the chicken livers and mix. Place the brisket on top and pour the wine, stock, and tomatoes over the meat.

Cover tightly and bake until very tender, stirring about once an hour and adding a little water if necessary, about 4 hours. Serve in slices with the pan juices.

POTATO LATKES

MAKES **4** TO **6** SERVINGS

6 large Idaho potatoes
1 onion, peeled and halved
1 egg plus 1 egg yolk, beaten together
2 teaspoons kosher salt
2 teaspoons freshly ground black pepper
1 tablespoon rendered chicken fat (optional)
2 teaspoons all-purpose flour
Vegetable oil

Preheat the oven to 400°F.

Peel the potatoes and, working quickly, grate them on the finest hole of a box grater into a stainless steel bowl. With your hands, firmly squeeze all the water out of the potato pulp (you'll want to work over the sink).

When as much liquid as possible has been squeezed out of the potatoes, grate the onion into the bowl and mix. Add the egg mixture, salt, pepper, chicken fat (if using), and flour. Mix together very well.

In a large frying pan, heat the oil until very hot but not smoking. Place heaping tablespoons of the potato mixture in the pan, flattening them until they are about ½ inch thick. Reduce the heat to medium and fry until golden brown on the bottom. Turn and repeat, cooking until well browned and cooked through. Drain on paper towels, then transfer to a baking sheet and place in the oven. Repeat with the remaining potato mixture. If necessary, add more oil to the pan between batches and heat thoroughly.

ITALIAN CHRISTMAS EVE MENU
CHRISTMAS DAY MENU

Crazy Seafood Soup, page 117

Beet and Lentil Salad, page 63

Roasted Calamari all'Ancona

Oven-Braised Fennel, page 92

Risotto al Barolo, page 152

Cotechino with Lentils

Franz's Roasted Veal, page 189

Sautéed Potatoes and Onions, page 98

Spinach Sautéed with Olive Oil and Garlic, page 95

THESE RECIPES WILL HELP YOU CELEBRATE YOUR HOLIday with great food, no matter what time of day you choose for the celebration. Some are classical, some are more rustic and Italian. Tradition in Italy calls for an all-seafood meal on Christmas Eve, and Crazy Seafood Soup is festive and fun to eat all together. For the traditional Christmas dinner, in addition to the roast or bird you usually cook, it's fun to include a dish from the Italian tradition like *Cotechino* with Lentils.

Lentils are often eaten on Christmas and New Year's because their shape symbolizes coins and wealth. It's a custom worth adopting: Even if you don't strike it rich, the worst that can happen is that you will have a great-tasting dish in your repertoire. Year after year, you will become rich in family traditions and memories.

ROASTED CALAMARI ALL'ANCONA

MAKES **6** SERVINGS

1 cup plain dried bread crumbs
1 clove garlic, minced
Salt and freshly ground black pepper
Pinch of hot red pepper flakes
½ teaspoon dried oregano
½ teaspoon dried thyme
2 teaspoons freshly chopped Italian parsley
1 tablespoon freshly chopped rosemary leaves
2 teaspoons freshly grated Parmesan cheese
1 lemon, halved
About ⅓ cup extra-virgin olive oil
6 whole medium-size cleaned squid (calamari),
   bodies and tentacles separated but left intact
2 plum tomatoes, minced
6 leaves fresh basil
2 lemons, cut into wedges

Heat your broiler to very hot (or preheat your oven to 550°F). Grease a sheet pan large enough to hold the calamari in a single layer.

In a bowl, combine the bread crumbs, garlic, salt and pepper to taste, red pepper flakes, oregano, thyme, parsley, rosemary, and Parmesan cheese. Squeeze the lemon and drizzle the olive oil over the mixture until just moistened.

Dip the squid into plain olive oil, then into the bread crumb mixture, pressing to coat lightly. Transfer each piece to the sheet pan. Broil or bake about 3 minutes, until the calamari is crisp and just slightly charred on the edges. Turn the calamari and repeat on the other side.

Place the tomatoes in a bowl. Tear basil leaves into small pieces and add to the tomatoes. Add 2 tablespoons olive oil and salt to taste and mix. Transfer the calamari to a serving dish and garnish with the tomato mixture and wedges of lemon.

COTECHINO WITH LENTILS

MAKES **8** TO **12** SERVINGS

2 large fresh *cotechino* sausages or French garlic
   sausages
1 pound dried lentils, preferably green lentils such
   as Castelluccio or du Puy. (If using non-green
   lentils, they need to be presoaked overnight
   in water to cover before using.)
1 carrot, diced
1 celery stalk, diced
1 red onion, diced
2 tablespoons extra-virgin olive oil, plus extra for
   serving
Salt and freshly ground black pepper

Put the sausages in a large pot and cover completely with water. Bring to a simmer until firm, about 1½ hours. Do not test with a fork; the skin must stay intact as the sausage cooks. Remove from the water to cool, reserving the cooking water. When cooled, cut into ½-inch slices.

Meanwhile, return the water to a boil. Add the lentils, carrot, celery, and ½ of the onion and boil until the lentils are tender but not mushy, about 30 minutes. Reserve 1 cup cooking liquid and drain the lentils. Set aside.

When ready to serve, heat the olive oil in a large skillet over medium heat. Add the remaining onion and cook until softened, about 3 minutes. Add the lentil mixture and ½ cup cooking water and stir. Heat through, stirring gently. Add the sausage slices and salt and pepper to taste. Bring to a simmer, adding more cooking water if necessary, until the sausages are heated through and the lentils have thickened. Serve in bowls, drizzled with extra-virgin olive oil.

INDEX